CW00536277

TEACHING
CHILDREN TO PLAY
GAMES

Text copyright © British Council of Physical Education, the National Coaching Foundation and the Sports Council 1992

ISBN 0 947850 85 6

First published 1992

Joint publishers:
British Council of Physical Education
c/o Liverpool Institute of Higher Education, P. O. Box 6, Woolton Road, Liverpool L16 8ND
The National Coaching Foundation
4 College Close, Beckett Park, Leeds LS6 3QH
The Sports Council
16 Upper Woburn Place, London WC1H 0QP

Designed and produced by
White Line Publishing Services
60 Bradford Road, Stanningley, Leeds LS28 6EF

Cover design: The Reid Watson Partnership
Illustrations (including cover): Neville Swaine
Diagrams: Chris Oxlade

Printed in Great Britain

This book is copyright under the Berne Convention. All rights are reserved. Apart from any fair dealing for the purposes of private study, research, criticism or review, as permitted under the Copyright, Designs and Patents Act, 1988, and apart from the exception specified below, no part of this publication may be reproduced, stored in a retrieval system, or transmitted in any form or by any means, electronic, electrical, chemical, mechanical, optical, photocopying, recording or otherwise, without the prior written permission of the copyright owner. Enquiries should be addressed to the National Coaching Foundation.

Users of this resource may photocopy the skill cards and the blank lesson-plan forms, provided that this is done solely for the purposes of teaching and coaching.

Teaching
children to play
Games

A resource for primary teachers

Compiled by:
Brenda Read and Phyl Edwards

5–11

BRITISH COUNCIL OF PHYSICAL EDUCATION
THE NATIONAL COACHING FOUNDATION
THE SPORTS COUNCIL

ACKNOWLEDGEMENTS

This resource could not have been produced without the enthusiasm, support and expertise of many people.

We wish to express our grateful thanks to:

The management team:

Elizabeth Murdoch (British Council of Physical Education)
Sue Campbell (National Coaching Foundation)
Elaine Burgess (Sports Council)

Representatives from national governing bodies:

Jake Downey (Badminton Association of England)
Greg Welch (British Baseball Federation)
Brian Coleman (English Basket Ball Association)
Bob Carter (National Cricket Association)
Robin Russell (Football Association)
Stephen Jones (British Handball Association)
Mike Hamilton and Carl Ward (Hockey Association/All-England Women's Hockey Association)
Sarah Barton (All-England Women's Lacrosse Association)
Mary French (All-England Netball Association)
Dave Dorrell (National Rounders Association)
Phil Larder (Rugby Football League)
Keith Bonsor (Rugby Football Union)
Karina Bowlby and Stuart Houghton (National Softball Federation)
Claire Chapman and Sue Woodhouse (Squash Rackets Association)
Richard Elmsley (National Stoolball Association)
Gail McCulloch and Diccon Gray (English Table Tennis Association)
Pauline Harrison and Phil Veasey (British Schools Lawn Tennis Association)
David Joy (English Volleyball Association)

I. M. Marsh Campus, Liverpool Polytechnic, for distributing questionnaires

Loughborough University for access to computers and servicing

and so many other people who have contributed to the preparation of this resource, especially the following:

Peter Boyer and staff (Middlewich County Primary School)
Peter Cooil and staff (Victoria Primary School, Runcorn)
Bruce Nash, Kathryn Parkin and Ray Potter (Thorpe Acre County Junior School, Loughborough)
Gill Simmonds (Godmanchester Primary School)
Claire Stretch (PE Inspector, Wirral).

Brenda Read and Phyl Edwards

Contents

CONTENTS

Introduction

Please read this introduction before turning to the later sections.

Teaching children to play Games is a guide to the planning and delivery of a games curriculum for pupils aged 5–11. It has been designed to make it easy for you to select the material needed to support the teaching of all ages and abilities within this range.

It is not intended that you should work through the resource page by page, nor that your pupils should experience any task only once.

Indexes are provided to lead you to specific material. For example, by looking up **throwing and catching**, you will be directed to all the games, tasks and skill cards which involve pupils in this activity.

This publication is presented in a loose-leaf format so that you can add materials of your own and build up a really comprehensive teaching resource.

How the material is organised

There are three main sections, forming a progression. They are colour-coded yellow, blue and green. The **yellow** section introduces different types of games equipment and concentrates on developing the core skills; the **blue** section deals with games-making and introduces formal games; the **green** section is devoted to the many mini-games which have been introduced by sport governing bodies.

You will also find **red**-coded pages such as this. These give guidance on the planning and delivery of lessons.

Follow the main yellow – blue – green route, but use the materials flexibly and design your own series of lessons in response to pupils' readiness to learn. If necessary, ignore age boundaries, and provide pupils with tasks that will encourage them to work up to, and even beyond, their individual skill thresholds at any given time.

Throughout the resource, we have included supplementary information to help teachers extend their own knowledge and understanding of games.

Definitions of terms

You will meet the following expressions frequently throughout this text:

Families of games Groups of games which share a common structure; for example, the *net* family includes badminton, tennis and volleyball. The other families are *invasion*, *striking/fielding*, *target* and *wall* games. Target games are not included at this stage of the curriculum. Details of the families are given in the blue section.

Formal games Games played to an agreed set of rules prescribed by the teacher alone or in negotiation with the pupils.

Games-making Giving pupils opportunities to devise their own games so that they learn to understand how games are structured and the significance of rules.

NGB The National Governing Body responsible for a game; for example, the Lawn Tennis Association.

NGB mini-games Modified versions of *regulation games* designed for children but played to a code of rules laid down by the NGB.

Regulation games Adult games played to a code of rules laid down by the NGB or International Rules Board.

Technique This refers to a particular way of performing a skill specifically and 'correctly'. For example, *throwing* is a core skill, but a *chest pass* is a particular type of throw — that is, a *technique* chosen for its potential to meet the specific game demand of throwing quickly and accurately over a short distance.

You will find technique-improvement cards (more briefly called **skill cards**) which provide information on techniques and their performance criteria.

Through their lessons, pupils should acquire the **skills** to play games and the **insight** to play intelligently. In addition they need to be prepared **physically** to meet game demands. So these three components contribute to a balanced programme: skill + insight + physical preparedness.

Teachers should enable pupils to:

- know the purpose, rules and conventions of games
- play fair and exhibit good sporting behaviour
- display alertness, agility and athleticism
- respond quickly, accurately and efficiently
- assume responsibility for their own decisions
- sustain effort over significant periods of time

Decision-making

The pupils have to learn to make good decisions. They will be able to do so when they can:

- recognize problems posed by different games
- consider possible solutions to those problems
- test those solutions
- remember what happened
- know what to do next time a similar problem arises

Key Stage suitability

The material in the yellow section will be suitable for pupils at Key Stage 1, but *Teaching children to play Games* is aimed primarily at national curriculum requirements for Key Stage 2.

These requirements apply to games in the invasion, net/wall and striking/fielding categories. They specify that pupils should — individually, with a partner and in small groups —

- explore and be guided to an understanding of the common skills and principles, including attack and defence

- be helped to improve the skills of sending, receiving and travelling with a ball

- be given opportunities to develop their own games practices, working towards objectives decided sometimes by themselves and sometimes by the teacher

- make up, play and refine their own games within prescribed limits, considering and developing rules and scoring systems

- develop an understanding of games created by the teacher as well as small-sided and simplified versions of recognised games

Core skills

The yellow section familiarizes pupils with different types of equipment, and focuses on the core skills of capturing a ball, making a ball move under control, and sending a ball. Building on this foundation, the pupils learn that **games give skills their meaning**. The skills are the means by which pupils act out their decisions.

Games-making

Pupils need to understand the purpose of games, their similarities and their differences, if they are to use their skills intelligently. **Games-making** in the blue section has a special contribution to make in this area of understanding, as has the material on **formal games**.

Introducing mini-games

Many sport national governing bodies (NGBs) have devised simplified versions of their games, to make them easily playable by younger children. These mini-games are featured in the green section.

THE GAMES CURRICULUM SPIRAL

The games curriculum spiral illustrates how skills are first established and later adapted or refined to respond to more complex games, tighter rules, faster play and the need for individuals to adopt specialist roles.

PROGRAMMES OF STUDY

AGE	KEY STAGE			PROGRAMMES OF STUDY
16	4		**SPECIALIZATION IN GAMES AND ROLE**	Adapt advanced strategies and tactics to players' strengths and weaknesses; performance of and analysis of advanced techniques; understanding of rules/laws and fair play; use opportunities to practise cooperatively to refine techniques; play different positions in competitive games and experience full recognized versions of games.
14	3		**NGB REGULATION GAMES**	Extend skills and principles to develop techniques, strategies and tactics specific to each game played; observe etiquette and rules/laws of games; make up, play and refine own games; work from simplified towards full recognized game in a variety of invasion, net/wall and striking/fielding games; play varied roles including officiating.
11	2	GREEN	**NGB MINI-GAMES**	Explore and be guided to an understanding of common skills and principles, including attack and defence, in invasion, net/wall and striking/fielding games; improve skills of sending, receiving and travelling with a ball for these games; develop own games practices; make up, play and refine own games within prescribed limits, considering and developing rules and scoring systems; within the categories of invasion, net/wall and striking/fielding games, develop an understanding of and play games created by the teacher and simplified versions of recognized games.
7		BLUE	**FORMAL GAMES GAMES-MAKING**	
	1	YELLOW	**SKILL CHALLENGE GAMES**	Experience using a variety of games equipment; experience, practise and develop a variety of ways of sending, receiving and travelling with a ball; experience elements of games play that include chasing, dodging, avoiding, and awareness of space and of other players; make up and play games with simple rules and objectives that involve one person and a limited amount of equipment, extending to working with a partner when ready.
5			**FAMILIARIZATION**	

AGE KEY STAGE

NATIONAL CURRICULUM REQUIREMENTS

Before teaching a series of lessons, take time to define your **intentions** or **objects**. What exactly do you expect pupils to achieve* by the completion of a task, a lesson, or a block of lessons? Once you have decided, choose the material and teaching styles to enable pupils to realize those intentions.

* *i.e. to know, to understand, and to be able to do*

Monitor and **assess** the pupils' progress, and finally compare **outcomes** with **intentions** (objects).

Try to follow these guidelines:

Do

✓ Work outdoors whenever possible

✓ Teach boys and girls together

✓ Make games accessible to all pupils by being prepared to modify rules, provide user-friendly equipment, reduce the number of players in a game, adjust the playing area

✓ Explain the purpose of games to pupils

✓ Help pupils to understand their roles within a game

✓ Encourage honest competition and the idea of doing one's best

✓ Provide for lots of activity and maximum involvement

✓ Relate skill learning to the demands of the game

Do not

✗ Play adult regulation games during lessons

✗ Spend a disproportionate amount of lesson time in the training of techniques

Here are some extra guidelines to help you when your class includes children with special needs.

Do

✓ Provide 'kinder' equipment if appropriate, such as a slower-bounce ball

✓ Encourage other pupils to share, help and work with the special-needs children

✓ Take account of the particular disability when making performance demands

✓ Be sensitive to cultural influences

Do not

✗ Involve pupils in physical contact if it makes them vulnerable

✗ Let them suffer in miserable weather if their activity rate is low

✗ Include them in large groups unless they can be fully involved

✗ Involve them in too much technique-focused practice

✗ Make their problems public

Assessment should provide evidence of attainment or lack of attainment. It must monitor and support learning, not intrude to its detriment.

The information gained by assessment should provide enough feedback to enable teachers to identify learning targets for individuals and classes.

This resource will help you to develop an 'informed eye' as you observe and monitor your pupils' progress in learning to play games.

Assessment: practical points

• Know what you are assessing and set appropriate tasks. Then step back for a brief period during each lesson to observe and record.

• Use simple check methods. Experience shows that a straightforward code, such as using ✚ (above average), ✓ (average) and ✗ (below average) as performance indicators, is quite adequate. To these markers should be added brief comments to pinpoint strengths and weaknesses and to guide future planning.

• Be systematic in your observation, to ensure that all pupils receive equal attention.

• If you are uncertain of a pupil's proficiency or understanding, unobtrusively set a task to give you further information.

• Take account of the pupils' effort and involvement.

• You may be able to identify a weakness common to many of the pupils, such as difficulty in leaping to catch a large ball, or being unable to time the release of a pass; this should receive particular attention in subsequent lessons.

• Use your performance indicators (see above) to help you organize pupils into ability groups which are mixed or matched according to need.

• Day-to-day observation should supply most of the information needed to measure achievement, but selected tests may be used to clarify or confirm your assessments.

• Many classes will include pupils who are interested in NGB skill award schemes. The tasks for these qualifications may be complemented by the work undertaken during lessons, but it is best to conduct the formal testing outside lesson time. However, selected NGB tests may be used informally during lessons, to help with the observation of performance in specific skills.

You, the teacher, should set a good example by wearing appropriate clothing and footwear whenever you are involved in games classes.

Require all pupils to wear clothing which permits freedom of movement, is comfortable, is suitable for the conditions, and is appropriate for the activity.

Encourage pupils to change their clothing so they can put on something dry and warm when they come back indoors.

Discourage pupils from wearing jewellery or wristwatches — apart from the risk of loss or damage, these items can cause injury.

Footwear must provide good grip, and must be capable of absorbing impact on landing. If the foot is to be used for striking, the uppers of the shoes should provide adequate protection.

Team identification

Provide distinctive small bibs or braids to identify the players belonging to a team, or those who have to carry out a particular role in a game.

Balls

Provide different types of balls. They may vary in size, shape, weight, texture and rebound. It can be useful to adjust the rebound of inflatable balls by altering their pressure, so if you are using these, keep an inflator handy.

Quoits and bean bags may be used in throw/catch activities, but they are not essential.

Have enough of one type of large ball and one type of small ball so that the majority of pupils can work individually when required.

Sticks and bats

Think about the size of the implements your class will need, and provide enough for the pupils to have one each. Remember that lightness and ease of grip are important in the early stages of learning to manage an implement.

Bats or rackets need to have short handles and wide faces. Longer implements for hitting a ball along the ground, such as hockey sticks or cricket bats, should not be so long that they cannot be manipulated easily.

Other equipment

Many items can be used as targets and barriers. It is useful to have a supply of hoops, cones, skittles, wickets, ropes, canes, posts, nets and plastic chairs available.

When playing a sport-specific mini-game, try to provide the recommended equipment. However, if this is not possible, don't be afraid to improvise.

Provide suitable containers for the storage and carriage of equipment. Keep these light enough to manoeuvre, and see that they have handles which pupils can grip easily.

Store equipment adjacent to the working area whenever possible. Trolleys should be used to move equipment over longer distances.

Count the number of items you take to a lesson, and ask the pupils to help you account for them all at the end.

During the lesson, do not place all the equipment in one spot as this will cause crowding when it is distributed or returned. Instead, divide the class into, say, four colour-coded groups, each with its own supply of equipment in its own coloured basket.

From time to time check the equipment for damage and wear, to ensure that it remains safe to use.

Playing surfaces

Make sure that the playing areas provide a flat, non slip surface free of obstructions and holes. This is especially important for games of the hockey and cricket type, where a poor surface can cause the ball to rise up unexpectedly.

Ideally, playing fields should always be cut and rolled. Whenever possible, try to ensure that the grass cuttings are removed.

Temporary marking of playing areas may be done in a variety of ways — use plastic cones, tape, chalk, or cans of spray paint. Bean bags or even old bibs can be used, but whatever you choose, make sure that it cannot slide or cause injury if stepped on.

It is helpful to have some permanent markings to facilitate organization and task performance. The use of different colours enables markings for different purposes to overlap without causing confusion. Some examples of ground markings follow.

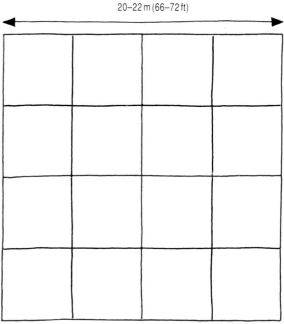

20–22 m (66–72 ft)

For games play this layout provides one large playing area, or two pitches side by side, or four grid squares (red). Further subdivisions (black) provide up to sixteen small work-stations for solo, pair or small-group tasks in skill development.

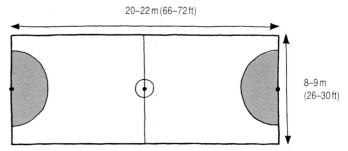

20–22 m (66–72 ft)

8–9 m (26–30 ft)

This is a suitable layout for games of the throw/catch, football or hockey types. The semi-circles may be used as no-entry zones or as areas to enter before shooting.

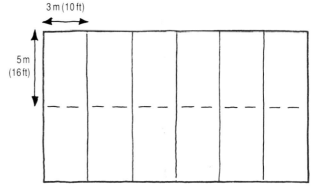

3 m (10 ft)

5 m (16 ft)

This layout is ideal for net games; you can use single lanes for 1v1 games, or double lanes (red) for 2v2 games.

Grids are particularly useful for invasion games, but if they are marked permanently on grass the area can become worn and muddy, thus creating a potential hazard in wet weather.

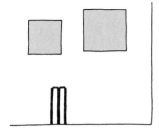 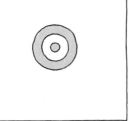 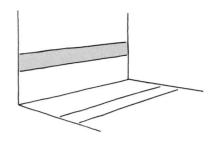

Targets may be marked on walls. Some examples are shown above.

If you are setting up temporary nets on posts, make sure that the posts are firmly weighted at the bottom and will not easily collapse if any load is put on the net.

Whenever there is any choice, and conditions permit, **work outdoors**. Most of the games described in this resource can be played on a variety of surfaces — playgrounds, courts, grass fields, artificial pitches or indoor areas.

Apparatus should be used inventively to provide barriers and targets, but do check that they are safe. You will find ideas about equipment under the various game headings.

We are aware of the diverse range of facilities and equipment in schools. Thus we have tried not to be prescriptive in our task-setting, but to offer sensible guidelines around which teachers can improvise and be selective.

ORGANIZATION AND SAFETY

Encourage pupils to become responsible for their own safety and that of others. Help them to **understand** what safety means when setting out their own equipment.

Insist that pupils respond quickly to instructions communicated by voice or whistle.

Instil care and anticipation in your pupils, especially when the class is using implements such as bats or sticks.

Eliminate foreseeable risks. For example, keep spare equipment well away from the working area.

Provide and maintain a clear working area which allows the pupils to move freely.

Don't put your pupils in situations where they are likely to run at speed into a wall. Make sure that there is sufficient space between the working area and any confining barriers — such as rails, walls and fences — to allow them to stop safely. Help

them to control their speed when close to obstacles and other people.

Organize the directional flow when pupils are repeating set tasks. Here are some examples:

"Go and return down the same track."

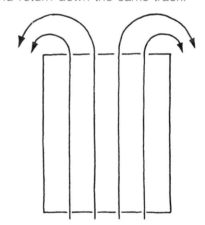

"Go and return around the outside."

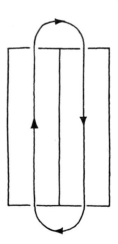

"Go and return down an adjacent track to form a circular route."

Be flexible in your task-setting, to maximize involvement and to individualize learning. Typical examples are:

1 The whole class works on the same activity at the same time.

2 Small groups of pupils work at different 'stations' doing different tasks, but all with the same theme.

3 The groups of pupils work at stations having contrasting activities.

Work-stations and circuits

A work-station is a space and/or set of equipment set out for the use of pupils in pairs or small groups. Several stations can be set out in the working area, and these may offer a range of activities or progressive tasks which the pupils perform in rotation. You may be used to calling such an arrangement a **circuit**.

Using stations flexibly

In examples 2 and 3 above, the tasks may be graded according to difficulty, and rather than rotating through all the stations, the pupils can be encouraged to choose a station which challenges their skill before moving on to another. When offering this choice, you may need to adjust the stations to accommodate fluctuating numbers, and must be prepared to increase the degree of difficulty as the pupils progress.

This type of flexible organization can be helped by siting a skill card at each station so that you will be freed to give attention to individuals.

How to cope with large numbers in restricted space

These are general guidelines, as circumstances vary considerably from school to school.

First, be certain that your class really does have to be in a relatively confined indoor space. Whenever possible, try to go outside and take advantage of a larger playing area. If it is not raining and the playing surface is safe, this is a much better option for active lessons. However, if you do have to stay indoors, or have access only to a small playground, here are some ways to make the best of it:

• You can divide a hall or gymnasium into a number of courts simply by suspending one long tape or rope, supported by intermediate posts where necessary, down the length of it. This becomes the 'net', and

individual courts are marked by tying coloured braids to it at suitable intervals. The net can be made more visible and realistic by draping bibs over it between the braids.

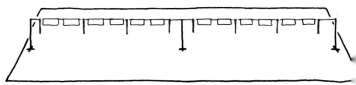

• When setting up several small courts, allow sufficent space for the players by offsetting the courts or providing a wide gap between adjacent end lines. The diagrams show some alternative layouts.

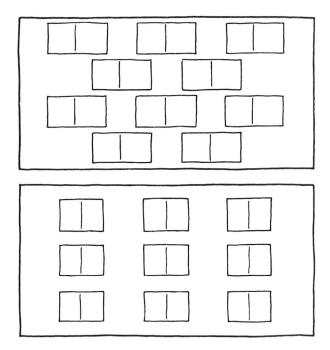

• When planning for invasion games, don't place goals back-to-back, or you will find that shots will go directly onto the next pitch or court.

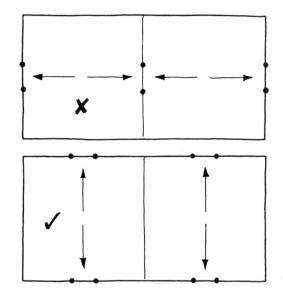

• If you simply cannot find enough space to allow every pupil to be active at the same time, then you may need to resort to rotating them fast between playing and waiting roles:

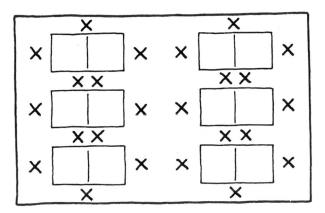

In net games, allot four children to each court; two pupils play, and they change with the waiting pair after, say, every three points or rallies.

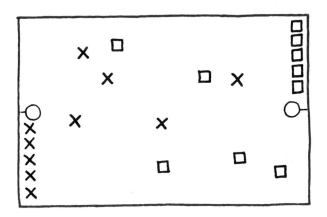

In invasion games, have one or two teams waiting at the side to switch with the participating teams each time a goal is scored or the ball goes out of play.

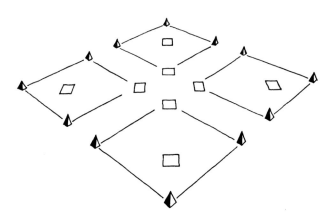

In striking/fielding games you can arrange several small games around a clear central zone, as shown in the diagram, so that the ball is hit outwards in each. This is especially safe if the ball is hit from a tee or self feed. If bowlers are involved, they must understand the need to be cooperative in not bowling so aggressively that the ball penetrates other games.

• When pupils are practising techniques, it is possible to halve the number of active pupils by working them in pairs, in which one uses a skill card to analyse and comment on his/her partner's performance before changing roles.

Always try to keep an acceptable balance between maximum involvement and safety.

Numbering system

The games and tasks are the core of this resource. Games are competitive: tasks are for practising skills. However, the distinction is not absolute — some tasks have a competitive element, and naturally skills are extended in playing the games.

For this reason all the games and tasks in the yellow and blue sections have been numbered in one continuous sequence to make them easy to find and to remember.

The numbering sequence does not continue into the green section; this contains the official NGB regulation mini-games, which are easily found under the game headings.

There are three ways to find a particular game or task:

• If you remember its number, look it up in the numerical list of games and tasks (see Contents page).

• If you know its name, you can use the alphabetical list.

• If you want to find a game or task that uses a particular skill, or that relates to a particular regulation game, look in the thematic index of games, tasks and skill cards.

An important aspect of safety lies in ensuring that the children are prepared both physically and mentally to meet the demands of the lesson.

Opening the lesson

• Set the scene for what is to follow, and focus the pupils' attention

• Be ready, so that you ensure purposeful activity right from the start

• Make sure that the pupils are ready physically to meet the demands of the lesson

Warm-up

Warm-up should be sufficient to build up the heart rate and increase the body temperature; its duration should reflect the intensity of the work to follow. In short lessons of 20–25 minutes' duration it would be exceptional for a warm-up to exceed 5 minutes. Warm-up activities must be organized quickly and easily with a minimum of explanation.

The following pattern is a useful one to follow:

1 Extend the pupils' natural activity level through running and then jumping.

2 Recapitulate an activity or a skill worked on in the previous lesson.

3 Offer tasks in which pupils work together.

4 Ensure that the tasks increase in vigour throughout the warm-up.

Warm-up dos and don'ts

✓ Do help your pupils to appreciate the changes occurring in their bodies as they exercise, e.g. feeling warmer, breathing harder, increased heart-rate.

✓ Make the warm-up enjoyable and relevant.

✓ Make it gradual.

✓ Monitor it carefully to ensure safe practice both in what pupils do and in how they do it.

✓ Encourage the children to assume more and more responsibility for aspects of their own preparation.

✗ Don't introduce serious competition during this preparation period.

✗ Avoid activities such as relays and tag games which require children to wait or to be eliminated — keep everyone involved all the time.

✗ Don't introduce high levels of challenge into warm-up activities.

✗ Don't allow too much freedom or unstructured activity.

Remember the three key words for warm-up: **purpose, activity, enjoyment**.

Gradually reduce the intensity of the exercise before pupils go to change. This **cool-down** stage is particularly important when they have to go back indoors after an outdoor lesson.

Familiarization

Equipment

You will need a range of balls of different sizes, shapes, weights, textures and rebound characteristics.

In the early stages, bats, sticks and other implements should not be too long or too heavy, and they should have relatively large striking surfaces.

Layout of the tasks

Usually the tasks are phrased as the teacher would say them to pupils. When you present them, don't rely on words alone — always **show** pupils what is expected of them too.

The notes in *italics* give guidance on lesson organization and teaching points.

Technical information on how to perform skills effectively can be found on the technique-improvement cards (skill cards).

This section introduces the following **core skills** which are central to games playing:

- travelling without a ball

- controlling a ball, leading to travelling with a ball

- sending and capturing a ball

Your pupils should be introduced to all these core skills, both through direct contact and by using implements such as sticks or bats. On completion of the tasks, they should **know** how different balls behave and should **be able** to control and exploit that behaviour. Throughout the sessions, individual practice should be interspersed with opportunities for pupils to exercise their developing skill with and against others.

Do provide opportunities for the children to devise their own tasks and to practise them, both working independently and in cooperative groups. You should always be available to advise, provide feedback and monitor safety.

TRAVELLING WITHOUT A BALL

Object: for pupils to develop the ability to start and stop under control, run quickly, change pace, change foot patterns and turn.

Task 1 Starting and stopping

Start with all pupils standing still.

"Get ready to run; run."

"Stop!"

Keep the children thinking about what they are doing. For example:

"Does it take you longer to start or to stop?"

"How can you start more quickly?"

"Show me three different ways of stopping." For example: turning sideways and braking with the lead leg; jumping into a stop; taking lots of little steps.

Task 2 Return dash

Start with all the pupils behind one of a pair of parallel lines, such as the side of a netball court.

"Run from this line and go straight to the far line. Touch the line and return."

Task 3 Fast and slow

"Run freely in the space. When I blow the whistle once, run as fast as you can; when I blow it twice, slow down again."

Task 4 Retrace your steps

"Run freely in the space. When I blow the whistle, turn round and go back on the same pathway."

Variation: As above, but modify the turning instructions, e.g. "turn to the left, then the right"; "make a quarter-turn" etc.

Task 5 Forwards, sideways and backwards

Start with a group of children facing you.

"Run towards where I point to, but keep your toes facing in their original direction."

CONTROLLING A BALL, LEADING TO TRAVELLING WITH A BALL

Object: In this series of tasks, the pupils learn to hold, move and travel with a ball, while keeping reasonable control.

The agility skills of dodging, swerving, jumping and leaping will become increasingly evident as pupils learn to respond to a moving ball.

CARRYING A BALL AROUND THE BODY

For these tasks, use a large ball at first and then move on to a smaller one.

Task 6 Rolling

"Try rolling a ball around your body. Can you find different pathways?"

Task 7 Round the waist

"Roll the ball around your body at waist level. Now make it go round the other way."

Task 8 Hands only

Repeat Tasks 6 and 7, "but now **pass** the ball using only your hands — don't let the ball touch your body."

Task 9 Timed circles

Repeat Task 8, but now "start with the ball in front of you and count how many full circles you can make in 10 seconds."

Task 10 Front and back

"Carry the ball up the front of your body, over your head or shoulder, down your back and through your legs to the front position."

Task 11 Back and front

"Can you now do this the other way, so that the ball goes up your back first and then down your front?"

Task 12 Figure-of-eight

"Stand with your feet wide apart. Pass the ball around your legs in a figure-of-eight path. Repeat as quickly as you can without dropping the ball."

BOUNCING A BALL ON THE GROUND

Make sure that your pupils try all the following tasks using both hands together as well as each hand separately. They will find this easiest with a large ball which bounces to a comfortable height. Later, let them try using a smaller ball and introduce a short-handled, light, large-faced bat.

Encourage the children to try to contact the ball before it reaches the top of the bounce — never to try to chase it when it is dropping down to the ground.

Task 13 Bouncing

"Bounce the ball on the ground continuously, keeping an even rhythm."

Task 14 Variable height

"Can you vary the height of the bounce?"

Task 15 Feet still

"Can you keep your feet still as you bounce the ball?"

Task 16 Around the body

"Can you bounce the ball right around your body?"

Task 17 Through the legs (1)

"Bounce the ball round your body and then through your legs. Can you bounce the ball through your legs from front to back?"

Task 18 Through the legs (2)

"... and from back to front?"

Task 19 Leg bounce

"Bounce the ball and lift one leg over it before it reaches the top of the bounce. Can you do it with either leg?"

Task 20 Travelling

"Can you travel as you bounce the ball?"

Remind the children to keep the ball out in front of them. If using a bat or racket the face needs to be angled in the direction of travel.

KEEPING A BALL OFF THE GROUND

These tasks should be done using any part of the body, or an implement (bat or racket).

Task 21 Keep it up

"Hit the ball repeatedly to keep it in the air. How long can you keep the ball moving without letting it hit the ground? Get a partner to time you, or count the number of times you hit the ball. If it hits the ground, restart from zero. What is your highest score?"

Let the pupils try **variations** of Task 21 by:

• using only hands

• using hands and arms

• using only feet

• using feet and legs

• using feet and hands in turn

• using the head (NB a soft, lightweight ball for this!)

Then use any combination of the following:

• open mesh rackets and bats of wood or plastic.

• sponge balls, table-tennis balls, tennis balls, airflow balls, shuttlecocks

Task 22 Keep it up (pairs)

Two players cooperate to keep a ball off the ground. Each player may be permitted only one contact at a time or be restricted to a certain number of contacts before the partner plays the ball.

Task 23 Balls and rackets

Where the expression 'racket' is used, it should be taken to include various types of bat or racket, both solid and strung.

"Balance the ball on the face of a racket. Try this in a variety of positions — sitting, kneeling, standing on one leg — and while changing position."

Task 24 Balance the ball

"Can you roll the ball around on the face of the racket without it falling off?"

Task 25 Balance and move

"Balance a ball on your racket and walk without it falling off ... then run without it falling off."

Task 26 Obstacle balance

Set up a variety of obstacles, such as benches, cones and markers.

Repeat Task 25, but change direction as you travel, and go over, along and around the obstacles.

Task 27 Transfer

"Hold the ball on your racket and let it roll off onto your partner's racket without letting it drop to the ground. How many times can you pass it back and forth without letting it drop and without using your free hand? Can you do this without letting your rackets touch?"

Challenge pupils to do the same tasks with different kinds of equipment; it is more challenging to balance a table-tennis ball on a small solid bat than a sponge ball on a strung racket.

BOUNCING ON A RACKET

Task 28 Bouncing

"Can you keep the ball bouncing for 20 seconds without it falling off? Can you keep the ball bouncing and vary the height of the bounce?"

Task 29 Different grips

"Can you bounce the ball holding the racket with the palm up? Now down? Now alternating, palm up, palm down?"

Task 30 Bounce and pass

"Can you bounce the ball on your racket and pass it to your partner's racket? Can you keep it bouncing four times before passing it?"

Task 31 Bounce tag

Mark out an area of play which will allow the children to move freely, but not to become too spread out. Divide the class into four teams, each identified by coloured bibs or braids. The pupils each have a racket and a ball. The object is for each child to 'tag' players in the other teams with a free hand, while keeping the ball bouncing on his or her racket.

Players who drop their ball or who are touched by the hand of an opponent must stand still and bounce their ball on the ground until a team-mate touches them and releases them back into play. The winning team is the one with most pupils in play when the teacher gives a signal.

Pupils who find it difficult to control the racket can hold it close to the racket head and use two hands if they wish. Large, light balls are easier for children to manage when first playing this game.

Task 32 Obstacle course

Set up lots of different obstacles for pupils to go along, over, around or through. They have to negotiate the obstacles while bouncing a ball or carrying one on their rackets. They have five lives, and forfeit one each time the ball is dropped.

Variation: Partners can time each other to see how long they can stay 'alive'.

You will be able to think of many types of obstacle. Here are some ideas for how the pupils can use them:

- Walk along a bench

- Jump from side to side of a bench while travelling its length

- Zig-zag along the bench by stepping up and down on alternate sides

- Kneel on a low box-top as you cross it

- Sit on a chair for six bounces

- Travel parallel to a wall, hitting the ball repeatedly against it and never allowing more than a single bounce

- Negotiate a course marked by cones

- Pass under ropes set at different heights

LEARNING TO JUDGE THE BOUNCE OF A BALL

Task 33 After the bounce

"Hold the ball on the racket; let it fall off the racket to bounce on the ground and then:

- catch it again on the racket

- or hit it forward

- or hit it up into the air."

Task 34 Bounce in the hoops

Lots of hoops are scattered on the ground.

"Travel among the hoops carrying a ball on your racket; drop the ball to bounce in a hoop and catch it again on the racket. Each time you do this successfully in a different hoop, you score a point. How many can you score in one minute?"

Task 35 Catching

"Toss the ball up from the face of the racket. Let it bounce on the ground as often as you like and then try to catch it on your racket. Can you catch it after only one bounce? Can you catch it before it bounces? Can you tap it up in the air again after the bounce?"

Task 36 Hit down

"Can you let the ball fall off the racket to bounce and then hit it down to the ground again?"

Task 37 Up-down-up

"Can you hit the ball into the air, let it bounce, then hit it down to the ground, let it bounce, hit it up again, and so on?"

23

Task 38 Pair catching

The children practise this in pairs:

"Let the ball drop off your racket and bounce on the ground for your partner to catch on his/her racket. S/he then drops the ball for you to catch after one bounce. How many times can you do this without ever letting the ball bounce more than once?"

Once your pupils have begun to master this task, move them a little further apart, ready for Task 39.

Task 39 Passing

"Can you pass the ball back and forth between you by hitting it after a single bounce?"

RUNNING WHILE CARRYING A LARGE BALL

Task 40 Touch down

"Run freely. When I blow the whistle touch your ball on the ground and go on running."

Task 41 Markers

This task needs a number of different-coloured markers spread throughout the playing area. Each pupil carries a ball.

"Run freely. How quickly can you touch a blue, green, red, yellow and white marker with the ball?"

Task 42 Finish line

Use the markers at different intervals to set out a course to a finish line.

"Run as quickly as you can from the start to touch your ball on the ground at the finish line."

Variation: Lay out parallel pathways and invite pupils to race against each other.

STEERING A BALL ALONG THE GROUND

Your pupils should try all these tasks using their feet and then using an implement such as a hockey stick. These two ways of propelling the ball make very different demands of the children.

Task 43 Pass to the right

"Travel along a line. If you meet someone coming towards you, go to the right to pass them, i.e. pass left-shoulder to left-shoulder."

Later, switch the task to passing to the left of the approaching player.

Task 44 Exchange

"Travel freely in the area. When you meet someone else, stop and exchange balls without either of you losing control."

The children can try different ways of travelling with the balls and use different types of ball if there are not enough of one type to go round.

Task 45 Tag

A task for pairs. Player **A** squats down with his/her back towards the start line. Player **B** shouts 'go' and crosses the start line to take a ball over the far line before s/he can be tagged by player **A**.

*Change over several times. Alter the difficulty of the task by requiring player **A** to start from a sitting position, or even lying down.*

Task 46 Moving the marker

Each pupil has a cone or similar marker which has to be placed a few metres from the start line. After a trial run, they have to judge where to place the marker.

"Travel from the line, go around the marker and return to the line as quickly as you can. You have eight seconds! Place your marker as far away from the line as you can manage and still get back to the start line before the eight seconds is up, and without losing control of the ball. Can you move it further away next time? What could you do to help you travel more quickly?"

Task 47 Gates

Place lots of gates throughout the area, each made up of pairs of markers set approximately 2 metres (6.5 ft) apart.

"How many gates can you steer your ball through in one minute? Keep moving; if someone else is blocking a gate you have chosen, go and find another one."

Task 48 Square

"Can you move your ball so that it 'draws' a square? Keep your feet facing in the same direction as you do so."

Task 49 Patterns

"Now try to draw other patterns in your working space — for example, a cross, a diagonal cross, your initials."

Task 50 Speed

In this task, the pupils discover more about the problems of keeping a ball under control at speed. Let them find out which method of travelling is quickest by challenging each other to races over a given distance.

"See how quickly you can travel with the ball."

This challenge can be tried using any method of travelling with the ball, for example:

* carrying the ball on the racket
* bouncing the ball on the racket
* bouncing it down using hand(s) or racket
* propelling it with the feet
* propelling it with an implement.

Provide different pathways, and encourage pupils to move quickly, change pace and change direction, always without losing control. Let pupils design their own pathways.

"It helps to keep the ball out in front of you when travelling in a straight line. What do you have to do to swerve or turn corners?"

SENDING AND CAPTURING A BALL

Object: for the pupils to develop the ability to send a ball to selected targets, using throwing and striking skills, and to capture a moving ball. Start by using a fairly small ball.

ROLLING A BALL ALONG THE GROUND

Task 51 Rolling and capturing

"Roll a ball towards a target marked on a wall. Collect the rebound. Have lots of turns and see how far away you can be and still hit the target."

"Now repeat the task, but see if you can collect the rebound without having to move from where you started."

Task 52 Roll and pick-up

This task needs a playing area with two parallel lines marked several metres apart.

"Travel across the area rolling the ball ahead of you. Run after it and pick it up; then roll it again. Now try to make three* pick-ups before you get to the other side."

* The number of pick-ups should be appropriate to the width of the area and the abilities of the children.

Task 53 Goal rolling

Set out two goals approximately 3 metres (10 ft) wide, facing each other and 8–10 metres (26–33 ft) apart.

"Can you roll the ball through your partner's goal? Score a point if you do. If you collect the ball rolled towards you cleanly, you also score a point. Who gets the highest score after six rolls each?"

Task 54 Roll and run

Work in pairs. Set up the task area as shown below. Each marker should be approximately 3–5 metres (10–16 ft) back from the line.

One pupil rolls the ball to cross the partner's line and then runs back around marker **A**. The receiver attempts to collect the rolling ball before it reaches his/her line and rolls it back before running around marker **B**.

"Can you roll the ball over your partner's line before s/he can recover to collect it?"

If the receiver misses the ball, the roller also scores a point.

SENDING THE BALL BY HITTING IT WITH A RACKET OR BAT

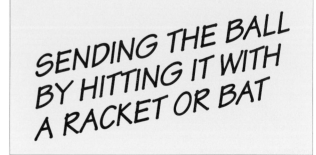

Use soft sponge balls when working in a free space.

Task 55 Hit and chase

"Hit your ball along the ground, chase it and hit it again. Repeat. Try to hit the ball into a clear space."

Task 56 Toss and catch

This task helps the pupils to learn to self-feed by using their hands to launch the ball.

"Can you toss the ball up gently with one hand, let it bounce, and catch it on the racket?"

"Can you catch the ball just after the top of the bounce? Can you catch it just before it hits the ground again?"

Task 57 Toss, bounce, hit

"Toss the ball up gently, let it bounce, and instead of catching the ball on the racket, try to hit it forwards."

If some of the children find that hitting after one bounce is too difficult, allow them to let it bounce more than once.

Task 58 Toss and hit

"Can you toss the ball in the air and hit it forwards before it bounces on the ground?"

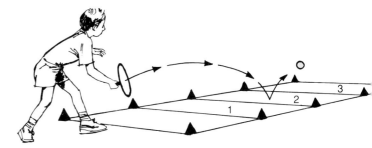

DEVELOPING ACCURACY IN SENDING

Task 59 Judging distance

Mark out a playing area as shown in the illustration.

"Can you hit the ball forward to pass between the cones?"

"Can you hit the ball and call the number of the area it will bounce in?"

After each attempt, the pupil should retrieve the ball and run back around the outside of the area to try again.

Make sure pupils attempt each of the three distances and that they keep the ball inside the markers.

Task 60 Above the head

Use sponge balls for this task.

"Can you hit the ball when it is above your head?"

Task 61 Toss and touch

"Toss the ball up and try to touch it with your racket before it drops below your head."

Task 4 Hoop

"Toss the ball up and hit it forwards and down into a hoop."

Task 5 Foot lift

"Trap the ball between the outside of your foot and the racket, and lift the ball with your foot and racket together. Then hit the ball upwards or forwards."

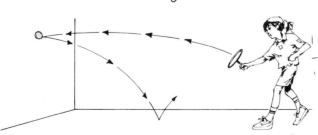

HITTING TO A WALL

Task 1 Bounce and catch

"Hit the ball against a wall; let it bounce as often as you like and then catch it again on your racket."

Task 2 Bounce rally

"Can you hit the ball against the wall, let it bounce once and then hit it back to the wall? Can you do this 10 times?"

It may help pupils with their timing if they say 'bounce' and 'hit' as the ball bounces and is struck. Also, encourage them to turn sideways-on as they hit the ball.

Task 3 High and low

"If you hit the ball high onto the wall, where does it bounce? If you hit it low, where does it bounce?"

Task 4 Back to base

"Can you hit the ball against the wall so that it bounces back to exactly where you are, ready for the next hit?"

Task 5 In the box

"Can you control the rebound so that the ball always lands in the box marked on the ground? Can you make the box smaller and still get the ball to bounce in there?"

Task 6 Two boxes

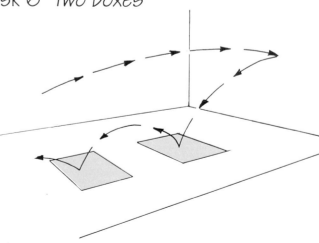

"Can you mark out a front box and a back box, and get the ball to bounce first in one and then in the other?"

Task 7 Line accuracy

Mark one horizontal line on the wall.

"Can you hit the ball above the line marked on the wall and then below the line?"

Now mark a second line parallel to the first.

"Can you hit the ball between the two lines marked on the wall? How many times can you do this in succession?"

Variation: *Provide lots of different targets, both on the ground and on the wall; make these of various sizes and shapes so that any pupil can choose a target which challenges his or her skill.*

Task 8 Forehand and backhand

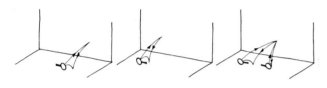

"Can you keep hitting the ball against the wall using just forehand shots? Now can you do it with backhand shots only?"

"Can you angle your hits to alternate between forehand and backhand?"

Learning to work in pairs is an important step towards playing racket games.

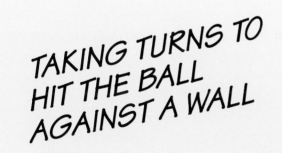

TAKING TURNS TO HIT THE BALL AGAINST A WALL

Task 1 Rally

Two pupils take turns to hit the ball against a wall, with just one bounce allowed each time, until the rally fails.

Providing a target on the wall will help the children to learn control. Also, encourage pupils to move out of the way to let their partner get to the ball.

ORGANIZING WORK-STATIONS

As the children develop a range of skills, you can set up and supervise a series of activities offering a variety of challenges. The best way to do this is by laying out work-stations, each with a different task, which pairs or small groups of pupils tackle in rotation.

● Have a card on display at each station, describing the task and explaining how to score.

● Give the pupils time to try out each activity first.

● Time each station for a suitable period — say, one minute.

● Let the pupils test themselves against the clock.

● Let them practise their skills, especially at the stations which have given them problems, before letting them re-test themselves against the clock.

● When there are large numbers of pupils, try to offer more than one working area at each station.

Here are some examples of suitable work-stations for racket activities:

Station 1 Volley over rope

Tie a rope between two chairs and drape a bib over it to form a 'net'. The pupils play in pairs.

"Send the ball over the rope from behind the line, using a volley. If the ball hits the ground or fails to go over the rope, or if your feet cross the line, you cannot count the hit. What is the best score of consecutive hits the pair of you can make in the time?"

Station 74 Single-bounce rally

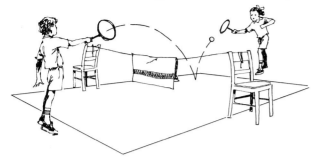

Tie a rope between two chairs and drape a bib over it as in Station 73.

"Play a single-bounce rally over the rope and count a hit if your ball bounces on the far side of the rope in the marked area. What is your best score of consecutive hits in the time?"

Station 75 Target and bounce

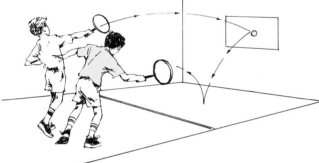

This task uses a wall with a target marked on it. Two pupils take turns to hit a ball against the wall alternately. It must hit the target and bounce within the marked area each time.

"Only count those hits which hit the target on the wall and then bounce in the marked area. How many did you score in the time?"

Station 76 Volley against wall

This is very similar to Station 75, but there is no target, and the children must volley the ball — if it bounces on the ground the hit does not count.

"Hit the ball against the wall alternately without letting it bounce on the ground. Keep your feet behind the line when you play the ball. What is the greatest number of times you can do this before the ball hits the ground or your feet cross the line?"

Station 77 Bench platform

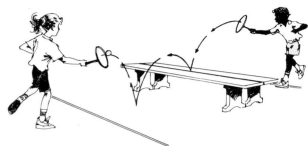

Set up a platform of benches between two parallel lines.

"Hit your ball from behind the line to bounce on the platform of benches. It can then bounce on the ground before your partner hits a return. What is your best score of consecutive hits in the time allowed?"

The previous set of tasks requires the pupils to cooperate with each other to achieve good scores. Emphasize that each pair is trying to better their previous score(s). Let pupils work with different partners. When it seems that the tasks may be getting too easy, think of ways of making them harder; for example, use one bench for a platform instead of two; reduce the size of wall targets; make the partners stand further apart. Always try to use your ingenuity to keep the tasks interesting and sufficiently challenging.

BOWLING AND PITCHING

Task 78 Wall targets

Use a wall with several different-sized targets on it.

"Can you toss the ball underarm to hit your chosen target?"

Encourage the children to attempt the more difficult targets and to move back further as their skill and accuracy develops.

Task 79 Ground target

Place a target on the ground with a series of lines different distances away; hoops may be used instead of lines.

"You have four tries to get your ball into the target. You may choose which line you start from; after each successful throw you move to a line or hoop which is further from the target."

Let the children have several attempts, always trying to improve on their previous performance.

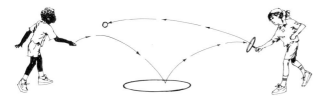

HITTING A BALL FED BY HAND

In all these examples of pairs exercises, make sure that each pupil has an equal opportunity to act as hitter and feeder.

Learning to feed well is important; good feeding provides a predictable ball for learners to hit in the early stages of trying to master a new technique.

Task 80 Bounce and return

"Use a gentle underarm throw to bounce the ball in a target area on the ground; your partner with the racket then hits the ball back to you."

Stress care and control.

Task 81 Hit to target

"Throw the ball underarm against the wall and let your partner hit it back to a target on the wall after one bounce."

Task 82 Feed and catch

"Gently toss the ball to your partner's racket so that s/he can play it back for you to catch before it bounces."

Variation: *Once your pupils are doing this fairly reliably, get them to repeat the task over barriers set at different heights.*

KICKING SKILLS

The children should use both left and right feet for these tasks. Any child will naturally prefer to use his or her dominant foot, but do encourage your pupils to kick with the other foot too. Also, let them try striking the ball with different parts of their feet.

Task 83 Goal gates

Use markers approximately 2 metres (6.5 ft) apart and scatter gates throughout the play area.

"Travel freely in the area and score a goal by sending your ball through a gate. Having scored through one gate, look for another gate and score again — you may not use the same gate twice. How far away can you be and still score?"

After a little practice, let the children see how many goals they can score in a given time — say, 20 seconds.

Task 84 Kick to wall

"Kick your ball against a wall, control the rebound and kick it back to the wall. Can you kick the ball back to the wall without controlling it first? How many times can you do this before the ball rebounds past you? Try working at different distances from the wall."

Task 85 Drop and kick

"Hold the ball in your hands, drop it and kick it into space. Can you kick it before it hits the ground (volley)? And just after it has hit the ground (half-volley)? Can you kick it to land in a target area?"

THROWING AND CATCHING

Throughout this section, secure catching with two hands should be emphasized, although pupils should also become adept at catching with either hand, as many games will demand that skill.

Unless the type of ball is specified all pupils should complete these tasks using both large and small balls.

Task 86 Throwing and catching

"Throw a ball up into the air and catch it."

This task can be made more difficult by introducing the following **variations:**

- send the ball further away
- catch with one hand instead of both
- catch with either hand
- catch balls of different sizes.

If pupils find the tasks too difficult, let them use soft, pliable balls or bean bags.

Task 87 Wall catch

"Can you throw a ball against a wall, let it bounce and then catch it? Now can you do it without letting it bounce?"

Be sure to try this task with a small ball.

Task 88 Clap and catch

"Throw your ball up into the air and clap your hands before catching it. How many times can you clap your hands and still catch the ball?"

Variations: Let the pupils do other actions before catching the ball. For example: sit down and stand up again; turn a full circle. Let the children devise other actions of their own.

Allow the ball to bounce once before it is caught.

Task 89 Widen the gap

"Throw the ball back and forth with a partner. Each time you catch it successfully, take a step back. If you drop the ball, take a step forward instead. How far apart can you get without dropping the ball?"

Task 90 Name catch

This needs groups of four children: one throws the ball into the air and calls the name of another of the group who must try to catch it before it touches the ground.

Task 91 Target catch

"Throw the ball up and away from you into an open space, run after it and catch it before it bounces. Now throw it so that when you catch it again you are in a marked area."

Task 92 Clock catch

Use four (or twelve) markers to indicate a clock face on the ground. The pupil stands in the middle, with a ball, facing '12 o'clock'.

"Throw the ball towards (say) three o'clock and catch it before it bounces."

You can let the children choose their own 'times' to begin with, and later call the time they are to attempt. Can they all manage six o'clock? As their skills improve, let them increase the size of the clock face.

Task 93 *Over your head*

"Can you make the ball go over your head by throwing it with one hand and catching it in the other? Can you do this in both directions?"

Task 94 *High bounce*

"Throw the ball down hard on the ground so that it bounces high, and leap to catch the rebound."

Task 95 *Chest pass*

This task (for pairs) requires a fairly large ball which is not too heavy.

"Stand 5 metres (16.5 ft) apart. Starting with the ball held with both hands at chest height, send flat passes between you five times. When you can do this without dropping the ball, each take a step back and repeat the passes. Continue doing this and see how far apart you can go and still send good flat passes."

Task 96 *Target bounce*

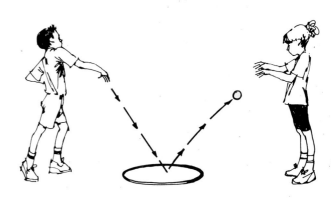

"Place a target on the ground between you — a hoop would be fine — and throw the ball to your partner by bouncing it inside the target. How far away can you move and still bounce the ball inside the target?"

Task 97 *Catch the rebound*

Two pupils stand behind a line 5 metres (16.5 ft) from a wall.

"Throw the ball against the wall so that your partner can catch the rebound before it hits the ground and without having to cross the line. Take turns at throwing and catching. How many times can the pair of you do this without dropping the ball or crossing the line?"

Variation: *Develop this task by requiring pupils to throw into both high and low target areas on the wall. This will give them practice at catching at all levels.*

Task 98 Rebound distance

"Throw a small ball at a wall and see how far it bounces away from the wall. Can you throw harder and increase that distance?"

Show the pupils that they will get the best results if they stand sideways-on to the wall when they throw. Encourage them to take the throwing arm well back as they start the action.

Task 99 Clock catch

 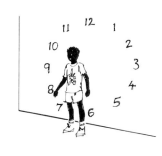

This task requires a clock face drawn on a wall. One pupil stands just in front of this, 'guarding' it. A partner throws the ball to each hour, starting at one o'clock and finishing at 12 o'clock, and the guard has to try to catch it each time.

Make sure that the children change roles frequently enough to give equal amounts of throwing and guarding.

After a while you can introduce **variations**:

- "Throw to any hour you like."

- "Guard, try to make all your catches without moving your feet."

This helps pupils to master catching at different heights and on both sides of the body. Encourage them to get to the ball quickly and to catch at full stretch.

Task 100 Passing on the run

This is a pairs activity. You can develop many variations of this basic passing task, according to the type of goals used and the size of the playing area. The pupils score points by throwing the ball into the goal.

"Travel with a partner across the playing area, passing the ball between you as you go. You must both touch the ball at least twice before either of you can score. Move onto the return route and repeat. Continue this circuit for a given period of time and keep a tally of your score. Keep trying, and think of ways of improving your scores."

Provide different types of goals or targets: some high, some low, some large, some small. Invite pupils to choose and place their own targets.

Remind each pair to change sides on each circuit so that they learn to throw and catch on both sides of their bodies.

As the pupils' skill increases, introduce them to the idea of costs and benefits. For example, should they risk shooting from a distance to cut the travelling time, or get close and be sure to score? Will lots of short, fast, flat passes be better than a few long, looping ones? They will also learn to pass the ball to a point just ahead of a partner, so that the forward movement is continuous.

Variations: Different conditions may be imposed on the passing. Here are some suggestions:

"Go as fast as you can, but:

- Don't let the ball hit the ground

- Bounce the pass to each other

- No more than two steps before passing

- Catch the pass and bounce the ball on the ground once before returning it

- Instead of catching the ball immediately, let it rebound off your hand(s) and then the ground before you catch and return it

- Don't make a forward pass; only pass the ball when you are ahead of your partner. You are allowed to run forwards for up to five strides before passing, and the final shot at the target can be forwards

- You must put the ball on the ground immediately you receive it, and then throw it from the ground back to your partner

- Touch the ball only with your feet; or only with an implement, such as a hockey stick for passes along the ground, or a racket for passing the ball through the air."

Let pupils challenge each other by thinking up their own conditions.

JUDGING THE FLIGHT OF A BALL THROUGH THE AIR

Several of the previous tasks require pupils to estimate how far and how fast a ball is travelling and so to make their movement coincide with that of the ball. The following tasks focus on this important skill.

Task 101 Long or short?

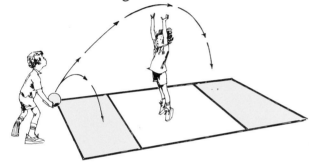

This needs two target areas, and a line marked on the ground.

One pupil, **A**, stands between the targets, and **B** tries to throw a ball into either of them from behind the line. **A** must try to catch the ball before it can land. **A** cannot move until the ball is released, and must try to anticipate whether it will be sent long or short.

You can operate a scoring method in which **B** scores a point for each ball which lands in the target and **A** scores a point for each ball caught.

Task 102 Dash to catch

This task needs two markers on a line parallel to a wall. **A** stands by one of the markers and **B** throws the ball against the wall from a position between the markers. **A** then has to dash to catch the rebound. **A** should start from alternate markers. Five tries, and then change roles.

The thrower must wait until the catcher is standing by a marker before throwing to the wall.

COLLECTING A MOVING BALL

Task 103 Rolling and chasing

The children roll a ball away and have to chase and recapture it before it stops. After a few attempts in unmarked space, let them try to send the ball into a marked area and recapture it there.

Let the children perform this task by rolling the ball by hand, kicking it and by hitting it with an implement such as a hockey stick. *They will soon learn to estimate how hard to send the ball to cover the required distance.*

FINDING OUT ABOUT SPIN

Task 104 Free practice

Encourage pupils to experiment with applying spin to the ball by turning it with their hands as they throw it. They should try rotating it towards their bodies as well as away from them.

Ask the children to observe how the spin affects a bounce. See if they can predict which way the ball will bounce when different spins are applied.

Task 105 Backspin

"Send the ball away from you, but with it spinning towards your body. Can you make it roll back towards you without touching it again?"

You will have to choose a size and type of ball which will give good results on the surface the pupils are using.

35

SENDING A BALL ALONG THE GROUND TO A TARGET

*All these introductory familiarization tasks will have begun to **develop individual competence** in your pupils. As their skills of control and consistency increase, you can introduce suitable games from the next section to test and challenge their developing abilities.*

These tasks may be performed by rolling the ball, kicking it, or propelling it with an implement. Let your pupils experience as many methods as possible.

Both tasks are for pupils working in pairs.

Task 106 Narrow gate

Use two markers to make a gate approximately 2 metres (6.5 ft) wide.

"Send the ball through the gate to your partner; gradually move further apart and see if you can still direct the ball accurately."

"Now stand a fixed distance apart (about 8–10 metres; 26–33 ft) and move the markers closer together after every 10 hits. How narrow can you make the gate and still get the ball cleanly through it every time?"

Task 107 Angled gate

Use the same gate as that in Task 106.

"Move around your gate after you send the ball each time. Try going anti-clockwise and then clockwise. See how the angle at which the ball goes through the gate changes as you circle it. Can you send the ball through the gate from a really tight angle?"

Skill Challenge Games

Skill challenge games shift the focus from **learning** skills to **using** skills in order to meet game demands.

This section provides examples of games under the following headings:

- avoiding and chasing games
- target games
- rebound games

Variations are given where different skills may be used in the same game structure.

AVOIDING AND CHASING GAMES ('TAG' GAMES)

In this group of games 'catchers' or 'taggers' try to touch other players for a variety of reasons:

- to remove them from the game (elimination games)

- to prevent them from crossing or entering a piece of territory (territory-defence games)

- to prevent them from acquiring 'trophies' (trophy-gaining games)

The skills most in evidence are running, dodging, swerving and travelling with a ball, as well as the positional skills of anticipating where to be and when to go there.

The size of the area used for games in this category should be appropriate for the number, needs and abilities of the pupils. Make sure that everyone gets a turn at being a catcher or tagger.

Tag games contribute to the development of agility and athleticism. They are physically demanding, requiring sustained effort, rapid acceleration and deceleration, and changes of direction. Often, you will also be able to select games from this group which incorporate ball handling and control skills.

Your pupils will find tag games exciting and exhilarating. Do ensure that they thoroughly understand the rules before they start, and build in the expectation that they will always own up to being tagged. This is a useful early introduction to honest competition.

ELIMINATION GAMES

Pure elimination games should be avoided: always aim to keep everyone involved. Here are some games which remove players from the game but enable them to be reinstated by their own teammates or to rejoin the game having completed a separate task.

Game 108 Ball tag

This game requires a main play area and a separate side space where several individual challenges can be set up as forfeits.

One-third of the class are taggers, and each has to carry a ball and keep hold of it throughout the game. The remaining two-thirds spread out in the main area and run and dodge to avoid being tagged. Players who are touched by a tagger's ball have to leave the main area to do a forfeit, such as bouncing a ball 20 times in a hoop, or dribbling a ball back and forth six times between two lines. Having completed the forfeit the pupil returns to the game.

"How many players can the taggers remove from the game at any one time?"

"How many of you can avoid being tagged?"

Game 109 Bounce tag

This game can be played on a marked area of almost any shape.

A quarter of the class wear bibs or braids to identify them as catchers, and spread out in the area. The remaining pupils each have a large ball which they have to bounce-dribble continuously. All the players have to stay within the area. If a catcher touches a bouncing ball, the owner of the ball has to stop immediately and keep the ball in his or her hand(s). These players must stay put for the rest of the play period, but they also become a form of catcher; they must keep one foot still but are allowed to pivot to touch the ball of any passing dribbling player.

"Who can survive for the longest time?"

Game 110 Gate tag

This game can be played on a marked area of almost any shape.

Pupils are divided into two clearly identified teams. Each player has a large ball, and the object of the game is for each player to tag members of the other team while propelling his/her own ball along the ground with the feet. Both teams travel freely in the area. Players who are tagged by a member of the opposing team have to pick up their ball and stand with their feet wide apart to form a 'gate'. They are released back into play when a teammate sends a ball through their gate.

The teacher blows a whistle from time to time: everyone stops briefly, and the team with fewest tagged players at that time scores a point.

Variation: If a player's ball goes out of the marked area s/he has to pick it up, move back into the area and form a gate, just as if s/he had been tagged. *This encourages players to keep control of the ball as they travel and change direction.*

TERRITORY-DEFENCE GAMES

In this set of games, catchers try to prevent other players from crossing or entering a piece of territory.

Game 111 Cross the gap

This game requires a marked rectangular play area, with a central 'gap zone' about 10–12 metres (33–40 ft) wide. The ends of the rectangle form 'start' and 'finish' lines.

Play starts with two or three catchers waiting in the gap, where they must stay. The rest of the class have to try to get from start to finish, crossing the gap on the way, without getting caught (touched by a catcher).

Those players who get to the finish immediately run round the outside of the play area and return to the start line to try again. Players who are caught join the catchers in the central zone.

"How many times can you cross without being caught?"

"Who survives the longest?"

Variation: Players crossing the central zone have to carry a soccer or rugby ball, and to catch them a catcher has to touch their hips with both hands simultaneously.

Game 112 Touching opposite lines

The playing area is a marked square or rectangle.

One-third of the class are identified as catchers. The remaining two-thirds each carry a large ball.

Play starts with all the class spread out throughout the area. The ball-carriers each try to score a point by touching their ball on any boundary line and then crossing the area to touch it on the line directly opposite. A point can only be scored when both lines have been touched and the player has not been tagged by a catcher on the way. The players can dodge and weave as much as they like to avoid being caught.

"How many points can each player score in a given time?"

TROPHY-GAINING GAMES

Game 113 Tails

This game can be played on a defined area of almost any shape. The duration is fixed beforehand.

Each pupil tucks a braid into the back of his/her waistband. They all travel freely in the area, trying to grab as many braids as possible. Captured braids must immediately be tucked into the back of the captor's waistband.

"Who can collect and keep the most braids before the whistle blows?"

Game 114 Take it home

This game is played on a marked square or rectangular area. You need four mats, one at each corner, to serve as 'home bases' and four hoops placed together in the centre, as 'stores'. Several balls are placed in each store. These should be of a variety of types, but each store should contain the same selection, e.g. a tennis ball, a soccer ball, a rugby ball and so on...

Divide the class into five equal teams. Four of the teams each have a home-base mat and a store, while the fifth is the 'tagging team', and free to roam the whole area at will.

Start the game with a whistle; as soon as it blows, all the players in the home-base teams rush to their stores in the centre and each attempts to take a ball back to base without being tagged.

A player who is tagged must hold his/her ball up high in the air and quickly return it to the team's store before going 'home' to start again.

"Which team can capture the most balls?"

Variations:

• Players can work together to carry the ball home, so that if the carrier is about to be tagged s/he can pass the ball to a team-mate.

• As well as simply carrying the balls, you can tell the children to bounce them home, dribble them with hands or feet, or propel them with an implement.

• You can attach a particular skill to each kind of ball, such as always having to bounce a basketball or dribble a football.

TARGET GAMES

In this group of games the pupils try to send objects to both stationary and moving targets.

Target games develop the skills of aiming, estimating distance and power, throwing, kicking and hitting accurately.

Game 115 Skittle fall

This needs a bench sited between two parallel lines, and a selection of target objects such as plastic cones, empty plastic bottles or even empty cereal packets.

Place three or four targets on the bench. Two pairs of children are each given a ball and take up positions behind the lines on opposite sides of the bench. Using just the two balls, the four players try to knock the targets off the bench as fast as possible. The two players on each side take turns to throw.

The children soon find that retrieving the ball quickly is almost as important as throwing accurately.

Game 116 Scoring goals

This is similar to Game 115, but the bench is replaced by cones marking out 5 'goals' carrying scores of 1 in the centre, 2 adjacent to the centre and 3 for each outside goal.

Two pairs of players kick the two balls from behind the lines to score as many points as possible within a given time. If a cone is knocked over, a player must run in and place it upright before another score can count.

Players take a risk when aiming to score 3, because if they miss to the outside they will score 0.

"Total your team score and try to beat it."

"Compare your team score with the other team's."

Variation: Use smaller balls, and strike them with implements instead of kicking them.

Game 117 Touch ball

This game needs a rectangular marked area and a supply of balls. These can be of any size, but **must** be soft.

Divide the class into three teams, **A**, **B**, and **C**. Each member of **A** and **B** has a sponge ball, and these teams spread out one along each side of the area, while **C** groups at one end, the start line.

The object is for the players in team **C** to run through the area from the start line to the safety line (the other end) while the other teams throw their balls to try to hit the runners below waist height. Each safe crossing earns a point. Runners may go as often as they like, but they must return to the start line by going around the outside of the area. Balls that remain in the marked area may be retrieved by the throwers, who must not interfere with the runners when they do this.

"Add up your team score."

The following games are for small groups of players. To involve the whole class, set up several stations for the same game, or — if this is not possible — set up stations offering different but related games (see pages 14–15 and 29).

Game 118 Protect the target

This game needs two targets marked on a wall, approximately 4 metres (13 ft) apart. Two lines run parallel to the wall at distances of about 2 metres and 6 metres (6.5 and 20 ft). *The distances are not critical — you may need to adjust them according to the skills of the players.*

The pupils play in pairs.

One player attempts to hit either of the targets by throwing a sponge ball from the 6-metre line. The other, with a racket, tries to stop this by blocking the targets from just in front of the 2-metre line. Change over after 10 tries.

"How many times did you hit a target?"

Variation: Mark a square on the ground between the two lines. If the defender can bounce the blocked ball into this area, s/he scores a point. A slightly harder ball may be used when playing this variation.

"Add your defending and attacking scores to reach your game score."

If the throws become too aggressive, limit throwers to underarm only.

Game 119 *Protect the legs (French cricket)*

This game **must** be played with a soft ball which will not hurt the legs. Also, the bowler may never bowl from within 3 metres (10 ft) of the batter.

At its most simple, this game is played in pairs: one child stands with his or her legs close together and protects them with a bat. The other rolls a ball along the ground to try to hit the batter's legs. The first ball is bowled from directly in front of the batter; after that it must be bowled from wherever it ends up.

At no time is the batter allowed to move his or her feet. Consequently, s/he must twist around to keep the bat facing the bowler.

The players change roles when the batter's legs are hit, when the ball is caught directly from the bat, or when six balls have been bowled.

Variation: Double up the number of players. Any of the three fielders may bowl, and they are also allowed to pass the ball between them to make it harder for the batter to follow.

REBOUND GAMES

This is a group of games in which the pupils have to react to a ball bouncing off the ground or a wall.

These games develop the skills of throwing, catching, hitting, kicking, judging ball flight, and making their movements coincide with those of the ball.

Rebound games continue to focus on the developing skills of individuals, though scores may be combined to contribute to a team effort.

Game 120 Keep it in court

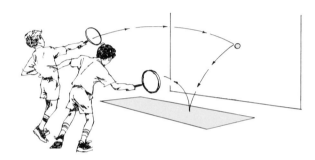

This pairs game requires a wall with a target area, approximately 4 metres wide and 1 metre deep (13 x 3 ft), marked on the ground a suitable distance in front of it. Each player has a bat; one of them starts by serving the ball to hit the wall and land in the target area, whereupon the other player hits it to the wall, and so on, alternately. A player scores a point when his/her partner fails to play the ball off the wall to land in the target area.

"Who is the first to score 5 points?" Start a new game at this stage.

Variations:

• Mark a target area on the wall, as well as, or instead of, on the ground.

• Dispense with the rackets and play the game as 'throw/catch' instead of 'hit'.

• Select and position the target areas on the ground to make the game either easier or more challenging. The targets may be sited closer to or further from the wall, and may be shaped differently, e.g. diamonds, squares, circles or triangles.

Game 121 Bounce score

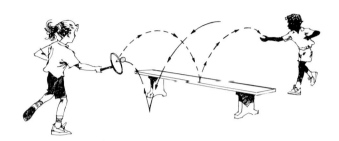

This is a cooperative game for pairs of players. The equipment required is a bench, a racket and a ball.

Player **A** tosses the ball to player **B** on the far side of the bench. Player **B** lets the ball bounce once and then hits it to land on top of the bench. If s/he succeeds a point is scored, and if **A** catches the rebound off the bench a further point is scored.

"Have ten tries and combine your scores, then change roles."

"Compare your best total with the scores of another pair. Try again and see if you can better your score." *This encourages pupils to cooperate in order to compete.*

Variations:

• Require **B** to hit the ball before it bounces.

• If necessary, you can make the task easier by placing two benches side by side, or by permitting up to three controlling bounces with the racket before the ball is returned to the bench.

Game 122 High ball catch

To start, player **A** stands touching the wall. Player **B** faces the wall, a couple of metres back from it, and throws the ball to bounce first on the ground and then against the wall. **A** must try to catch the ball after it rebounds from the wall, but is not allowed to move until that first bounce on the ground. Each catch scores a point.

"Take six turns and change over. Who can make most catches?"

Variations:

• If a player catches every rebound, make him/her adopt a starting position which will delay movement to the ball; for example: "sit with your back to the wall", or, "stand facing the wall until you hear the ball hit the ground".

• Try a large ball and a small ball, a slow-bounce ball and a fast-bounce ball.

• If no wall is available, you can get the pupils to bounce the ball against a bench placed on its side.

Game 123 Angle ball

This is a relay game for pairs of players.

Mark a goal 2 metres (6.5 ft) wide at the foot of a wall. Set two markers, **X** and **Y**, about 8–10 metres (26–33 ft) from the goal and 12 metres (40 ft) apart.

Starting at **X**, player **A** dribbles the ball a short distance and takes a kick at the goal. S/he then traps the rebound and carries on to dribble it around marker **Y**, and takes another kick at the goal on the way back to **X**. **A** then passes the ball to player **B**, who repeats the whole process.

"How many journeys can the pair of you make before you miss the goal or fail to collect the rebound while you are still between the markers?"

Variations:

• Play the game using hockey sticks or similar, and a small ball.

• Mark a target area higher on the wall and use a throw/catch combination.

• Make the task harder by reducing the size of the target, and/or requiring the attempt at the target to be made while the player is outside the markers rather than between them.

Where games encourage it, some pupils will begin devising their own strategies to help them succeed, such as finding the best way of keeping away from a catcher. As soon as they are ready, pupils should increasingly play games which require them to solve problems both individually and collectively.

Here is an example of a simple problem-solving game:

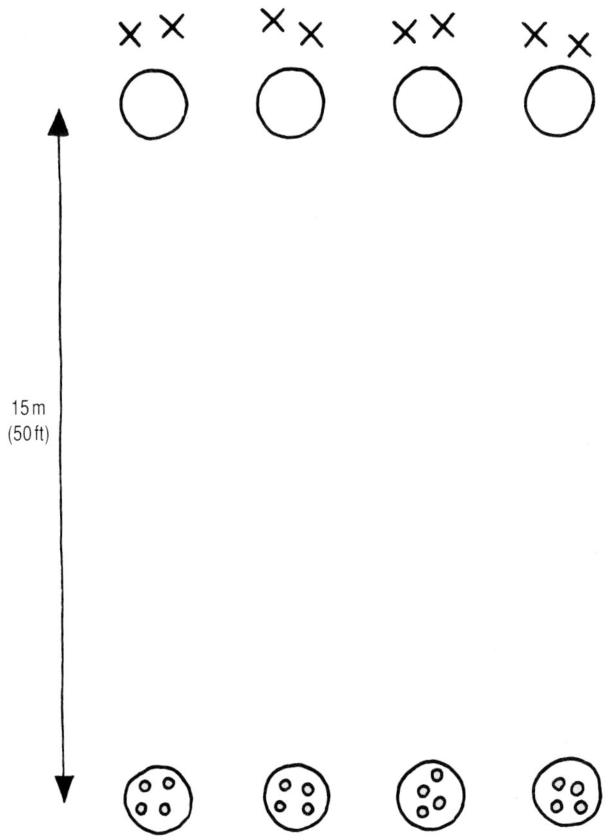

Game 124 Fill the hoop

This game requires as many hoops as there are children, and twice as many balls (or bean bags). The class is separated into teams of two.

The hoops are laid out a metre (3 ft) or so apart, in two rows, with about 15 metres (50 ft) between the rows, as shown in the diagram below left. Each of the hoops in the far line contains four balls. At the start of the game, a pair of children stands by each of the empty hoops. Their problem is to transfer all the balls from the far hoop to their empty hoop and then back again as quickly as possible. The only specific rule is that a player is allowed to touch only one ball at any time.

Will the children run in pairs and carry the balls? Will the pairs split and throw the balls between them? Will some choose to roll the balls to each other?

"All start at the same time when I give the signal, and put your hands up when you have completed the task."

After the first attempts, allow the pupils some practice time to test their new ideas before repeating the competition.

Variations:

The problem can be altered by changing the conditions; for example:

• No throwing

• Both players must touch each of the four balls on the journey out and on the journey back

• A team may move only one ball at a time

Skill variations may be introduced in many ways. For example, by requiring that small balls be transferred using rackets or striking implements, or large balls by using hands for the journey out and feet for the journey back.

15 m
(50 ft)

MOVING ON

This yellow section has introduced your pupils to the core skills needed for games playing, and helped them to appreciate the importance of agility and athleticism. They have also met the concept of simple game strategy. The blue section (pages 61–172) moves on to more formalized games in which pupils learn to adapt and use their developing skills to win competitions, both individually and as members of teams.

LESSON PLAN 1

Intention: by the end of this lesson pupils should be able to travel with pace and change of direction while bouncing a large ball, and should be able to throw an accurate flat-chest pass a greater distance than before.

Pre-lesson organization: have large balls ready to give out as the pupils enter the playing area; place markers (enough for one between two) in a basket to take into the area; put large hoops together (enough for one between two). Take two empty baskets out to receive spare balls during the lesson.

Organization for Task 1: give each pupil a large ball as s/he enters the working area; if the balls are too few for one each, work pupils in pairs taking turns.

Task (What pupils do)	Observations (What to look for)	Points to remember
Warm-up and revision "Run around the area bouncing your ball as you go. Now stop and bounce your ball on the spot, keeping the bounce at the same height. Now vary the height. Travel again."	Does the hand **push** the ball rather than **slap** it? Are they remembering to look up and avoid other players?	Let pupils use their dominant hand or even two hands if contact is poor.

Bridging organization: join up in pairs; one pupil puts his/her ball away in a basket while the other puts his/her ball down, collects a marker and stands on an outside line facing into the area; the pupil with the marker takes 12 paces from the line, puts the marker down, collects the ball, and then returns to the line; the second player runs to stand behind his/her partner. Make sure all the players are spread out along the line.

New work Player **A** (the front pupil of each pair) runs from the line bouncing the ball, turns around the marker, and runs back to the line to hand the ball to player **B**, who repeats the process. **Progressions:** "Go round the marker so that the hand bouncing the ball is nearest the marker. Now go round with the bouncing hand on the outside. Which is quickest?"	Do they push the ball out in front when travelling straight? Can they anticipate closing in on the marker and keep close to it when they go round? Do they realize which way is best to go round the marker, depending on whether the bouncing hand is nearer to the marker or further from it?	It does not matter that the markers may be different distances from the line.

Bridging organization: put the markers to the side; divide the class into three groups of pairs; ask one group to put their balls to the side, to put on braids, and to spread out in the area.

Revision Game 109 Bounce tag (page 38).	Do pupils switch the ball to the hand furthest from a threatening player to keep it away from him/her?	Change the group in braids twice to let each pupil act as a catcher. Time 3 equal periods.
Task 95 Chest pass (page 33).	Are they stepping into the throw as the arms extend? Do the arms and fingers extend to add power to the ball?	Make sure the pupils cannot step back into each other.

Bridging organization: get them to remove the braids and return to their pairs along a line with markers placed 12 paces out as before. They then put a hoop on the line opposite each marker.

New work Player **A** bounce-travels with the ball to go around the marker, and makes a chest pass to player **B** who is standing in the hoop. Player **B** catches the ball and bounce-travels out to repeat, passing to **A** who now stands in the hoop. How many journeys can the ball complete in one minute? If the ball is not caught in the hoop, that journey does not count.	Can the bounce-travel be quick, and yet the turn be close to the marker? Is the throw strong and accurate for direction?	Help the pupils to realize that the ball can travel quicker when thrown than when a player is travelling with it. Thus it should be quickest to throw as soon as they have gone around the marker.

Closing organization: each child is to collect a piece of equipment and put it to the side.

Cool-down

"Jog gently in the area; now walk; now stand in a space with your feet apart, raise your hands above your head and circle them forwards (slowly), now backwards. Walk to collect your piece of equipment and go to place it by the store room."

LESSON PLAN 2

Familiarization and skill challenge

Intention: by the end of this lesson pupils should be able to throw with increased power and catch a high ball safely, and should be better at judging the flight of a ball they have thrown.

Pre-lesson organization: distribute enough small balls for one per pupil between three baskets.

Organization for Task 1: on arrival in the working area each pupil takes a ball from a basket.

Task (What pupils do)	Observations (What to look for)	Points to remember
Warm-up "Hold your ball in one hand and jog in the area, changing direction as you go. Now bounce the ball on the ground and catch it as you travel. Now throw it above your head and catch it. Can you throw it up and catch it without having to stop or run faster to make the catch?"	Do pupils look up to avoid others? When throwing the ball up, how many can match their throw to coincide with their movement? Help them to throw the ball ahead and to move forward to catch it.	**Enabling idea:** have bean bags and slightly larger balls available.

Bridging organization: divide the class into three fairly equal groups. Send group 1 to a wall, group 2 into a clear space and group 3 to an area with two lines with a 5–10 metre (16–33 ft) gap between them. Provide a card at each station to set the task, or let the pupils play freely at their station while you visit each in turn to set the task.

Revision **Station at the wall:** task 97 Catch the rebound (page 33). After a few practice turns at throwing, insist that the rebound is caught.	Do the pupils get sideways-on and take the hand well back as they prepare to throw? Does the elbow come away from the body as they throw? Does the hand follow through after the ball?	If pupils throw underarm, ask them to try overarm and to see which is the most powerful.
New work **Station in free space:** task 88 Clap and catch (page 32).	Do pupils watch the ball throughout? Which throw goes highest—underarm or overarm?	Let pupils invent their own 'tricks' to perform while the ball is in the air.
New work **Station with two lines:** task 91 Target catch (page 32). Throw the ball from behind one line across the gap and run to catch it on the far side of the second line.	Do they move smoothly into the run from the throw? Can they judge the flight of the ball for height and length, and arrive in time to catch the dropping ball?	**Easier variation:** reduce the gap, and gradually extend it again with practice.

Rotate each group through each station with an equal period of time on each.

Bridging organization: for the task that follows, only permit all the pupils to work freely at the same time if the space is large enough. Alternatively, require pupils to work in the same direction across an area so that all the throws are in parallel.

New work Player **A** with the ball says "go" and counts out loud from one to five. On "go" player **B** runs as far away as s/he can while staying within the boundaries of the area. When player **A** shouts "five" player **B** has to stop and stand still. Player **A** throws the ball towards **B** and runs to catch it. How many throws does player **A** need to take before s/he can catch the ball, stand still and reach out to touch his/her partner with the ball? The ball must not touch the ground. Change over.	Do pupils wait for a space before throwing? Can they judge line and length? Help pupils to appreciate the relationship between power, trajectory, and the time the ball takes to cover a given distance.	If space is limited, be prepared to work the pupils in groups one after the other, in one direction, with recovery back round the outside of the area.

Closing organization: "From where you are, see how few throws/catches you and your partner need to make before you can place your ball in a basket. If the ball touches the ground you go back and start again."

Cool-down
"Gently jog on the spot with the toes only just leaving the ground; make each step lower until neither foot is leaving the ground, though each is being stretched as the weight goes up onto the toes and down again. Stand still and then walk slowly back to your classroom."

Planning and Teaching

All the sample lesson plans in this resource use a common format, and we suggest that you use the same format in your own planning. On the following page a blank lesson plan form is provided for you to photocopy as often as you need. Draw your own horizontal lines where necessary to enclose your notes on bridging organization.

Preparing your plan

Use a step-by-step approach to planning:

1 Decide what you want pupils to learn from the lesson, and then complete the sentence, 'By the end of this lesson pupils should ...' in the space headed **Intention**.

2 Each lesson should include:

• warm-up
• revision
• new work
• cool-down

Consider if any tasks previously experienced are suitable for inclusion in this lesson as revision work. In addition, make sure pupils experience some games-playing in every lesson, thus keeping a sensible balance between practices and competition.

Keep in mind that the patterns of lessons should vary; you do not always have to follow the traditional pattern of warm-up – skill training – game – cool-down. Mix in games and practices together. For example, following the warm-up with a game can help pupils understand why the skill practice to follow should improve their game.

3 Organize the chosen tasks in logical progressions and write them into the task column. Sometimes allow your pupils time to practise what **they** want to practise.

4 Choose warm-up activities which are relevant and which prepare the children for what is to follow. See the guidance on preparing pupils for their lesson on page 16.

5 Identify what you will be looking for when the pupils are working, and note it in the second column ('what to look for').

6 Fill in the third column ('Points to remember'). For example, decide whether you will need to provide any skill cards; if you will, make a note in the third column. Add any additional memory-joggers, e.g. that a pupil missed the previous lesson and may need additional help.

7 Look through the tasks, and — taking account of the number of pupils — decide how much equipment you will need. If you do not have enough, consider using alternatives or setting up more than one station to allow various pieces of equipment to be used at any one time.

8 **Pre-lesson and bridging organization:** Decide what will need to be done to prepare the working area for each task and for smooth movement between tasks, and write this in as shown in the sample plans. Keep safety requirements clearly in mind.

9 Decide how best to collect the equipment together and return it to the store at the end of the lesson. Note this under 'Closing organization'.

10 Choose a suitable cool-down activity to calm the pupils down and reduce their activity level before going back to the classroom.

11 Finally, read down the task column and check the flow and progression of your lesson. Look particularly to see if there is a balance between high- and lower-intensity activity.

LESSON PLAN

Intention: by the end of this lesson pupils should

Pre-lesson organization:

Organization for Task 1:

Task (What pupils do)	Observations (What to look for)	Points to remember
Warm-up		

Closing organization:

Cool-down

With experience some aspects of organization will become second nature and need not be written into the lesson plan. However, it is **essential** always to plan lesson content thoroughly, to keep a record of completed work and to evaluate the pupils' performance in anticipation of the next lesson.

The technique-improvement cards (usually referred to more briefly as **skill cards**) cover many specific points of games technique. You can use these cards by encouraging pupils to check their performance against simple **key criteria** shown on a card in words and pictures.

Children vary in their needs and learn at different rates. While some pupils may have developed precise, consistent techniques, others will need more practice time or further help. This is the disadvantage of always teaching the whole class the same technique to a single standard. Using skill cards, on the other hand, enables you to **individualize** learning: at any time pupils can work on their techniques at their own level.

The drawings on the skill cards illustrate what you should see when a pupil is performing the technique 'correctly' — that is, in the most effective way. The written criteria that accompany the drawings are designed to tell the teacher what to look for and which points to tell the pupils to pay attention to.

By endeavouring to copy the techniques shown on the cards, pupils will develop consistency and greater control of their actions. Later, when they have mastered the basic techniques, they can

learn to adapt them to meet the varied demands of the situations arising in actual games.

Photocopy as many cards as you need. If necessary, you can modify them to suit your own needs, or design your own cards for additional techniques.

You will probably be using the skill cards frequently, so either laminate them for durability or slip each card into a transparent plastic sleeve.

You can use the skill cards in a variety of ways:

For the whole class

Have the relevant cards on display for all the pupils to refer to as they wish.

An example skill card

At work-stations visited by different groups of pupils

Display the appropriate cards beside each station.

For pairs work (older pupils)

One pupil practises while the other checks his/her performance against information on the card, and then gives praise and constructive criticism as appropriate.

Pupils who observe and comment on the actions of a partner learn how to analyse performance, and thus gain an insight into the activity. This frequently pays dividends when their own turn comes to perform. It also helps them to develop communication skills and to recognize the needs of others.

For individual work

Individual pupils move to the side and use a skill card to check their own performance during practice.

Used flexibly, skill cards offer an ideal way to individualize learning.

Younger pupils

The written criteria as printed are not appropriate for younger pupils, so you should copy the drawings and replace the text with a few simple **key words** to guide their performance. By reducing the detail in this way, you can enable younger pupils to benefit from those skill cards that are suitable for them — the ones showing simpler techniques.

Teacher enthusiasm is a vital ingredient in games lessons, but enthusiasm alone is not enough; all the other elements of effective teaching are needed too:

- Businesslike management

- Well-directed observation

- The confidence to leave a lesson plan temporarily in order to respond to pupils' needs

- The appropriate provision of feedback and correction

- The art of making lessons purposeful yet fun

Using lesson time efficiently

It is important to use the lesson time allocated to games as fully and productively as possible. So, from time to time, it is helpful to reflect on your teaching and compare what you **actually** do with what you **might** do.

After a typical lesson, try asking yourself the following questions about your own performance as a teacher:

- Am I speedy and efficient in setting up the working area?

- Do I explain the purpose of each task and help the pupils to know what is expected of them?

- Do I check that the pupils are doing what they have been asked to do?

- Do I think about adjusting a task if the class response is inappropriate?

- Can I identify individual problems and give helpful feedback or correction?

- Do I remember to praise pupils and tell them why they are improving?

- Do I know when a task has exhausted its potential and it is time to move on?

- Do I give pupils time to practise, or do I talk too much?

- Do I keep pupils in the same place or at the same type of practice for too long?

Many more questions could be asked, but because teaching is a systematic process which regularly involves teachers in the same procedures, it is possible to provide a model of these procedures against which to compare your teaching performance. The model **systematic teaching cycles** on page 53 illustrates the process.

In this model the **grey** or **go-forward route** describes what the teacher does when everything is running smoothly and the pupils are progressing. The **red** or **stop-and-go-back route** (recapitulation) sends the teacher back to a previous procedure in order to maintain a safe and suitable work setting, keep pupils on task and promote learning.

SYSTEMATIC TEACHING CYCLES

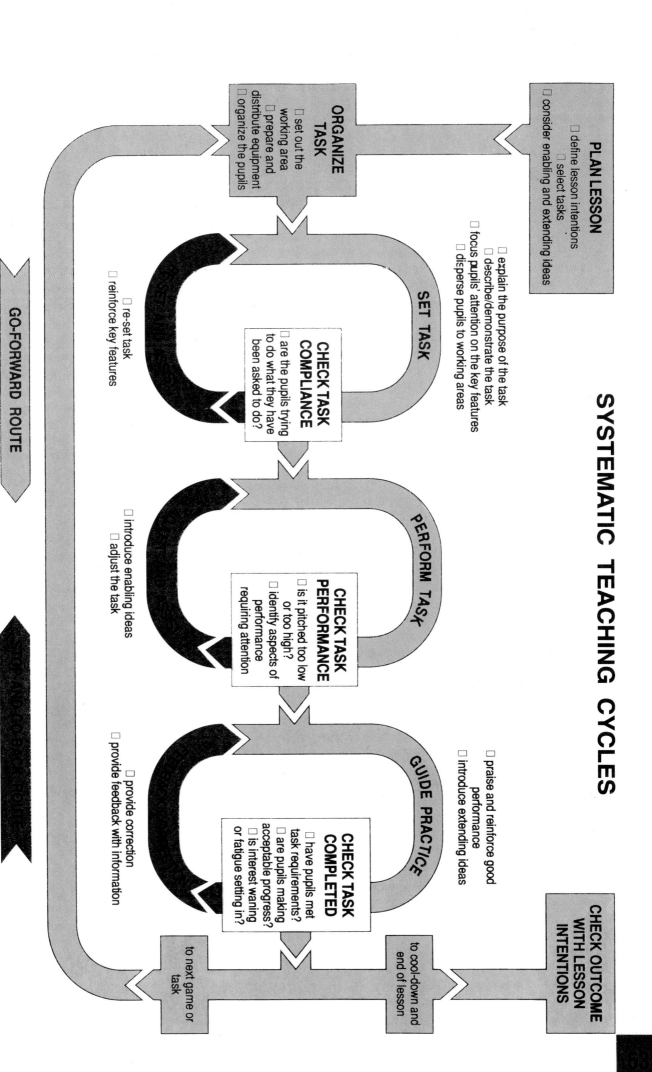

PLAN LESSON
- ☐ define lesson intentions
- ☐ select tasks
- ☐ consider enabling and extending ideas

ORGANIZE TASK
- ☐ set out the working area
- ☐ prepare and distribute equipment
- ☐ organize the pupils

SET TASK
- ☐ explain the purpose of the task
- ☐ describe/demonstrate the task
- ☐ focus pupils' attention on the key features
- ☐ disperse pupils to working areas

CHECK TASK COMPLIANCE
- ☐ are the pupils trying to do what they have been asked to do?

- ☐ re-set task
- ☐ reinforce key features

PERFORM TASK

CHECK TASK PERFORMANCE
- ☐ is it pitched too low or too high?
- ☐ identify aspects of performance requiring attention

- ☐ praise and reinforce good performance
- ☐ introduce extending ideas

- ☐ introduce enabling ideas
- ☐ adjust the task

GUIDE PRACTICE

CHECK TASK COMPLETED
- ☐ have pupils met task requirements?
- ☐ are pupils making acceptable progress?
- ☐ is interest waning or fatigue setting in?

- ☐ provide correction
- ☐ provide feedback with information

to next game or task

to cool-down and end of lesson

CHECK OUTCOME WITH LESSON INTENTIONS

GO-FORWARD ROUTE

GO AND GO-BACK ROUTE

From time to time pupils should be invited to make up their own tasks and games.

DEVISING THEIR OWN PRACTICES

Being able to make up their own practices, either working alone or with the support of other pupils, indicates an understanding of game demands and how to meet those demands. Here is a typical example for a pair:

"Make up a practice between the two of you which will help you to pick up a rolling ball and then throw it accurately to a target."

The task can be guided by asking them to decide on the shape, size and location of the target and how far away they will be when they throw to it.

A further possibility would be for the pupils to plan a practice within a specific type of game such as rounders. Quite often these practices can be shared with other pupils, and if they prove useful they can be added to the general repertoire of tasks.

GAMES-MAKING

Left to their own devices, children enjoy making games. These will not be the formal games introduced and developed through the physical-education curriculum, but modified and adapted versions, as well as games unique to their creators.

In games-making, teachers need to present tasks which are not too open-ended, for so often these lead to poorly structured and unsatisfying games. Provide guidelines, and a few restrictions, so that your pupils are given some direction and sense of purpose. Then you will be acting as a **facilitator** — supporting, guiding, questioning and helping the children to develop their ideas.

You may introduce games-making tasks within directed lessons, or plan a short block of work with games-making as the main theme. In any event pupils should have this experience before they are involved in formal games played to a code of rules laid down by the national governing body. Later,

games-making tasks can be used from time to time to focus on a particular feature of games (e.g. scoring, ball out of play) or to stimulate tactical ideas.

Games-making through the formal harnessing of this childlike activity **enables** pupils to:

• be involved in self-generated activity

• understand how rules make and shape a game

• appreciate and plan tactics

• find out how techniques can be used within a game

• share ideas — this involves communication and give and take

• appreciate and understand the strengths and weaknesses of others

Games-making is **not**:

• abdicating all responsibility to the pupils

• to make good shortfalls in the creativity of staff

• a spur-of-the-moment activity

Games-making **requires**:

• structuring within the overall programme

• careful management

• constant monitoring to make sure the activity is purposeful

• assessment to measure the pupils' progress in understanding game structures and the significance of rules

What the teacher needs to do

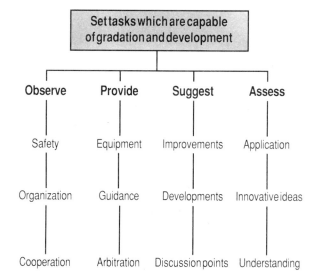

Set tasks which are capable of gradation and development			
Observe	**Provide**	**Suggest**	**Assess**
Safety	Equipment	Improvements	Application
Organization	Guidance	Developments	Innovative ideas
Cooperation	Arbitration	Discussion points	Understanding

Establishing a balance

The success or failure of games-making is largely dependent on establishing a good balance between direction by the teacher and the freedom of the pupils to explore, to experiment, and to accept and reject ideas.

Some children who are not particularly skilful at playing may come into their own by offering ideas, leading discussion, and helping their friends to discover how changing a rule can improve or impair the game.

Writing out the game

The pupils can make notes about the game as they are developing it, or afterwards in the classroom. Either way, this is a particularly helpful introduction to the framing of rules. The rules of mini-games could be used as examples; it will be best to choose simple, straightforward ones for this purpose.

Games which work well can be written out, with illustrations, and inserted into this resource. If you can, divide these into **original games** *and those which belong to a particular* **existing family of games.**

What the pupils need to do

As the pupils devise their game, they will need to cover the following elements:

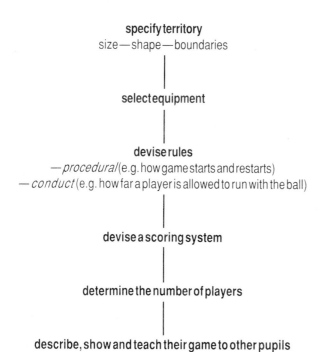

specify territory
size—shape—boundaries
|
select equipment
|
devise rules
—*procedural* (e.g. how game starts and restarts)
—*conduct* (e.g. how far a player is allowed to run with the ball)
|
devise a scoring system
|
determine the number of players
|
describe, show and teach their game to other pupils

Decisions to be made

Here are some examples of decisions which may need to be made. According to local conditions any or all of these decisions could be made by the pupils:

playing area
size
shape
siting of boundaries where needed
how it is marked out
placement of targets, barriers etc.

equipment
selection available
orthodox or modified usage

players
how many are needed?
how are they organized?
do they have names or numbers?
do some have special roles? (i.e. can some do things others can't?)
can everyone go anywhere, or are there restrictions on players' movements?

game structure
how is the game started?
how do players score points or goals?
how does the game restart after a score?
if the ball goes out of play, how is it brought in again?

conduct
how may players play the ball?
if the opposition have the ball, what can players do to get it back?
what may players **not** do ?

penalties
if players break the rules, what happens?
how is the game restarted after an infringement?

game time
when does the game end? (e.g. time-limit, or when a certain score is reached)
is the game continuous, or are there any breaks?
are there any time rules or restrictions?

Rules and laws is a useful cross-curricular topic which can be expanded to embrace the laws of the land, school rules, and rules agreed at home, as well as rules that govern games.

57

NOTES

NOTES

Introducing Formal Games

Moving on from the yellow section, pupils should now be introduced to formal games. These provide two different forms of competition, and initially the numbers competing are kept quite small:

Directly competitive games

These are one-versus-one games, in which pupils rely entirely on their own resources.

Cooperatively competitive games

This heading covers all games in which pupils contribute their skills to a cooperative team effort. The games include small equal-sided games starting with 2v2, as well as weighted games such as 3v1 and 4v2.

RESPECTING THE RULES

Formal games are played to an agreed set of rules stipulated by the teacher. Normally all players are expected to conform to these rules in order to compete on equal terms. However, from time to time you may adjust a rule either to help disadvantaged players or to provide a greater challenge to better players.

Games-making

Refer back to the section on games-making (pages 54–55). This gives general guidance on how to provide opportunities for your pupils to devise and negotiate their own rules, so that they will better understand how rules make and shape a game.

In addition, panels giving specific games-making tasks have been provided throughout the blue section.

Regulation mini-games

Regulation mini-games are introduced in the green section. The rules of these games are determined by the relevant national governing body or international rules board, and are published on their behalf.

FINDING YOUR WAY AROUND THE BLUE SECTION

The materials are grouped under three families of games:

- Net and wall games
- Invasion games
- Striking/fielding games

Information about each family of games is organized into the following sections:

- an introduction to the common features of games within that family
- competitive games, with complementary skill-development tasks and skill-card references
- sample lesson plans.

Use the materials and add your own ideas to construct lessons, always making sure that you respond to pupils' needs. Vary the lesson formats, and ensure a high level of involvement for every pupil. Include both revision and new work in each lesson.

Ensure that your programmes of study provide a balanced mixture of games from each family, as required by the national curriculum.

Family tree of formal games

The family-tree diagram on the facing page shows in graphical form how the regulation games whose skills are covered in this resource relate to each other and to the mini-games described in the green section.

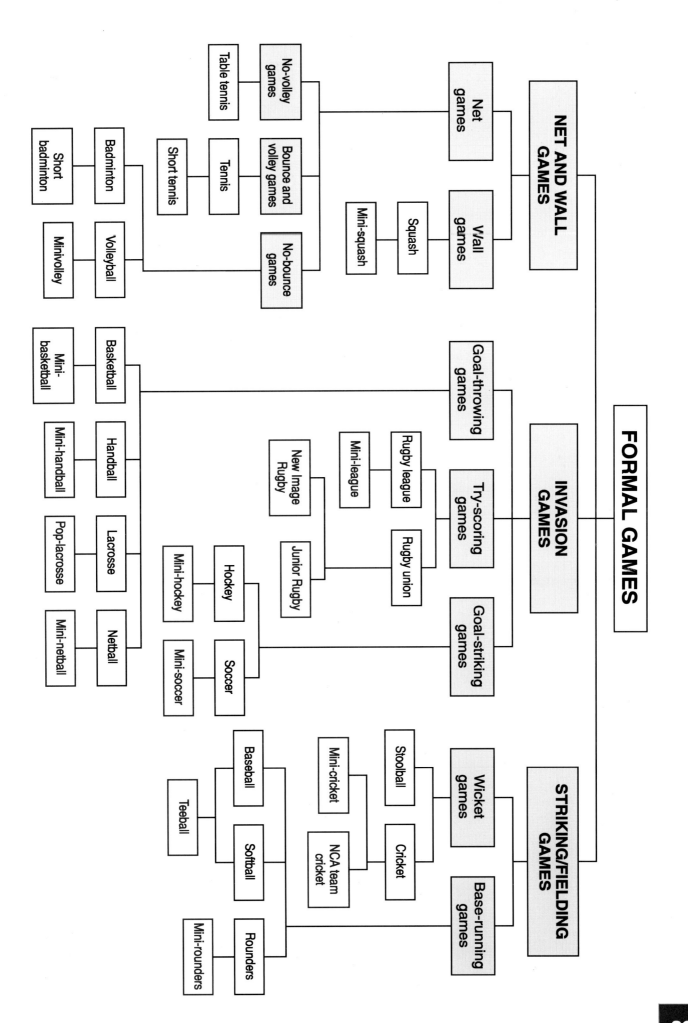

NOTES

Net and Wall Games

The basis of this family consists of the net games, such as tennis and volleyball. Games which are played against a wall or walls are included too, because they use the same core skills. The regulation games can be classified as follows:

• Net games in which the ball may be played before or after it bounces, e.g tennis.

• Net games in which the ball must not be volleyed, e.g. table tennis.

• Net games in which the ball (or shuttle) must not bounce, e.g. badminton and volleyball.

• Wall games, in which the ball is rebounded into a shared court, e.g. squash.

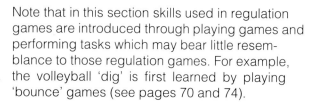

Note that in this section skills used in regulation games are introduced through playing games and performing tasks which may bear little resemblance to those regulation games. For example, the volleyball 'dig' is first learned by playing 'bounce' games (see pages 70 and 74).

Pupils begin by playing 'bounce' games, where they learn basic hitting skills and tactics, move onto 'bounce and no-bounce' games, where volleying is introduced, and finally play 'no-bounce games'. Additional specialized skills are covered in the remaining three sections on volleyball, table tennis and squash.

NUMBERS OF PLAYERS

Net games are played either as singles (1v1) or as doubles (2v2), with the exception of volleyball, which in its regulation form is played in teams of 6v6. Volleyball teams of this size are not suitable at this stage of your pupils' development, so keep to 3v3 — as in minivolley (page 170) — or 4v4.

PLAYING AREAS

When children are learning these games, don't be afraid to change the conditions to suit their needs. Courts may be altered in size and shape; nets or other dividing barriers may be varied in height and depth to make different demands of the players. Here are some examples:

• A long narrow court, to encourage both long and short hits, so that the pupils learn to exploit depth.

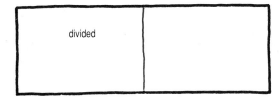

divided

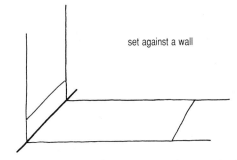

set against a wall

• A short wide court for encouraging angled hits, to exploit width.

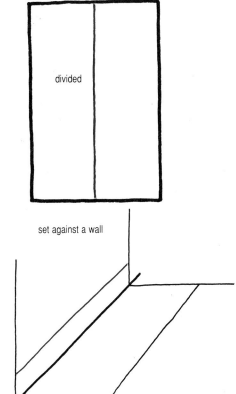

divided

set against a wall

• A court with no net, but instead a central no-entry zone which no player may enter and in which no ball may bounce. This helps the pupils to focus on line and length.

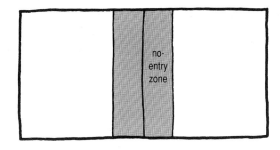

no-entry zone

• Lowering the net or wall line makes the game faster.

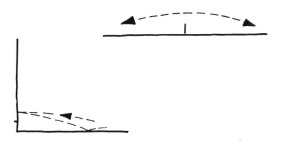

• Raising the net or wall line slows the game down.

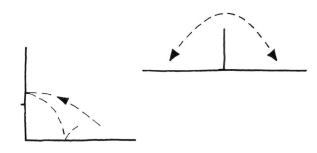

OBJECT OF THE GAMES

In all net games the players have the same object: to score by hitting the ball into the opposing court so that it cannot be returned to land in their own court.

Similarly, the object of wall-games players is to score by hitting the ball so that it bounces correctly on the wall and rebounds back into the court in such a way that the opponent cannot return it via any permitted route.

All these games make similar **demands** of players. They are fast-reaction games calling for:

- alertness
- anticipation
- judgement
- agility
- athleticism
- technical control of the ball.

Vocabulary

Rally The series of hits made by alternate players between *serves*.

Server The player who is allowed to play the ball first.

Feed To send the ball in a controlled manner for a player to hit.

SCORING POINTS

To win a game, players need to score more points than their opponents. The illustrations show how points may be scored in this family of games. Help your pupils to understand this aspect of the rules by displaying photocopies of these sheets in the classroom so that they can study them.

At this stage, a point is scored after each rally, regardless of which player served. The concept of winning a rally to gain service, as in squash or badminton, is not introduced until later (see page 168).

Basic scoring in net games in which the ball may bounce (table tennis and tennis)

1 Into the net

If your opponent's **service** does not go over the net, you score a point.

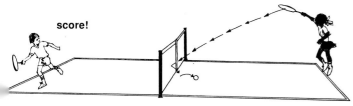

2 Service out

If your opponent's **service** does not land in the correct area, you score a point.

This demonstrates how serving gets the game started and how easily points can be won or lost on the serve.

3 Out

If your opponent hits the ball out of court during a **rally**, you score a point.

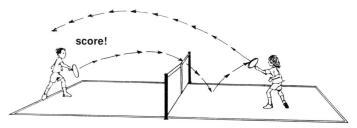

4 Into the net

If your opponent hits the ball into the net during a **rally**, you score a point.

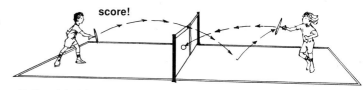

5 Double hit

If your opponent hits the ball twice in succession during a **rally**, you score a point.

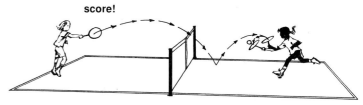

6 Second bounce

If during a **rally** your opponent hits the ball after a second bounce, you score a point.

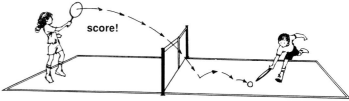

7 Winning shot

All the points shown so far were scored because the opponent made a mistake. Points can also be scored by making a **winning shot**. This is a hit which bounces in the opponent's court but which s/he cannot contact.

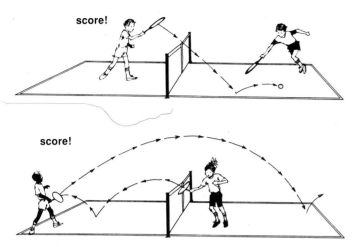

Basic scoring in net games in which the ball may not bounce (badminton and volleyball)

Where the term **ball** is used in this section, it should be taken to apply equally to a shuttlecock.

Although no-bounce games are similar to bounce games in that points are lost if the ball fails to clear the net or land in the correct part of the opposing court, there are some important differences:

• In no-bounce games, to score a point for a ball which lands out of the service area or out of court, the receiver must leave it to bounce. If the ball is played, the rally continues, regardless of whether it was obvious that the shot would have landed out. Your pupils will have to learn to judge whether a ball is going to land in or out of court, and this will require practice.

• A winning shot is made wherever a player makes the ball clear the net correctly and then touch the ground in the opponent's court. This is called 'grounding the ball'.

Basic scoring in wall games (squash and racketball)

In these games a line on the front wall of the court fulfils the same purpose as the net in net games. Returning the ball correctly to bounce on the front wall above the line is a feature of all the games in this sub-family. There may also be a higher line which the ball must clear during service.

Here are the ways in which points are won and lost. First see how your opponent gives you a point:

1 Service out

If your opponent's **service** does not go above the line on the front wall or land correctly in your half of the court, you score a point.

2 Out of bounds

If, during a **rally**, your opponent hits the ball onto the wall above the lines on the side walls, you score a point.

3 Too low

If during a **rally** your opponent returns the ball to the front wall but below the line, you score a point.

4 Double hit

If your opponent hits the ball twice in succession during a **rally**, you score a point.

5 Double bounce

score!

If during a **rally** your opponent lets the ball bounce on the floor twice, you score a point.

6 Winning shots

As in net games, all the points so far were scored because the opponent made a mistake. Points are also scored by making **winning shots**. These are played to bounce correctly in the court, and to be too difficult for the opponent to return.

TACTICS FOR WINNING POINTS

Encourage your pupils to think about tactics at an early stage. Introduce them to:

• Hitting the ball so that the opponent will be lured to a position that will leave space for your next shot to be a winning one. For example, hit the ball to the back of the court and then place the return to the empty front court.

• Forcing a mistake by disguising the power of a shot or using spin, so that the opponent cannot judge its flight.

• Placing yourself in a good 'ready' position from which you can move to all parts of the court and be comfortably placed to play the ball. This denies your opponent space in which to place his/her return shot.

DEVELOPING INSIGHT

Encourage your pupils to consider that what they do determines what their opponents can do. Every stroke is a tactical move designed to lead to a winning shot or to force a mistake.

Within formal games, pupils should learn how important it is to weigh up each game situation so that they can make good choices about the next move.

This **situation model** describes what a player should consider and what a teacher should look for during competitive play.

The stroke cycle

Net and wall games are relatively simple, as only a limited number of shots are possible in a given situation.

Even when pupils can recognize game situations and know what to do, they need to use controlled techniques to carry out their intentions. The model at the top of page 70 demonstrates the importance of the travel phase, during which the player moves into position to be comfortably placed to play the ball, and highlights the cycle of making the stroke.

Initially, encourage pupils to say "Ready, prepare, hit, recover" as they perform each stroke cycle, until it becomes second nature. Too many players hit the ball and then stand and wonder why they cannot play the next shot.

69

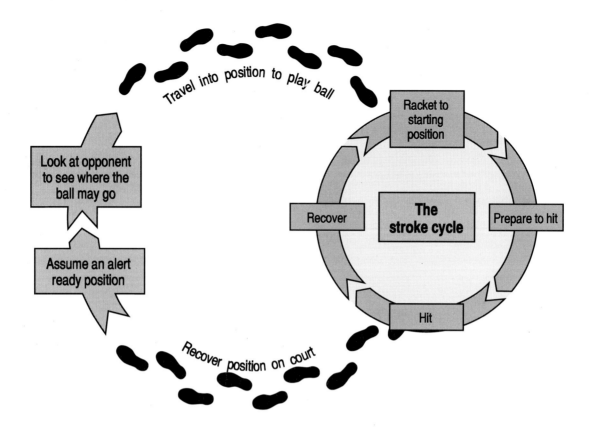

By analysing and correcting faults in the phases of the stroke cycle, you help your pupils to acquire the economy, rhythm and fluency needed for good stroke production. The skill cards referred to within this section show you what to look for.

LESSON CONTENT

Remember the three components of games performance:

- skill
- insight
- physical preparedness

Try to include in each lesson:

- tasks which help pupils to control their hitting

- tasks which help pupils to understand how to outwit their opponents

- tasks which help pupils to develop their agility and athleticism

A single lesson may focus on one type of game, such as no-bounce, or offer a variety of game types. It is important sometimes to let your pupils choose whether to play a no-bounce game, a bounce game, or one that combines the two.

VOLLEYBALL: A SPECIAL CASE

Volleyball features in this family of games because it has the same **objects** as other net games, and many of the techniques are of value in learning racket games. However, volleyball is different in two important ways:

- Players use their hands to play the ball.

- In the regulation game, players may pass the ball to each other before returning it over the net.

As well as being a help in learning racket games, volleyball techniques will be good preparation for when your pupils start playing minivolley at a later stage.

Although regulation volleyball is a no-bounce game, it is acceptable to allow pupils to play the ball after the bounce at this stage. This is a good introduction to the 'dig' technique.

The 'dig' — playing a ball below head-height: skill card 6

The volley — playing a ball above head-height: skill card 9

Volleyball and beginners

In games such as volleyball, where the hands are used instead of a racket, make sure that the ball is large, light and kind to the hands on contact. Sponge balls are ideal, and you can obtain special volleyballs for youngsters. Balls which are heavy or which could sting the hands must not be used.

APPLYING DIFFERENT TECHNIQUES

Throughout this section, symbols are used to indicate where techniques of other games may be used.

V indicates that volleyball techniques may be used in games and complementary practices.

TT is used where the special requirements of table tennis apply.

It is quite acceptable to plan lessons which involve pupils in multi-skill games and practices drawn from the wide variety within the family of net and wall games. This is especially helpful when you do not have enough of one type of equipment to share it among the whole class.

ORGANIZATION

When choosing the size of court and dividing it up, remember the following guidelines:

• Ensure that the side and end lines are marked, or easily located as an imaginary line between two markers.

• For bounce games, start with the net at approximately the height of the children's waists. Later, it may be lowered to speed up the game, or raised to slow it down.

• The net needs to be higher for no-bounce games — try shoulder-height at first.

• When setting out several 'courts', allow generous clearances between them.

• Do not let pupils run into, or across, other courts to retrieve a ball.

• Be especially watchful when pupils are choosing their own court shape and size. Help them to establish acceptable clearances.

NET GAMES

Throughout this section, the term 'net' is used for any type of court division. These can be improvised from benches, box tops, high-jump stands and tape, chairs and ropes, and so on.

SCORING

For each game, choose a scoring system based on those described under **Scoring points** on pages 67–68. Keep it simple.

Whatever system you choose, you can adjust it as necessary. For example, for less-able pupils, you might decide to simplify a game by permitting the ball to bounce twice before being returned.

In some games you may choose between:

• letting both the server and receiver score

• letting only the server score.

In addition, you may decide that the service has to be returned before scoring starts.

The winner can be either the first player to reach an agreed score, or the one with the highest score after a given period of time.

Once the pupils become familiar with scoring systems, the games can be extended into 'sets' of say five points, with the winner being the first to win two sets.

SERVING

The service is essential to get the game started. There's no need to be too rigid about it for beginners — there are many possibilities. The following variations may be considered when making rules about serving:

• **Where from?** Serve from anywhere on court, or from behind a mid-court line, or from behind the endline, or from the centre of the endline, or from the right or left, or from alternate sides.

• **Where to?** Serve over the net to any part of the opposing court, or into a marked area.

• **How?** Serve using underarm action, or using overarm action; hitting the ball before or after the bounce.

ACCOMMODATING PLAYERS WITH DIFFERENT ABILITIES

With a little flexibility and ingenuity, you can accommodate pupils of different abilities so that they all gain enjoyment from playing together. For example, to ensure equal competition it is not necessary for both players in a 1v1 game to:

• Play to the same rules. For example, the weaker player may be permitted to let the ball bounce twice before returning it.

• Play in the same size of court as the opponent. The illustration shows how the weaker player may play in a court which is smaller than the opposing court, thus giving him/her a larger target area to aim into and a smaller target area to defend.

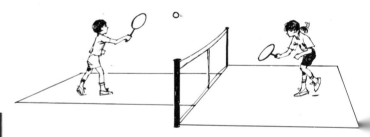

• Use the same type of racket. The weaker player can use a racket with a shorter handle and larger face.

THE BASIC 1V1 BOUNCE GAME

Game 125 Bounce

One player serves a ball into the opposing court. The ball has to be returned over the net after one bounce and the rally continues with each player hitting after one bounce until a point is scored.

Easier variations: If you need to make the game easier, waive the single-bounce rule and allow the players to hit the ball after two bounces. Alternatively, raise the net so that the ball is in the air for a longer period.

THE BASIC 1V1 BOUNCE GAME
COMPLEMENTARY SKILL-DEVELOPMENT TASKS

To play a 1v1 bounce game over a net, pupils need to be able to:

• Control the direction, height and power of a shot so that a chosen target can be hit with reasonable consistency.

• Do this both from a self-feed and when returning a ball hit from the other side of the net.

Easier variations: if necessary, make the task easier by providing larger target areas or lowering the net.

Extending variations: provide smaller targets; move the targets further away from the net.

UNDERARM SERVICE

Task 126 Into the hoop (novices)(V)

Object: to serve the ball to land consistently in a target area.

Work in pairs.

Place a large hoop on each side of the net. Each player takes turns to serve the ball from his/her own hoop to land in the opposite one. After each serve the partner collects the ball by hand or racket.

Task 127 Target choice (novices and intermediate players)(V)

Object: to increase the length of the service while still controlling where it bounces.

Work in pairs.

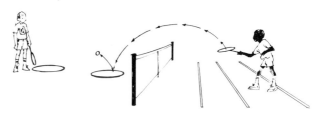

Place two hoops on one side of the net, one close in and the other further back. On the other side, mark three parallel lines at different distances from the net. The server chooses the line to serve from and calls out "near" or "far" to identify the target in which s/he aims to land the ball. Let pupils try lots of variations of distance and choice of target. Encourage them to try to make five accurate services in a row.

"Can you hit the ball from the furthest line into the furthest target?"

> *Racket underarm service: skill card 1*
>
> *Volleyball service: skill card 2*

OVERARM SERVICE

The overarm service should be introduced at this stage, but in games your pupils should be permitted to serve either underarm or overarm according to ability.

> *Racket overarm service: skill card 3*

HITTING A BALL AFTER THE BOUNCE

When rackets are used, these tasks should be attempted using both the forehand and the backhand.

The volleyball 'dig' may be substituted (skill card 6) where (**V**) is shown.

Task 128 Throw and hit (novices)(V)

Object: to hit the ball over the net after the bounce.

Work in pairs.

One pupil feeds by using an underarm throw to send the ball over the net; after the bounce, the other hits the ball towards the hands of the feeder, who catches it and repeats.

"Change roles after five tries."

Task 129 Change the length (novices)(V)

Object: to control the length of the hit.

Work in threes.

Use markers or lines, as shown in the illustration, to indicate front, middle and back target areas on one half of the court. Start the task by deciding who is to be feeder, hitter and receiver.

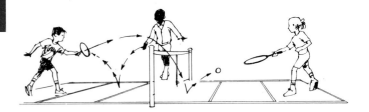

The feeder bounces the ball underarm to the hitter, who sends the first shot to the front court, the second to the middle court and the third to the back court. The receiver attempts to catch each ball and serves it back to the feeder. *As skill develops, the receiver can hit the ball directly back after one bounce.* Change roles at frequent intervals.

Variation for intermediate players: Let the hitter choose the court in which s/he intends the ball to land, by calling out as it bounces on the feed: bounce—"back!"—hit.

Variation for advanced pupils: Turn the task into a game by letting two players attempt to maintain a one-bounce rally. They can nominate the type of rally: e.g. every shot into the middle court, or a continuous sequence of front, middle, back, front, etc. The third player keeps score. The players change over at regular intervals, so that each of the three possible pairings accepts the same challenge. Then let a new pairing decide the next challenge.

> *Racket forehand: skill card 4*
>
> *Racket backhand: skill card 5*
>
> *Volleyball 'dig': skill card 6*

COMBINING SERVICE WITH HITTING AFTER THE BOUNCE

Task 130 Hit-and-touch (intermediate players)(V)

Object: to learn how to move quickly into position after playing a shot.

Refresh your memory about positioning by checking the stroke cycle illustrated on page 70.

Work in pairs.

Use a divided court of convenient size and place a marker such as a cone on each corner of the court.

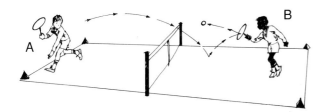

Player **A** serves from the centre of the endline and then dashes to touch one of the markers and get back into position in time to play B's return. Play continues as a normal single-bounce cooperative rally until someone makes a mistake. Then **B** serves and touches a marker. Alternate service and cooperative rally.

Variation for advanced pupils: the players have to touch a marker after every stroke, instead of just after service.

Task 131 Diagonals (intermediate players)(V)

Object: to achieve directional control.

Work in pairs.

Divide the court by a line marked lengthways down the centre. Each player starts in his/her right-hand court. Play a service followed by a single-bounce rally during which the ball has to be hit alternately into the left-hand and right-hand courts.

Extending variation: Once the pupils become adept at this, introduce the idea of trying to send the ball to the side of the court away from where the opponent is positioned.

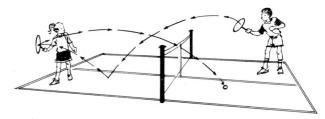

Variation: When dealing with pupils of mixed abilities, have two players on one side of the net and one player on the other. Only one player now has to cross the court to take shots to the left-hand and right-hand courts.

Task 132 Doubles diagonal serve (intermediate players)(V)(TT)

Object: to develop the skills of anticipation, rapid positioning and awareness of other players' movement around the court.

Work in fours.

Divide the court lengthways down the middle, with two players on each side of the net. Start by serving from behind the endline into the diagonally opposite court. Play out a single-bounce rally, with each player taking alternate shots regardless of where the ball falls in court. Play cooperative rallies, with service being rotated through the four players.

TEACHING TACTICS

THROW/CATCH GAMES OVER A NET

To help pupils grasp the tactical principles of net games it is sometimes helpful to dispense with the rackets and play throw/catch games. Children do not necessarily find throwing and catching easier than hitting, but it does slow a game down, and is particularly useful in giving players time to consider where to direct their next shot. It can also be a good way of introducing a scoring system.

Game 135 on page 77, *Near and far*, which teaches pupils how to exploit both long and short shots, is a good example of when it may be useful to substitute throw/catch before returning to racket play.

Throw/catch is particularly helpful in games leading up to volleyball. See the progressive examples on page 83.

THROW/CATCH GUIDELINES

With a small ball:

• Normally, allow pupils to throw only from below the shoulder.

• Throwing from above the shoulder may be permitted when a 'no-go' zone is marked out in front of the net.

• Do not allow pupils to take more than two steps before throwing.

• After a trial game, impose a time limit on how long a ball may be held before being thrown.

With a larger ball:

• Encourage pupils to use both hands to throw and to catch.

• Permit the underarm throw, and introduce the throw with two hands from above the head.

• Gradually restrict how far the ball may be taken back during the above-the-head throw. Eventually it should not be taken back behind the head at all, so that the thrower can see it throughout the action.

• Do not allow pupils to take more than two steps before throwing, but do allow them to jump when they throw.

• When playing in small teams, e.g. 2v2, 3v3, introduce the possibility of passing the ball to a team-mate before it is returned over the net. This introduces the idea of moving the ball closer to the net before making an attacking shot into the opposing court.

With a bean bag:

• In no-bounce games a bean bag may be used, as some pupils will find it easier to grip when throwing and catching. Quoits may also be used, but these are relatively difficult to grasp.

THE BASIC 1V1 BOUNCE AND NO-BOUNCE GAME

Game 133 Bounce or volley (V)

Object: for pupils to realise how returning a ball before it bounces gives the opponent less time to play it.

One player serves the ball from behind the endline to bounce anywhere in the opposing court. The service must bounce before being hit, but for the rest of the rally the ball may be hit **before or after the bounce**. Service rules may be varied.

Game 134 Near and far (V)

Object: to use a long high ball to the back court or a short low ball to the front court to attack vacant space; to use volley and overhead strokes.

The court should be long and narrow, with the net at waist height. The service may land anywhere in the opposing court, and must bounce once before being played. For the rest of the rally the ball may be played before or after the bounce.

Help players to understand how much easier it is to play an attacking volley or overhead shot from near the net, especially if the ball is high.

Game 135 Diagonal serve (V)

Object: to familiarize players with serving into the court diagonally opposite; to learn to play shots which draw an opponent wide so that the ball can then be played into the vacant space.

The court should be relatively wide, with a net at waist height; there should be a mid-line parallel to the sidelines.

One player serves the ball from behind the end-line to bounce in the diagonally-opposite court. Let players have a second service if the first is unsuccessful. The service must bounce before being hit, but for the rest of the rally the ball may be hit before or after the bounce.

Help pupils to discover how important it is to recover to the mid-line of the court, ready to move to the next shot.

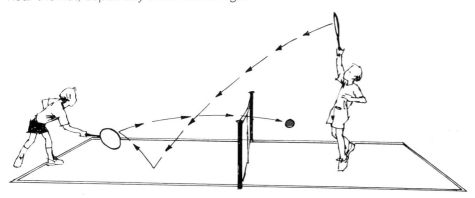

THE BASIC 1V1 BOUNCE AND NO-BOUNCE GAME
COMPLEMENTARY SKILL-DEVELOPMENT TASKS

With the introduction of no-bounce tasks the symbol (**B**) for badminton appears where a shuttlecock may be substituted for the ball.

To play a 1v1 bounce and no-bounce game over a net pupils need to be able to:

- hit the ball before the bounce

- angle the face of the racket to send the ball to a chosen target

- hit the ball either long and high or short and low after the bounce.

THE VOLLEY

You are strongly advised to use a sponge ball when introducing the volley.

Task 136 No man's land (novices)(V)(B)

For three players, one with a racket, and one ball.

The player with the racket stands in 'no-man's land', marked by two lines in the centre of the court. From opposite ends of the court, the other players throw the ball to each other, trying to avoid the racket of the player in the middle. If the ball goes dead in 'no-man's land', the middle player serves the ball to one of the throwers and the activity continues. Change places frequently.

Extending variation: using underarm throws only, to try to hit the body or legs of the middle player.

Task 137 Stretch the volley (novices)(V)(B)

Object: to keep the ball off the ground while passing it.

For two players, each with a racket. No court markings are necessary.

The players start about 4 metres (13 ft) apart and volley the ball gently to each other.

"How many times can you do this without letting the ball bounce?"

"Now, can you move further apart and still keep the ball off the ground?"

Task 138 Volley catch (intermediate players)(V)(B)

Object: to learn to direct a volley.

For two players, one with a racket. They play on a court with a net at waist height. Use a slow sponge ball at first.

One player throws the ball underarm for the other to hit back over the net so that it can be caught. Change roles each time the ball hits the ground.

"How long can you do this and keep the ball off the ground on both sides of the net?"

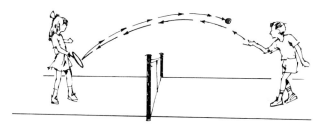

As skills improve, encourage the feeder to move freely to both left and right within his/her court so that the volleyer has to vary the return.

Extending variations:

1 (for advanced players) Place a pair of markers on the feeder's side of the net. These should be about 3 metres (10 ft) back and 4 metres (13 ft) apart. The feeder has to throw from one marker and run across the court to catch at the other. Can the hitter stay in the middle and direct the shots accurately?

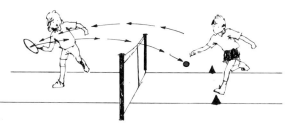

2 Play Task 138 and variation 1, but with both players using a racket; this is more difficult.

Racket volley, forehand: skill card 7

Racket volley, backhand: skill card 8

Volleyball volley: skill card 9

THE LOB

The lob is a shot which sends the ball high and long.

Task 139 Over the middle (novices)(V)

Object: to hit a ball after the bounce so that it goes high and lands in the far court.

For six players with rackets, playing on a court marked with a broad central zone and no net.

Divide the players into three pairs. The pairs at the endlines each have a ball, while the third pair occupies the central zone and tries to block shots sent by the pairs at the ends.

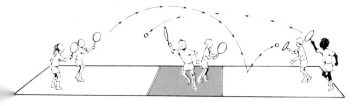

To play, one of each end pair feeds an underarm ball for his/her partner to hit after the bounce.

The hitters try to send the balls over the blockers to land in the far courts. If a blocker touches a ball with the racket, s/he changes place with the hitter. If a hitter hits the ball out of court three times, s/he swaps with a blocker.

The end players take turns to be hitters and feeders.

Extending variation: how many consecutive shots can be played over the blockers to land in court? The rally ends when a blocker touches the ball.

Task 140 Bounce and lob (intermediate players)(V)

Object: to play a long high shot after the bounce.

For two players, with rackets. Use long narrow courts with central nets.

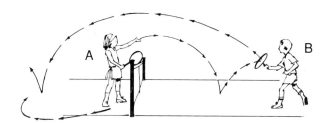

Player **A** stands close enough to the net to touch it. S/he serves the ball underarm to the opposing back court. Player **B** tries to hit the ball after the bounce to land the far side of **A**. When the ball has passed over his/her head, **A** may run back to try to play the return after the bounce. Each player scores if s/he is successful.

"After six tries each, compare your combined score with that of a neighbouring pair. Change partners and try to improve on the previous scores."

Variation for advanced players:

Player **A** serves the ball from the endline into the opposing court and then runs forward to touch the net. After the bounce, player **B** returns the ball over the head of **A**, to land as close to the endline as possible while remaining in court. If the ball can be returned by **A**, play continues with a normal bounce and no-bounce rally.

Whenever the ball goes 'dead' the player nearest the ball serves to restart play.

Racket lob: skill card 10

THE OVERHEAD SHOT

Initially, sponge balls must be used in these tasks.

Task 141 *Down and in (novices)(V)*

Object: to introduce pupils to the controlled overhead hitting action.

These exercises are best performed against a wall with a line at about waist height. High netting, similarly marked, can also be used. The pupils each need a racket and a ball, and should stand about 6 metres (20 ft) from the wall.

"Throw your ball up, and when it is above your head catch it in your hand."

"Throw your ball up, and this time reach up high to touch it with your racket."

"Now hit it to strike the wall above the line."

The players must start further away from the wall when they begin to use harder balls with greater rebounds.

Extending variation:

"Now hit the ball forwards and down, so that it bounces on the ground just in front of the wall. Can you block the rebound with your racket?"

Task 142 *Move in (intermediate players)(V)*

For three players, two with rackets.

Object: to get into position to hit high balls forwards and downwards.

Use a court divided by a low net.

Player **A**, without a racket, stands close to the net on the same side as player **C**. Players **B** and **C**, with rackets, start on the endlines. As **A** feeds a high ball into **B**'s front court, **B** moves forward to hit the ball from as high a position as possible, so that it goes over the net and lands in **C**'s court. **C** plays the return after the bounce, and the point is played out in a no-bounce or bounce rally.

At the end of each rally, **A** feeds the ball again to **B**. This continues until **C** is unable to return the ball: then it is retrieved and each player moves round one place to play a new role.

> *Racket overhead: skill card 11*
>
> *Volleyball overhead: skill card 12*

THE BASIC 1V1 NO-BOUNCE GAME

Game 143 No bounce (V)

Object: to ground the ball on the far side of the net while preventing it from landing on your own side.

For two players on a court divided by a relatively high net.

One player starts by serving the ball underarm across the net. The rally continues until the ball hits the ground, fails to clear the net, or lands out of court.

Try raising and lowering the net to see how this alters the pace of the game. Try also different types of balls and rackets when appropriate.

Game 144 Shuttle volley (B)

Object: to introduce the game of badminton.

Game 144 is the same as Game 143, but played using a shuttlecock.

Although by now familiar with the basic racket techniques, your pupils will find hitting the shuttle-cock quite different from hitting a ball. Make sure they start with rackets which are light and which offer a reasonably large striking area.

Variations:

Try some of the other suitable no-bounce games and practices (**B**), using a shuttlecock instead of a ball. Refer to the green section (page 169) for specific practices for short badminton.

Games-making task 145
Over the barrier

"With one, two or three other players, make up a game in which a ball crosses a barrier. Put your barrier in place, and draw out the size and shape of your 'court'."

"What will players be allowed to do when they play the ball? How will points be scored or taken away? How will your game be won or lost?"

VOLLEYBALL GAMES

Volleyball is a no-bounce game.

Early introductions to volleyball games can include throw/catch games using a large, light ball which is comfortable to hit. For guidance on playing throw/catch games, see page 76.

Apart from using the hands instead of a racket, the other two most significant features of volleyball are:

• more than two players can make up a team (six in the regulation game)

• these players may pass the ball between them before sending it over the net (three touches are allowed in the regulation game).

Volleyball games may be adapted for novices to produce satisfying play while introducing the concepts of cooperation and organization.

Game 146 1v1 volleyball (novices)

Object: to learn how to position to receive service and to direct the 'dig' and the volley across the net.

Play on small courts divided by nets at head height.

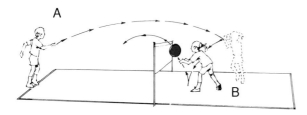

From behind the endline, player **A** throws underarm to serve the ball over the net into the opposing court. Player **B** controls the ball by receiving it on both hands, which are held in front of the forehead; the ball is then allowed to drop from the hands, and the rebound off the floor is hit back over the net. This second shot is called a 'dig'. The point is played out as either a no-bounce or a one-bounce rally.

Easier variation: Let the server throw the ball from mid-court.

Extending variations: The server hits the ball, rather than throwing it; s/he starts from the mid-court area and moves to behind the endline as his/her skill improves.

Game 147 Catch-throw-hit volleyball

Objects: to develop a throw/catch game into a hitting game; to learn how getting the ball high and close to the net can lead to a powerful attacking stroke.

For four players — three on one side of the net and a server on the other.

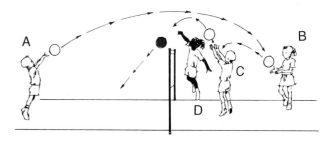

Player **A** serves the ball by throwing it underarm to be caught by player **B**, who then throws it to player **C**. **C** immediately throws it so that **D** can hit it over the net and down into the opposing court. If **A** can catch and return it, the ball remains in play and the sequence is repeated, though the three players **B**, **C** and **D** may play the ball in any order.

Remember — only **A** may **throw** the ball over the net. **B**, **C** or **D** must **strike** it over with a throw from another player.

Scoring: The server wins a point if the opposition let the ball hit the ground, send the ball to bounce out of court, or if they play the ball into the net. The server loses a point if s/he serves into the net or fails to catch or return the ball.

Extending variation: After a little practice, the server can be required to hit the ball rather than throwing it, and the catch/throw can be restricted to the player who receives a ball which has crossed the net. The other players have to hit the ball cleanly at the first attempt.

If a player catches the ball when it should have been hit, or throws it over the net instead of hitting it, the point is replayed.

VOLLEYBALL GAMES
COMPLEMENTARY SKILL-DEVELOPMENT TASKS

Task 148 Bounce-turn

Object: to improve alertness and to develop quick movement to the ball.

Played by groups of three in free space. Two balls are used.

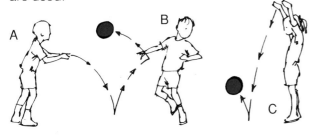

Player **A** throws the ball underarm to bounce in front of player **B**. **B** plays it back to **A**, who catches the return and feeds again. Player **C** stands behind **B**, with a ball held above his/her head. At intervals **C** drops the ball. On hearing the bounce **B** must turn and hit the dropped ball up into the air before it bounces again.

Can player **B** cope with both balls? Change roles regularly.

Task 149 Volley throws

Object: to control the height and direction of the volley.

For two players with one ball, in free space.

"Sit on the floor facing each other and try to throw the ball back and forth from just above forehead-height."

As the players become familiar with the action, speed it up, gradually reducing the contact time until it becomes a soft hitting action.

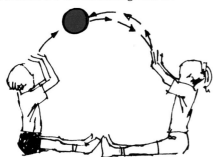

"How many consecutive hits can your pair make before the ball hits the ground?"

Extending variations:

• Sit astride a bench and repeat Task 149.

• Stand either side of a high net and repeat the task.

"Now, how many consecutive hits can your pair make before the ball fails to cross the net?"

Task 150 Clap-bounce

Object: to judge the flight of a ball.

For two players with one ball, in free space.

Start standing about 3 metres (10 ft) apart. With an underarm throw, player **A** lobs the ball towards player **B**, who has to clap hands when the ball is at the top of its flight and then get positioned so that the ball can bounce between his/her legs, before turning to capture the rebound off the ground.

A and **B** take turns to throw.

Extending variations:

• Can **B** turn and play the ball up into the air instead of catching it?

• Can each player hit the ball so that it serves as a feed for the other and play continues non-stop?

83

TABLE-TENNIS GAMES

Basic racket-game techniques will need considerable adaptation if they are to be effective on a table-top. However, with a little ingenuity, children can be taught a lot using only the simplest equipment.

Equipment

If you do not have regulation tables, try using:

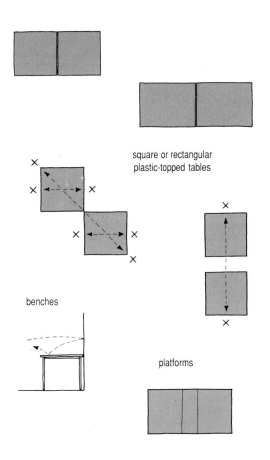

square or rectangular
plastic-topped tables

benches

platforms

Experiment with different ways of setting these out.

'Nets' may be improvised from card or plastic blocks, or just by marking a central strip on the table in which the ball may not land.

Normal table-tennis bats and balls are used for the games and tasks.

THE BASIC 1v1 TABLE GAME

Table tennis is unusual in that **the service has to bounce on the server's side of the net first.**

Game 151 Single bounce (intermediate players)

Object: to play the ball off the bat with sufficient control to keep it on the table.

Set up tables with dividing nets.

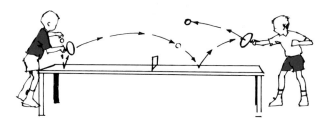

One player starts by dropping the ball onto the table and playing it over the net. Keep a single-bounce rally going until the ball misses the table or fails to clear the net.

"Serve until you lose a point."

Game 152 Full service (advanced players)

Object: to introduce the table-tennis service.

This is similar to the previous game except that the server has to hit the ball as it is dropped from the hand so that it bounces first on the server's side of the table and then on the far side. Once the ball is in play, the scoring is the same as in Game 151.

Table-tennis service: skill card 13

TABLE-TENNIS GAMES

COMPLEMENTARY SKILL-
DEVELOPMENT TASKS

Grip and control

A good grip controls the angle of the bat, which in turn controls the height, length, speed and direction of the ball. In later stages grip also plays a part in the amount of spin given to the ball.

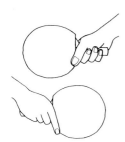

Teach your pupils the 'shakehands' or 'western' grip (see diagram); the alternative grips are not suitable for beginners.

Task 153 Bench bounce (intermediate players)

Object: to control the line and length of a ball off the bat.

Two players sit facing each other astride a bench with a 'net' between them. The server drops the ball onto the bench and plays it over the net using the backhand. The receiver catches the ball after it has bounced once and then serves back to the first player. Play continues, with the players taking turns to serve.

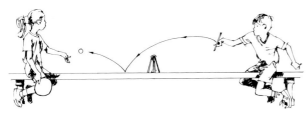

Extending variations:

• As above, but now the receiver hits the ball back to the server after one bounce. The server catches it. Change the roles after a set number of turns.

• (advanced players) As above, but keep a single-bounce rally going until the ball misses the bench or fails to clear the net.

"How far apart can you be and still keep the ball on the bench?"

Task 154 Target serve (novices)

Object: to serve accurately to a target area.

Chalk targets on each side of a table. Player **A** drops the ball onto the table and hits it to bounce in the far target area. Player **B** catches the ball and serves it to the target area nearest to **A**. Change ends after a set number of turns.

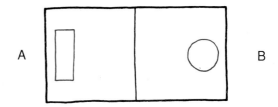

Easier variation: Let the players draw the target area they will aim into. Encourage them to make this smaller as they improve.

Extending variations:

• Use forehand and backhand on alternate services.

• (intermediate players) Place a 'net' across the centre of the table.

• (advanced players) Mark two targets on each side of the table, to the left and right of the mid-line. The players have to serve into each target alternately.

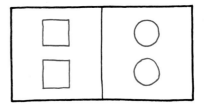

This task with its variations offers several different levels of difficulty without needing to adjust the placing of tables. Explain how each variation increases in difficulty, and let pupils choose which to attempt. Make sure that they are all striving to move up to the next level; for example: "When you can serve the ball into that target four times in succession, you can try again with a net across the table."

Task 155 *Obstacle dodge (novices)*

Object: to keep facing the table while moving quickly.

Use any suitable table with a dividing net. Place a chair about a metre (3 ft) from one end of the table.

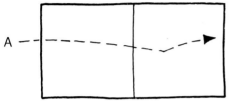

To start with, this is a throw-and-catch exercise: player **B** sidesteps round the chair, facing the table all the time, and as s/he gets to the far side of the chair, player **A** throws the ball (underarm) over the net. Player **B** has to try to catch the ball before throwing it back to **A** and moving round the chair again for another try.

The pupils change roles after several turns. At first, they may need to practise dodging around the chair without the ball being thrown.

Extending variations:

• (intermediate players) The task can be made a little harder if player **A** uses a bat and serves the ball over the net.

• (advanced players) Both players use a bat and try to maintain a rally with player **B** continuing to move round the chair. "How many shots can you manage before the rally breaks down?"

Task 156 *Wall-bounce rally (novices)*

Object: to maintain a rally and increase accuracy.

Place one end of the table against a wall. If the table is long enough it can be flush to the wall; if not, a gap may be left. Mark a rebound zone by chalking a line across the other end of the table, approximately 60 centimetres (2 ft) from the edge.

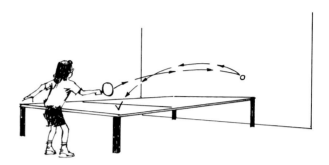

"Keep a rally going against the wall, and try to hit the ball so that it always bounces into the rebound zone."

Extending ideas:

• Keep the rally going on the forehand.

• Keep the rally going on the backhand.

• Alternate forehand and backhand.

• (advanced players) Join with a partner and take alternate shots.

Playing the ball against a wall is a useful way for pupils to practise most racket games because they can feed a ball to themselves and so repeat the strokes they wish to improve. Soon, they will be able to use their racket skills to play 'rebound games'.

SQUASH GAMES

These games may be played using tennis rackets and balls, but ideally squash rackets and balls should be introduced.

For complementary practices, let the pupils play all these games as cooperative rallies before making them competitive.

Game 157 Into the other half (novices)

Object: to develop accuracy; to rebound the ball off the front wall at such an angle that it lands in court.

A game for pairs, played against a flat wall.

A horizontal line is marked on the wall approximately 1 metre (3 ft) above the floor, and a court area is marked out on the ground. The court is divided down the centre by a line at right angles to the wall.

Each player takes either the left or the right court area. The player on the right serves the ball underarm to strike the wall above the line and land in the left court. The rally continues, with each player trying to hit the ball to bounce above the line and into the opposite court. Play as a single-bounce game, with alternating service. Change sides after five points.

Scoring: a player scores a point when the opponent fails to return the ball to hit the wall above the line, or if the rebound lands out of court or in the wrong half.

Extending variation: Allow volleys; players may hit the rebound off the wall either before or after it hits the ground.

Allowing volleys requires the players to judge the flight of the ball and to estimate whether or not it will land in court. They soon learn that a volley speeds up the return and can catch an opponent unprepared.

Game 158 Above the line (intermediate players)

Object: to control the angle and power of shots so that the ball stays in court but away from the opponent.

The game is essentially the same as Game 157 above, except that only the service must land in the opposite court; during rallies, the ball may land in either half of the court without penalty. If a player impedes an opponent who is moving to the ball a 'let' is given and the point is played again. Players serve alternately.

Scoring: a player scores a point when the opponent fails to return the ball to hit above the line, or if the rebound lands out of court.

Players should try to return to the mid-court after each stroke and be ready to move in any direction. They should keep checking the positioning of their opponent, both to avoid him/her and to wrong-foot him/her with the return stroke.

Game 159 Double trouble (advanced players)

Object: to work cooperatively with a partner; also as for Game 158.

This is a game for two pairs: **A1** and **A2**, **B1** and **B2**. The court is a larger version of that used in the previous two games. The players should have space to move about freely.

Each pair occupies one half of the court. Player **A1** serves into the opposite court for player **B1** to make the return. The rally continues in the sequence **A1–B1–A2–B2–A1–B1** and so on, until a point is scored because the ball was hit below the line on the wall or out of court, or was played twice in succession by the same player.

Game 160 Corner game (intermediate players)

Object: to judge angled rebounds by playing off a side wall.

Play the game on a court where two walls join at right angles. Mark a line 1 metre (3 ft) above the ground on one wall to indicate that it is the 'front' wall. *Whenever possible, pupils should experience playing this game with a left-hand side wall and with a right-hand one.*

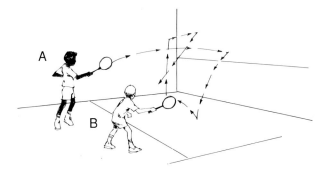

Player **A** serves from outside the court. The ball must hit the front wall and bounce in court. Player **B**'s return, and every shot for the rest of the rally, must hit the side wall, either before or after hitting the front wall, before bouncing back in court.

Scoring: you score a point if your opponent's shot fails to hit the front wall above the line, fails to hit the side wall once service is completed, or sends the ball out of court.

Easier variation: the court markings may be ignored.

Games-making task 161 Wall bounce

"With a partner, make up a game in which one or more balls bounce off a wall. You can choose the type of ball and the number of balls. You decide how the game will start, how the ball may be played, and how points are scored. What decides when the game is finished?"

Encourage the pupils to use any available equipment as part of their game.

LESSON PLAN 3

Intention: by the end of this lesson pupils should understand why it is important to move an opponent forward and back, and should be able to control the length of forehand and backhand strokes in order to set up a winning shot.

Pre-lesson organization: place baskets of rackets, balls and markers in three corners; each pair collects two markers, finds a clear section of line, and places the markers opposite each other approximately 3 metres (10 ft) either side of the line — this is their court. Benches, chairs and ropes or posts and nets will be needed to form the barriers.

Task (What pupils do)	Observations (What to look for)	Points to remember
Warm-up "Jog around the outside of the area. On command, slip-step to the left or right, stop and turn to run in the opposite direction."	Are they taking small steps? Can they keep their bodies upright? Are they looking out for others and avoiding them? Are they using their head and shoulders to lead into the turn?	Help those who are struggling to set out their markers. Check that pupils are joining in the warm-up as soon as they are ready.

Bridging organization: when a pupil passes a basket s/he collects a racket and goes on running to catch up with his/her partner. On command, one of the pair goes to collect a ball and the other goes to the court. Set the next task when both players are standing by a marker.

Revision "Play a single-bounce rally across the line, trying to make the ball bounce as close to the far marker as possible. Now add another marker on each side approximately 2 metres (6.5 ft) behind the first marker. Now try to rally so that the ball bounces alongside the back marker. Now can you alternate short, long, short, etc.?"	Do they recover to a good ready position after each shot? Can they maintain the full stroke and ease up on the speed to play the shorter ball, or do they check the swing and 'prod' at the ball?	Remind pupils about the stroke cycle (see pages 69–70).

Bridging organization: set out a net or barrier on the line, and if possible mark out two sidelines approximately 4 metres (13 ft) apart using ready-made lines, chalk or markers to make a long thin court. If the barrier is narrow it might be enough to say that the ball must go over it and so avoid the need for marked sidelines.

New work Game 125 Bounce (page 73). "See if you can play the ball into the back court to keep your opponent away from the net and then surprise him/her by playing the ball into the front court so that it cannot be returned to land anywhere in your court. If you do this you score 1. Out of court is beyond the back marker or over a sideline. Serve alternately.	Are they looking across the net to see where their opponent is positioned? Can they be patient and wait for a chance to play the shorter stroke into the front court? Are they trying to disguise the shorter stroke? Are they aiming the ball into a free space?	Have skill cards 1, 4 and 5 ready for underarm service and forehand and backhand drive. Have slow-bounce balls available. Change pairings to vary the challenge.
New work **Games-making:** Free play 1v1 competitive bounce game. Let pupils agree their own rules for serving and scoring points.	Are pupils actively trying to move their opponent away from where they expect to play a winning shot? Guide pupils to discover that if their opponent is drawn close to the net, the ball can be hit over the top of him/her to land in the back court.	Have skill card 10 available for those players ready to learn how to lob the ball over an opponent's head. Encourage independent practice before returning to the game.

Closing organization: ask the pupils to dismantle the courts and return the equipment to a collecting area or store.

Cool-down

"Walk gently throughout the area, taking care to avoid others. Stand and reach up tall, hands above your head. From this position bend over at the waist and gently reach down to touch your knees with your hands. Stretch up again, lower your arms and walk in."

LESSON PLAN 4

Net games
(no-bounce)

Intention: by the end of this lesson pupils should understand that no-bounce games are about grounding the shuttlecock or ball on the opposite side of the net while keeping it off the ground in your court.

Pre-lesson organization: fill three or four baskets with a mixed selection of rackets, shuttlecocks, small balls and large balls. Set up one long net at about the pupils' chest height, with braids tied to mark sections of the net as courts. If possible have a back-line to each small court. Separate courts may be used instead.

Organization for Task 1: set each basket out in a different corner of the working area. Each pupil collects *either* one large ball *or* a racket with a shuttlecock or small ball.

Task (What pupils do)	Observations (What to look for)	Points to remember
Warm-up and revision "Jog freely in the area (avoiding the nets), *either* carrying a large ball *or* resting a shuttlecock or small ball on your racket as you go. Now travel and keep your shuttlecock or ball in the air by hitting it with your hands or racket. In a space, can you keep your shuttlecock or ball in the air while sitting down and getting up again? Now travel again and when you meet a friend exchange equipment but do not let it touch the ground. Continue on to meet someone else and repeat the procedure."	Do the pupils look about them and avoid other pupils? Do they hit the ball up just far enough to keep control of it? Is the racket-head firm? Do the hands push the ball rather than slap at it?	Have skill cards 9 and 6 ready for the volleyball volley and dig.

Bridging organization: "Go and stand with the person nearest to you. When you have a partner, go to the net and position yourselves with one player on each side facing a gap between two braids."

Task	Observations	Points
New work "Using the large ball, play throw/catch and later strike across the net using underarm throws only. Using the rackets and shuttlecock or small ball, hit back and forth. Try to keep a rally going for as long as possible."	Do they help each other by hitting the ball fairly high? Are the pupils alert and ready to play the shuttlecock or ball?	Let pupils change their equipment from time to time if they wish.
New work Repeat the previous task, but now add a marker at the centre of the back-line on each half-court. Each time a shot is played over the net, the hitter has to run around the marker in time to play the return. "Try to help each other to keep the rally going." When ready, the pupils remove the markers and play a competitive no-bounce game: Game 143 No bounce or Game 144 Shuttle volley (page 81).	Do the pupils keep their eye on the shuttlecock or ball as they run around the marker? Are the hands or racket held ready to use? Do the pupils look for a space in the opposing court and try to hit the shuttlecock or ball into it?	**Easier variation:** bring the marker nearer to the net. Let pupils play against different opponents once a game is completed.

Closing organization: the pupils are to return the rackets, shuttlecocks and balls to the baskets. Remove the net and braids.

Cool-down

"Walk into a space and stand with feet apart and hands on hips. Keep your feet still and twist your body to the left, now to the right, and so on. Stand with feet together, and bend your knees so you go into the crouch position, making yourself as small as possible. Now, without hurrying, uncurl and stretch up tall. Relax. Walk in and change."

Invasion Games

INTRODUCTION

Invasion games are those in which two teams compete within a shared area. There is considerable diversity in the family, which includes association football (soccer), basketball, handball, hockey, lacrosse, netball, rugby league football and rugby union football. This section will help you to introduce your pupils to this diversity.

To avoid unnecessary repetition, the games have been grouped into those having a similar structure and related skills:

• **Goal-throwing games**, including basketball, handball, lacrosse and netball.

• **Try-scoring games**: the two codes of rugby football.

• **Goal-striking games**, including hockey and soccer.

All the materials presented in this section will prepare pupils for the specific requirements of the invasion mini-games featured in the green section.

The competitive games described are all even-sided ones. Information is given on progressing from simple to more complex games, and on how rules may be manipulated to change the pattern and flow of play.

The complementary practices include modified games which are designed to help your pupils understand simple tactics.

Three games-making tasks are provided on page 135.

COMMON PRINCIPLES

All these games require variations of the following skills:

• travelling with a ball

• sending

• receiving

• marking and intercepting

• challenging the player in possession

Different techniques may be used in the games, but it is important for pupils to understand the common principles underlying them all.

Passing is a typical example: whether throwing, hitting, or kicking, an effective pass depends on these combined skills of sender and receiver:

• The sender needs to exercise good judgement about who or where to pass to, which technique to use, whether to disguise the action, when to time the release, the direction of release, and how much power to use?

• The receiver has to judge where to be available, how and when to get away from an opponent, whether to attempt deception, and what to do if the ball does come.

INVASION GAMES

THE OBJECTS OF INVASION GAMES

The objects of invasion games are:

• to score by sending or carrying the ball to a special target or targets through territory defended by the opposing team

• to prevent the opposing team from scoring

• to have the higher score at the end of an agreed period of play

The means of success

Teams succeed in achieving these objects by:

• keeping possession and moving the ball

• countering the actions of their opponents, through individual and team action

• having the agility and speed to respond to game demands, and the stamina to sustain effort throughout play

• recognizing game problems, considering possible solutions, and making best-bet choices

Introduce pupils to the following basic principles at an early stage:

Principle 1 Get possession of the ball and use it intelligently.

Principle 2 If the opposition have the ball, stop them from moving it towards the target they are attacking, and try to regain possession yourself.

How these principles are used in regulation games will vary in accordance with the particular rules of each game. At this stage, you can temporarily modify game rules to help your pupils to understand the principles and exploit them. However, pupils will have to conform to the discipline of codes of rules when they start to play the regulation mini-games described in the green section.

THE DEMANDS OF THE GAMES

Always bearing in mind the three components of games performance — **skill**, **insight** and **physical preparedness** — try to follow these guidelines:

• Invasion games are essentially running games, so avoid practices which require pupils to stay in one place for any length of time.

• Keep team sizes small, so that at any moment each player has relatively few options. Also, the resulting intensive activity allows each pupil maximum contact with the ball.

• Players are required both to cooperate and to compete. Help pupils to know when it is best to accept support from others.

• Be flexible and sensitive when grouping pupils into teams.

• Skilful, quick or physically strong players should learn how to use their advantage in the best interests of the team.

• Encourage your pupils to note what proves successful and what lets them down.

• Exercise your judgement in teaching on the one hand that winning is not everything, but also that it is important to strive to win.

PLAYING AREAS

When deciding the size and shape of a pitch or court, give due consideration to the number of players, their skill levels and how big they are.

Because they are played in a shared area, invasion games allow players to challenge their opponents in an attempt to disrupt their play. When skill levels are relatively low, reduce this pressure by giving the players a reasonable amount of time and space in which to think and act.

On the following pages you will find many suggestions for altering the demands of a game to provide effective play at different levels of skill. By dividing your class up into appropriate groups and providing playing areas of different sizes, you can accommodate mixed abilities. If you use a different set of coloured markers for each playing area, you can direct players easily to their locations: "Your group to the blue area", "Your game to the yellow area", etc.

GOALS AND SCORING

All invasion games require players to score by sending or placing a ball into or over some form of goal. Goals are usually placed on or near the endlines of the playing area. There is a wide variety:

• rectangular, at ground-level and defended by a goalkeeper: handball, hockey and soccer

• small and sited off the ground: basketball, netball

• large and sited off the ground: rugby

• just a line: rugby, again

You can vary the difficulty of scoring into any particular goal by requiring players to:

• shoot from anywhere

• shoot only from inside a marked area

• shoot only from outside a marked area

Whatever type of goals you are using, start with a size which is large enough to encourage scoring, and gradually reduce the size as shooting skills improve.

Rugby — a special case

When introducing any of the rugby-based games, it is important to concentrate on scoring by carrying the ball through or around the defence and on over the **try-line**, rather than on kicking goals from free play.

Positioning goals for effect

You can use a lot of flexibility when deciding on the size and position of goals. With a little thought, you can help your players to progress much more easily than if they are restricted to the use of regulation goals. Here are some suggestions which apply to any basic equal-sided invasion game:

If you do not want a goal to be easily defended, you can:

• Put a 'no-go' area in front of it. No-go areas cannot be entered by attackers, and can be entered by a defender only when retrieving a dead ball. If any other player enters a 'no-go' area, the ball is awarded to the opposing team.

a large skittle or cone in a circle or semi-circle   a larger goal with a line across the playing area to make an 'end zone'

• Make it too wide for one player to cover.

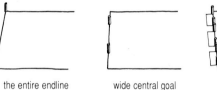

the entire endline   wide central goal   multiple goals

• Place the goal high enough to be out of reach, yet low enough for players to score in.

Some posts suitable for netball- or basketball-based games are adjustable so that the ring can be raised and lowered. Certain designs also allow it to be tilted towards the court.

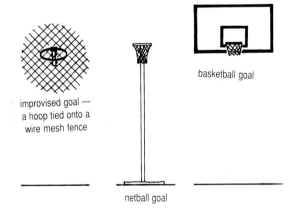

improvised goal — a hoop tied onto a wire mesh fence

basketball goal

netball goal

If you want to encourage the players to use the full width of the playing area:

• Avoid using single central goals. Because the goals in regulation games are usually sited in the centre of each endline, players tend to crowd into the middle of the playing area. Exhorting them to "spread out" or "stay wide" usually has little effect, so try these variations:

 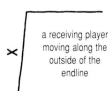 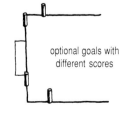 

diagonal goals   a receiving player moving along the outside of the endline   optional goals with different scores   optional goals with different scores

FORMING TEAMS

Given a free choice, children will usually form teams from among their friends. Often this is fine, but from time to time you will have to organize the membership of teams to:

• ensure that teams are evenly matched in competitive games

• group pupils according to ability and offer graded practices or games

• group pupils according to size and strength, especially when physical contact is likely

• ensure that a skilled player is included to help a group of less-able players

How many players in a team?

You need to get the number of players in your teams just right. This is because choosing (decision-making) is an essential skill in team games, and your pupils must learn which choices to make. Should they:

• keep the ball?

• pass the ball?

• travel with the ball?

• shoot?

If there are too many players in a team, they may become confused by the range of possibilities.

If there are too few players in a team, they may not have enough possibilities from which to choose.

Small-team activity

It is common to play 2v2 games, because they offer lots of involvement and are easy to set up. However, they give the ball-carrier only one choice of receiver.

What does this mean in practice? It depends on the rules of the game:

If the ball-carrier cannot travel with the ball (as in netball), progress relies on the team-mate being available to receive a pass. With only one possible receiver, the game frequently breaks down if that one receiver cannot get away from an opponent (see illustration at head of next column) ...

... or if the second opponent, knowing that the ball-carrier has to pass, joins in marking the one receiver.

If the ball-carrier is allowed to travel with the ball (as in most games) the game is still limited by having only one possible receiver, but the ball-carrier has many choices:

• to attack the goal

• to move to open up space for a pass

• to delay making a pass in order to give time for the team-mate to evade a marker

• to draw a defender away from a route to goal or from your team-mate.

2v2 has its uses, but it also has limitations, so increase the team size as players learn:

• not to chase after the ball all the time

• to respond to a change of possession and recognize when their team is on the offensive or the defensive

• to scan the playing area in their search for a receiver

(When carrying the ball, novices tend to look in one place, or at players nearest to them. They also can be confused by pleas from team-mates, all of whom want to be chosen as the next receiver.)

• to speed up the process of scanning, choosing and responding

- to send the ball accurately over longer distances

- to receive with control

The most important guideline is to choose team sizes which keep every player involved.

Remember, playing in increasing team sizes is not a linear progression. From 5v5 games pupils should, from time to time, return to smaller games such as 3v3 to focus on a particular skill. Even international teams do that!

By changing or suspending certain rules, you can easily alter the nature of a game. This can be a useful way of introducing pupils to the significance of rules in preparation for the time when they are invited to devise their own games.

Here are some examples. First, a look at games in which the travel of the player with the ball is restricted. In these games, usually:

- The ball-carrier must release the ball within a time limit (e.g. three seconds), or it is given to the opposing team.

- The player with the ball cannot be tackled — the opposition must gain possession by intercepting passes.

In games where players **are** allowed to travel with the ball, any or all of these rules may apply:

- Tackling is allowed.

- The body may be used to shield the ball from an opponent.

- The player in possession must either keep moving or pass; no stopping and re-starting is allowed.

- Travelling with the ball is allowed only on certain areas of the court or pitch.

Try applying or suspending any of these rules as appropriate, and ask the pupils to decide if the changes improve the game or spoil it.

You will find it useful to build up a repertoire of practice patterns which can be applied to a wide range of techniques.

A typical simple pattern is **unopposed passing in pairs**:

Two players travel side by side to a marker, passing to each other as they go. When they reach the marker, they switch sides and return.

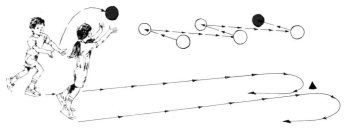

Variations can easily be introduced: this time one player runs straight forward and the other passes and runs behind to make a weaving pathway.

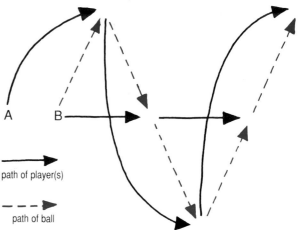

Clearly a practice pattern like this can be followed by pupils throwing and catching a ball, or kicking it, or hitting it with an implement. For example, the following task could easily be adapted for soccer or hockey.

Task 162 *Deft dodge*

Object: to speed up throwing and catching, and to encourage nimble footwork.

Work in threes.

Two markers are placed about 6 metres (20 ft) apart. Players **A** and **B** each have a ball and each stands by a marker. Player **C** starts about 5 metres (16 ft) in front of **A**. To play, **A** passes to **C**, who immediately returns the pass and then runs across to accept one from **B**. Player **C** continues sprinting between the two throwers until ten passes are completed or a ball is missed. The players then rotate through the three roles.

Extending variation: use one ball; when **A** or **B** receives the return pass from **C**, s/he passes it to the other, who then tries to beat the running **C** with the speed of the next pass.

USING RELAYS FOR PRACTICE

Relays offer a lot of practice possibilities. They are easy to organize, offer a controlled practice situation, and accommodate relatively large numbers in a small area.

There are three basic relay patterns, illustrated at the foot of the page.

All the core skills of travelling with or without a ball may be practised using relays.

Although relays give the impression of intense activity, remember that, in a team of four, only one pupil is actually active at any one time.

Relay dos and don'ts

✓ **Do** keep team numbers small — treat four as the maximum.

✓ **Do** choose a distance which gives pupils enough time to focus on their techniques.

✓ **Do** occasionally let pupils set their own distance by seeing how far they can go 'there and back' in a given time. The challenge then is to increase that distance with practice.

✓ **Do** use markers to vary the pathways to be followed by setting them at different intervals, and not necessarily in straight lines. This encourages changes of pace and footwork.

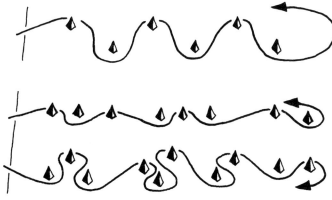

✓ **Do** focus pupils' attention on how to speed up their progress by refining their techniques. Giving feedback and guidance makes relays valuable as well as fun.

✗ **Don't** make every relay a competition against adjacent teams — sometimes let teams repeat relays to see if they can improve their own scores within a given time.

✗ **Don't** position the courses so that children may run into walls, fences or other potential hazards.

✗ **Don't** fall into the trap of talking to the pupils after every run — let them have lots of turns before you focus their concentration on how they are working.

Remember! Relays are good for practising, but they do not promote maximum involvement. Use them sparingly.

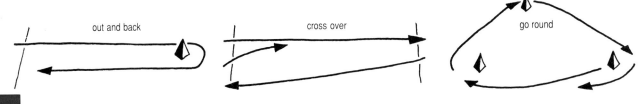

RULES FOR GAMES DESCRIBED IN THIS SECTION

Take care!

Teachers sometimes join in play with the children. There are many good reasons for this — it may be to distribute the ball, to involve neglected players, or to help a weaker team. Take care when joining in that you do not use your size, strength or speed to endanger or intimidate any pupils.

The following rules apply to all games unless otherwise stated:

• The ball is returned into play by a member of the team opposing that of the player who last touched it.

• When a goal is scored, the game is restarted from the centre of the court or pitch. It is usual for the restart to be made by the team that conceded the goal, but you may allow them to take turns, or alternatively a player from each team may compete for the ball (e.g. a throw-up).

• If a rule is broken, a free pass is awarded to the opposing team at the place where the foul occurred.

• A shot at goal may not be taken directly from a free pass or when returning the ball into play.

Unless otherwise stated, the goal-throwing games can be adapted for kicking and striking activities.

GOAL-THROWING GAMES

This group includes basketball, handball, lacrosse and netball.

There are two types of games within the group: those where the ball-carrier's movements are limited, and those where players are allowed to travel freely with the ball.

Games 163 and 164 illustrate these two basic types.

Game 163 Restricted travel (novices and intermediate players)

Object: to help players choose the best option out of two or more possible receivers and decide whether it is best to pass or to shoot.

Play this as 3v3 for novices, increasing to 4v4 and 5v5 as skills improve.

Use a marked rectangular court with a centre spot or line. Site a goal which is not easily defended in the centre of each endline. Identify the two teams by coloured bibs or braids. Use either a medium-sized ball, or a large light one.

Special restrictions: players may throw to a team-mate or into goal, but can take no more than **three steps** when holding the ball. *This forces players to keep a good look-out and* **choose** *a receiver, rather than going solo.*

Rules:

• Players may stand wherever they like at the start of play.

• Play is started by a pass from the centre of the court.

• The ball may not be touched when being held by an opponent.

• The ball may be regained by interception or by capturing a loose ball.

• The ball may not be held for more than five seconds (pupils may count up to five out loud).

Game 164 Free travel

Object: for pupils to learn whether it is best to travel with the ball or pass it to a team-mate.

2v2 or 3v3 for novices; 4v4 or 5v5 for intermediate players.

Play in a rectangular court with markings and goals as in Game 163. Use a ball with a good rebound. It can be medium-sized, or larger but lighter.

Special restrictions: players may throw to a team-mate or into goal, and may travel with the ball by bouncing it on the ground as they go (**dribbling**). The body may be used to shield the ball from an opponent's challenge.

Rules:

• Players may stand wherever they like at the start of play.

• The opposition may get the ball by intercepting a pass, by knocking the ball away as it is bounced, or by capturing a loose ball. They may not take or knock the ball from the hands of an opponent.

• Any player who stands holding the ball must pass within five seconds.

• No restarts: a player who dribbles and then stops and holds the ball may not start the dribble again.

Game 165 Half-court (advanced players)

Object: to help players to learn to switch from defence to attack and vice versa.

3v3 or 4v4.

The game is played on a half-court, with just one goal. A marker is placed on the mid-line of the court, at least 15 metres (49 ft) from the goal. Use a ball with good rebound. It can be medium-sized, or larger but lighter.

Special restrictions: Both teams try to gain possession and score, but during every attack the ball must be taken around the marker before the team in possession can shoot at goal. This game works best if the players are allowed to dribble.

Rules:

• Start play by giving the ball to one team at the marker.

• Neither team may attempt to score without starting from the marker or travelling around it with the ball.

• When a team scores, the other team restarts play from the marker.

Extending variations:

Increase the team sizes. To make sure every player is involved, insist that each member of a team has to touch the ball at least once before a shot at goal can be attempted. This can work well until the opposition realizes that one particular player has yet to touch the ball and they deploy all their team to mark him/her out of the game. An alternative is to require a team to make at least three passes before being allowed to shoot at goal.

Game 166 Mark the player (novices)

Object: to introduce the concept of person-to-person marking.

3v3 or 4v4.

Use a square or rectangular playing area; no goals are required. Any two opposing sides are designated as the goal-lines. Use a ball with good rebound; it can be medium-sized, or larger but lighter. Two sets of colour-coded, numbered bibs designate the teams.

The players are paired, so that number 1 in one team marks number 1 in the other, and so on.

A goal is scored whenever the ball is passed to a player who is positioned beyond the opponent's goal-line. Thus any player may become a 'goal'.

Players may travel with the ball by dribbling, and may also pass it to team-mates. They may re-start a dribble even after having stopped and held the ball. The body may be used to shield the ball from an opponent's challenge.

Rules:

• The game is started by a pass from one endline.

• A player may challenge and mark only his/her direct opponent.

• The opposing player may gain possession of the ball by touching it at any time, including when it is being held. As soon as the ball is touched, possession is lost, and it must be handed to the challenger, who can then dribble or pass.

• To score, the ball must be **passed** to a player over the goal-line; it may not be dribbled over the line.

• Only one player from each team is allowed over the goal-line during a scoring attempt. A penalty goal is awarded if two defenders are over the line against one receiving attacker: if two attackers go over, their team is penalized by possession being awarded to the defenders.

Extending variation:

After gaining possession, every player in the team must touch the ball at least once before a goal may be scored.

Game 167 Speed-pass (intermediate players) (throwing only)

Object: to speed up passing skills, and to find the best technique for keeping possession.

3v3 or 4v4.

Playing area: any square or rectangular space.

The teams spread out at random in the playing area. Each team aims to make five consecutive passes without the ball being intercepted by the other side. These five passes score as one goal. After each successful five-pass series, the ball is given to the other side. If the ball is intercepted, the side gaining possession immediately tries to make five passes in a row. Play is continuous.

This game is not strictly an invasion game, because the players do not attack and defend goals in shared territory. It can help your pupils to avoid opponents when passing, but you need to watch out for the tendency for the players to crowd together and make short passes. Use the game sparingly as an exercise to help your pupils develop quick handling and the ability to scan the possibilities and choose a free receiver.

Game 168 Dribble in (intermediate players)

Object: to demonstrate how three players working in triangular formations can pass more effectively than if they operate in straight lines.

3v3.

Played in a rectangular area with wide goals at each end. Use a ball with good rebound; it can be medium-sized or larger but lighter.

Players may travel with the ball by dribbling it. They may stop, restart and pass at will. The body may be used to shield the ball from an opponent's challenge.

Rules:

• A goal is scored when a player dribbles a ball through the goal and over the endline. It must be under the control of the dribbler and may not be thrown.

• Players may stand wherever they like at the start of play.

• The game is started by a player passing or dribbling the ball from the centre of the court.

• An opposing player may gain possession of the ball by touching it at any time, including when it is being held. As soon as the ball is touched, possession is lost, and it must be handed to the challenger, who can then dribble or pass.

• The player with possession also loses it if s/he:

— stands holding the ball for more than five seconds;

— takes more than three strides with the ball in the hands;

— runs into an opponent and causes body contact.

In each case the ball is given to the opposing team.

• After a goal, the game is re-started from the centre by a player from the team conceding the goal.

Game 169 No-entry zone (advanced players) (throwing only)

Object: to introduce zone defence and encourage a fast break in attack.

4v4 or 5v5.

The playing area is as for Game 168, but no-entry zones are marked out by lines across the court 5 metres (16.5 ft) in front of each goal. Use a medium-sized ball with good rebound — larger than a tennis ball but smaller than a netball.

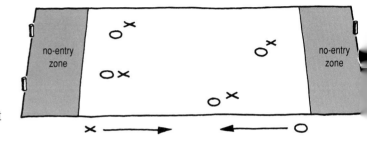

Rules:

Except for scoring, the rules are as for Game 168, with three additional rules concerning the no-entry zone:

• A goal is scored when an attacker throws or rolls a ball into the goal from outside the no-entry zone.

• No player may enter the no-entry zone.

• If the ball goes dead in the no-entry zone, or goes out over the endline, the defending team restarts the game with a pass from the zone-line.

Tactical tips:

• The defenders may retreat and form a 'wall' by standing shoulder-to-shoulder at the zone-line.

• The attackers should act fast to get into a shooting position before the defenders can block the route to goal.

• The attackers may leap to throw the ball over the wall, or pass the ball up and down in front of the wall to open up a space for a shot.

Extending variations:

• Increase the size of the no-entry zone to 7 metres (23 ft).

• Widen the goals and introduce goalkeepers. At first confine them to working within the no-entry zone, then later let them cover the whole court. This really encourages rapid changes from defence to attack and vice-versa.

COMPLEMENTARY SKILL-DEVELOPMENT TASKS

Good passing is the key to success in invasion games. This series of tasks will help your pupils to learn effective principles and practical techniques.

Unless stated otherwise, all these passing practices are equally suitable for throwing, kicking or striking activities, with very slight modifications.

TRIANGULAR PLAY

Attacking teams need to create at least two possible passes for the ball-carrier to choose from.

Game 168 (page 100) introduced an important principle: **triangular formations increase passing options**.

Show players with the ball how to **pivot** to keep it safe and to open up a new direction for a pass.

Triangles should be fluid: a player can run across the space, with or without the ball, and still preserve the essential triangular formation.

Rotating the triangle can take defenders away from the goal, and enable the attacker with the ball to peel off and go in for a shot at goal.

By contrast, a straight line is very limiting, as the illustration **left** demonstrates.

To introduce the idea of support play, teach your pupils to position themselves where they can receive a pass in front of or behind the ball-carrier, or to either side.

UNOPPOSED OR OPPOSED?

P actices can be either **unopposed** or **opposed**.

Unopposed practices are not very game-like and therefore soon become boring. They lack the essential ingredient of play! Use them sparingly.

However, unopposed passing practices remove the pressure and disruption caused by the presence of opponents, so they can have their uses. They enable the pupils to concentrate on:

• learning a range of techniques for sending and receiving

• developing control of power to send short and long passes

• speeding up the catch/throw sequence

• coordinating a pass with the movement of a team-mate.

Adding challenges can make unopposed practices more fun. For example, "How many passes can you make in 30 seconds?" or "How quickly can you go from here to the far line, making four passes on the way?".

Better still, try to make skill-development tasks game-like by introducing one or more opponents and by including some form of scoring into the practice.

Teach attacking play and defensive play at the same time. Invasion games depend on this constant interplay between defence and attack. The players need to think: "If I do this, what will my opponent do?", or "If s/he does that, how should I respond?" Help pupils to appreciate that effective play in games is about planning how to outwit the opposition as well as being able to outrun them or demonstrate better skills.

UNOPPOSED PASSING

Several unopposed practices can be operated at once if the pupils work in pairs. Two or three markers are all you need to set out the pattern for each practice.

Task 170 Pass ahead (novices)

Object: to pass ahead of a running player.

Work in pairs.

Set two markers approximately 10–12 metres (33–39 ft) apart.

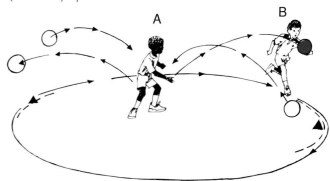

Player **A** stands between the markers holding the ball. Player **B** runs clockwise around the outside of the markers. **A** throws the ball over a marker to coincide with **B**'s run. **B** returns the ball to **A**, who turns ready to pass back to **B** at the second marker. "Time the release and control the strength of the throw so that **B** runs comfortably to the ball."

When playing this as a throwing exercise, require **B** either to dribble briefly before returning the pass (as in basketball) or to stop still within two steps before passing (as in netball). Change roles and direction frequently.

When playing this task as a kicking or striking activity, **A** sends the ball to the side of the marker ahead of **B**.

Task 171 Running passes (intermediate players)

Object: to pass ahead of a running player.

Work in pairs.

Set two markers approximately 5 metres (16 ft) apart.

Both players run around the outside of the two markers in a clockwise direction, continuously passing the ball to each other. "Can you direct your passes so that you can both keep up an even running speed?"

Change direction frequently.

This practice is also very useful for developing the swing pass in rugby.

Task 172 Pass and dribble (novices)

Object: to judge passes to a running player.

Work in pairs.

Set out two markers approximately 8 metres (26 ft) apart.

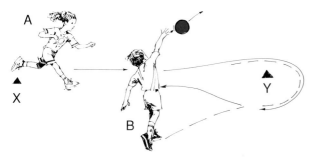

Player **A** runs from marker **X** towards marker **Y**. Player **B** stands to one side between the two markers and throws the ball so that it can be caught by **A**, who dribbles it around **Y** and passes it back to **B**. The task is then repeated in the opposite direction. Change over after a set number of passes.

Extending variation: Add a third marker **Z** about 2 metres (6.5 ft) beyond marker **Y**. The ball must now be passed so that it is caught while **A** is between these two markers. **A** dribbles the ball around **Z** and to where **B** was standing, and the players switch roles; the practice is continuous. After a few exchanges, move the thrower to the other side of the row of markers, so that the catch has to be made from the left as well as from the right.

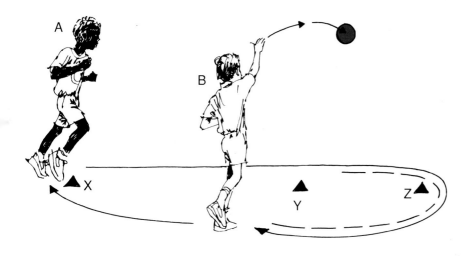

Task 173 Rapid return (novices)

Object: to receive a pass and return it immediately.

Work in pairs.

Set out two markers approximately 10 metres (33 ft) apart.

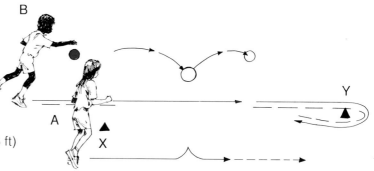

Player **A** starts just behind marker **X**. Player **B** has the ball and starts alongside **A** but a few metres away. **B** dribbles the ball past the marker and passes to **A**, who receives it and immediately passes it back to **B**, who carries on to dribble around marker **Y**. They repeat the task travelling the other way.

Change roles after a set number of turns.

Extending variations:

"Can **A** receive and return the pass without stopping or slowing?"

"Can you reduce the gap between the markers so that you have to speed up the 'give and go'?"

Task 174 Parallel pairs (advanced players) (throwing only)

Object: to judge long and short passes.

Work in pairs.

Use a large rectangular area. If necessary, use markers to define lanes.

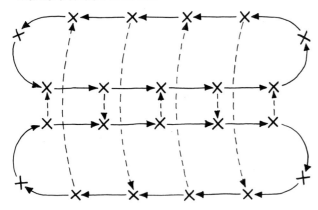

The pairs travel lengthways as shown in the diagram. They start by making short passes while going down the centre; on reaching the end, they peel off to left and right to send long, high passes over the pairs coming up the centre. Play is continuous. Change direction from time to time.

Start with the centre lanes quite close together, and gradually increase the gap.

Task 175 Pass it out (advanced players) (throwing only)

Object: to control the ball and to pass on a signal from a team-mate.

For groups of pairs.

Use several square areas with sides approximately 10–12 metres (33–40 ft) long. Three or four pairs of players occupy each square, with one ball to each pair. In each pair the player with the ball dribbles it freely in the area, which needs to be 'busy', so that the dribblers have to thread their way around the others. A dribbler has to keep control until his/her partner dodges outside the square and signals to receive a pass. If the pass is successful the receiver dribbles back in and play continues. Passes cannot be made over the same sideline twice in succession.

Extending variation: Add an extra player (a tagger) into each square, who tries to touch any bouncing ball. S/he takes possession when successful; the previous dribbler becomes the tagger and a new pairing is made.

Task 176 Speedball (novices)

Object: to return passes quickly, so that catching and throwing appear to be one movement instead of two separate actions.

For groups of six players.

Five pupils, standing about 2 metres (6.5 ft) apart, form an arc. The sixth stands about 6 metres (20 ft) in front of them and throws the ball to the player on the end of the line, who returns it as quickly as possible. Continue down the line and back. Try racing adjacent groups.

Task 177 Race the ball (intermediate players)

Object: rapidly to receive from one direction and pass to another.

For two teams of three.

Set out three markers to form a triangle with 8-metre (26-ft) sides. Team **A** places a player at each marker, with a ball at marker 1. Team **B** assembles in a line behind marker 1. On an agreed signal, team **A** starts to pass the ball around the triangle, and the first player from team **B** starts a relay run right around the outside, each of the team having to touch the next at the end of each lap. Can team **A** send the ball around three times before team **B** completes three circuits?

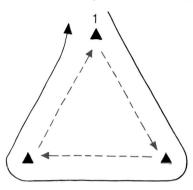

Extending variation: As passing skills improve, see if the ball can be passed around the triangle to beat a single runner who starts one marker ahead of the ball and who thus runs along only two sides of the triangle.

Task 178 Triangulate (advanced players)

Object: to learn how to make and maintain triangular formations when passing.

For groups of three.

The three players start in a triangle. Player **A** passes to player **B**, and then runs forward between **B** and **C** to make a new triangle. As **A** runs, **B** passes to **C** and runs in turn. Play proceeds, keeping up the rhythm: catch—pass—run between the other two players.

Extending variation: The receiver can pass either to the standing player or to the runner.

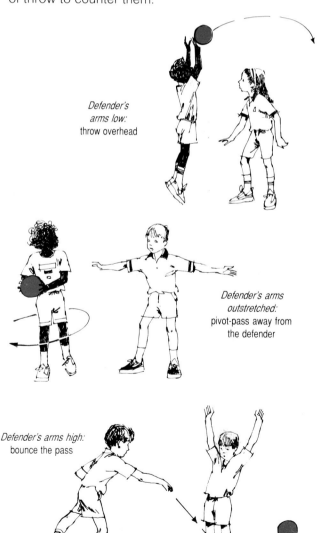

OPPOSED PASSING

All competitive invasion games involve players in opposed passing. The following practices enable your pupils to focus their attention on one or two aspects of passing without the pressure of a competitive game. If you wish, scoring may be introduced to offer incentives, to help pupils monitor their progress and to retain the element of **play**!

Countering defence

In throwing games, defenders need to make the best use of the three basic defensive arm positions, and attackers have to select the best choice of throw to counter them:

Defender's arms low: throw overhead

Defender's arms outstretched: pivot-pass away from the defender

Defender's arms high: bounce the pass

Task 179 Triangle block (intermediate players) (throwing only)

Object: to choose the most suitable throw for passing to a team-mate when an opponent is blocking the way.

For groups of three.

Set up three markers to form a triangle; place them about 5 metres (16 ft) apart to start with — you can increase this later.

Players **A** and **B** are inside the triangle; **A** stands in the centre with the ball. Player **C** remains outside the markers, but can run in any direction. **A** has to stay in the centre of the triangle and pass to **C**, while **B** tries to block every pass. When **C** catches the ball cleanly s/he runs into the centre of the triangle and **A** moves to the outside. If **B** gets the ball, s/he switches with the thrower.

Extending variation: Incentives can be introduced by allowing players to build up personal scores: give one point for every successful pass sent or received, and one point every time the ball is won through blocking.

> *Overhead pass: skill card 14*
>
> *Pivot and chest pass: skill card 15*
>
> *Bounce pass: skill card 16*
>
> *One-handed pass: skill card 17*
>
> *Two-handed swing pass: skill card 18*

Task 180 The harrier (novices) (throwing only)

Object: to improve the skills of marking and getting free; learning to time the release of a pass.

For threes.

Player **A** has to try to pass to **B**, while **C** acts as the harrier, attempting to spoil or intercept the pass. To start, **A** throws the ball up into the air and jumps to catch it with both feet off the ground. On landing, s/he must pass to **B** within three seconds — encourage the players to count out loud. **C** scores a point if the ball is held for more than three seconds, two points if s/he touches the ball and three points if s/he catches it. If **B** successfully receives the pass s/he now throws the ball up and **C** marks **A**. Play continuously, but rotate roles from time to time, so that all the players act as the harrier for the same number of turns.

Task 181 Border raiders (intermediate players)

Object: to keep the ball moving towards the goal by avoiding the defenders and passing to fellow attackers.

For groups of 16, divided up into four defenders and four teams of three attackers ('raiders').

This task can be adapted to any of the invasion games. The teacher decides which **conduct rules*** will apply: for example, it may be appropriate to allow the players to run with the ball in their hands, or you may decide to allow dribbling only. After a few practice runs, you may give the children the opportunity of setting the conduct rules themselves.

*Conduct rules determine how players may play the ball and what they may do to gain possession.

Mark two 'courts' as shown in the diagram. Each group of three attackers has a ball.

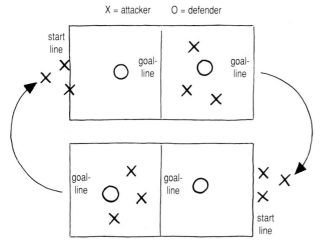

X = attacker   O = defender

One defender occupies each half-court, while two groups of three attackers assemble at each start line. On each court, one group of attackers at a time has to try to play the ball past the defenders, who must stay in their own court-halves. The attackers score when one of their team gets into position over the far goal-line and catches a pass over it from a team-mate. The defenders prevent the attackers from scoring by touching either the ball or the player holding it.

A team can set off as soon as the previous one has completely cleared the half-court next to the start line. Play is continuous, with the attackers moving down one court and up the other.

Encourage attackers to devise their own strategies for getting past the defenders, rather than just rushing forward and hoping for the best. Point out how passing in a triangular pattern opens up passing options.

At regular intervals, each defender changes places with a player in an attacking team, so that everyone takes turns at defending.

> *Getting free forward or back: skill card 19*
>
> *Getting free to either side: skill card 20*
>
> *Marking facing the ball: skill card 21*
>
> *Marking facing the player: skill card 22*

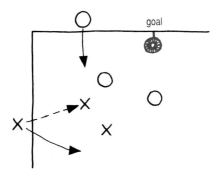

Task 182 *Scoring dash (intermediate players)*

Object: to give a pass and reposition quickly for the return.

For groups of five players.

Mark two parallel lines at least 12 metres (39 ft) apart, to form a central zone.

Identify the players as three attackers and two defenders. Two of the attackers and both defenders stay within the lines, while the remaining attacker starts outside the lines and passes to a team-mate. S/he then runs to cross both lines while the team-mates pass the ball between them as often as they like. When the first attacker has crossed to the far side of the central zone, the ball can be passed to him/her to complete the run. If a defender gets the ball, the attackers fail to score and the ball is given to an attacker to start again. Rotate all the roles frequently.

Extending variations:

You can introduce many variations into this task. For example, if you have previously allowed unlimited dribbling, restrict the ball-carrier's travel to a pace or two — or perhaps ban it altogether. Alternatively, limit the time for which the ball may be held; or restrict the passing techniques allowed, for example "No overhead passes" or "Use bounce or overhead passes only".

Task 183 *Quarter game (advanced players)*

Object: to rehearse marking and getting free; to respond to changes of possession.

For two teams of three.

Mark the area as shown in the diagram, or use the corner of an existing court. Place a goal on one of the sides.

Designate one team as the attackers, the other as the defenders. The attackers have to try to get the ball into the goal, while the defenders try to gain possession.

One player from each team starts outside the marked area: an attacker, with the ball, behind the sideline, and a defender behind the goal-line; the other four players are inside.

Play starts with the outside attacker passing to a team-mate. As soon as the ball is passed, the outside defender may enter the play from behind the goal-line. The game is played out until either the attackers score a goal or the defenders are able to intercept the ball and pass it over the sideline to a team-mate. (The receiver has to cross the sideline to receive the pass.)

You are free to set rules according to the skills of the players. For a throwing game, limiting travel to two steps and requiring the receiver to pass within three seconds works well. Don't allow tackling by taking the ball from the hands of the player in possession.

Extending variation: If possible, change the position of the goal after a while, so that the pupils can play both left-hand and right-hand versions of the task.

SHOOTING SKILLS

Good passing skills need to be backed up by good shooting skills. It is frustrating if a strong attack fails because of poor shooting. Accuracy can be improved through practice, and a good way to arrange this while keeping the pupils' interest is to organize a shooting circuit.

Many techniques are appropriate; shots may be one-handed or two-handed.

Shooting circuit

Goals in throwing games can be wide and low (handball), or small and high (basketball, netball). These practices deal mainly with shooting into small, high targets. The circuit challenges each pupil to realise his/her own potential and to build up the highest possible score in the available time.

• Pupils work in pairs and build up combined scores.

• Four pairs work at each station.

• Pupils rotate around the circuit: first to practise, and then to see how many points they can score in one minute at each station. (Allow more or less time if you wish.)

• At any station, pupils can switch to higher or lower scoring targets part-way through their allotted time if they wish.

• A partner may retrieve the ball after each shot and feed it back to the shooter.

The station activities given below are only suggestions: be prepared to improvise and to use substitute targets.

Standing one-handed shot: skill card 23

SHOOTING CIRCUIT

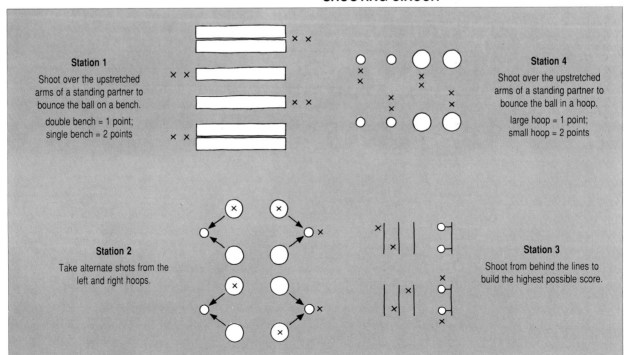

Station 1

Shoot over the upstretched arms of a standing partner to bounce the ball on a bench.

double bench = 1 point; single bench = 2 points

Station 4

Shoot over the upstretched arms of a standing partner to bounce the ball in a hoop.

large hoop = 1 point; small hoop = 2 points

Station 2

Take alternate shots from the left and right hoops.

Station 3

Shoot from behind the lines to build the highest possible score.

LESSON PLAN 5

Intention: by the end of this lesson your pupils should know how to mark an opponent and how to get free when being marked. They should also be better able to coordinate a pass with the actions of a team-mate.

Pre-lesson organization: set up four playing courts as described for Task 183 Quarter game on page 107. The goals should each be approximately 5 metres (16 ft) in from the corner. Provide enough balls for one between three pupils. Use bibs to identify one-third of the class.

Organization for Task 1: pupils go and spread out in the playing area.

Task (What pupils do)	Observations (What to look for)	Points to remember
Warm-up "Jog freely in the area. On command, sprint to touch a line and then go on jogging. Stop, and on the spot bounce on both feet; when I clap my hands sprint away, bounce again, sprint, and so on."	Are the pupils alert and light on their feet? Do they drive with their arms when sprinting?	Provide plenty of space. Ask pupils to keep watching and listening for commands.

Bridging organization: pupils form threes with one of them wearing a bib. One player collects a ball and the second and third players find space in which to work.

Task (What pupils do)	Observations (What to look for)	Points to remember
New work Task 180 The harrier (page 106). The player in the bib acts as defender. Each attacking pair has eight passes before an attacker changes places with the defender. Everybody takes a turn at defending. Compare scores.	**Attackers:** When trying to get free of the defender, do they wait to make their moves until their partner has caught the ball and is ready to throw to them? Do they pretend to go one way but quickly sprint in the opposite direction? Do they indicate where they want the ball? **Defenders:** Do they watch and respond to the movements of the attackers? and move quickly to intercept the ball once it has been released?	Rehearse short, quick sprints and sudden stops.

Bridging organization: each trio sets out two markers approximately 12 metres (40 ft) apart (lines of a grid may be used if the playing area is already marked out).

Task (What pupils do)	Observations (What to look for)	Points to remember
Revision Modified version of Task 172 Pass and dribble (page 103). Involve three players; two start at marker **X**, with the passer standing to one side between the markers. The pair run simultaneously, and the ball can be passed to either of them. They then dribble and bounce-pass it between them around **Y** and back towards **X**, to which the original passer has moved. During the return, one of the pair dribbles the ball off to one side, ready to become the passer. The other runs to **X** to form a new pairing which sets off back towards **Y**. Play continuously, rotating roles throughout.	**Passing:** Is the ball sent **ahead** of the running players? Is it thrown at a comfortable height? **Receiving:** Do the receivers indicate where they want the ball?	

Bridging organization: remove the markers. Double up the trios to make groups of six, with half wearing bibs (expand groups to eight or reduce to four to accommodate varied numbers). Set up a demonstration with six pupils. Gather the class to watch.

Task (What pupils do)	Observations (What to look for)	Points to remember
New work Task 183 Quarter game (page 107). Switch defending and attacking teams after four or five turns. Later switch opponents.	Check on the skills of marking and getting free. Watch shooting skills.	Have skill card 23 available for independent practice. Look out for teams which are poorly matched and make adjustments if needed.

Closing organization: the pupils remove the bibs, return the balls to the side and then run freely in the area. One team is given the task of collecting the bibs.

Cool-down
"Stand in a space, feet apart. Gently slide both hands down your right leg. Go as far as you can slowly, then straighten up and repeat with the left leg. Keep your legs straight. Repeat several times. Stand up and shake out. Walk in, trying to make yourself as tall as you can."

TRY-SCORING GAMES

These are the rugby-based group of games; at this stage no distinction is made between rugby league and rugby union. The games are played with an oval ball, and the primary way of scoring is by carrying the ball and placing it over a line. To familiarize pupils with the handling skills needed, you can use several of the games and practices featured in the goal-throwing games section, and simply:

• replace a round ball with a rugby ball

• allow pupils to run carrying the ball instead of dribbling

• modify rules where necessary.

No passing forwards!

Once pupils have become familiar with handling the oval ball, introduce this essential feature of these games:

The ball cannot be passed forwards, so pupils must **run forwards and pass backwards** to carry the ball towards the goal-line.

The ball may be **kicked** forwards, but although this can gain ground it often results in a loss of possession. Use kicking sparingly in the early stages, and when it is used make sure it is used constructively.

Physical contact — important safety note

Physical contact skills, including tackling, breaking a tackle, the hand-off and contested scrummaging, are **not** recommended for inclusion in rugby-football lessons at this stage unless you are sure that the pupils have the necessary skill and control.

Tackling is a particularly important feature of rugby league, and BARLA, the national governing body of the game, encourages teachers to introduce it early **if they are capable of teaching the skills competently and safely**. If you do decide to introduce physical contact, please refer to the guidance given in the green section (pages 161–216). If physical contact is not taught, then two-handed touch-tackling provides a satisfying substitute for pupils of this age range.

Touch rugby can be played on a playground, but **it is strongly recommended that grass surfaces be used for practice and competition, even when physical contact is not permitted**.

Playing area and equipment

It is assumed that all these games are played on a rectangular pitch divided into two halves by a centre-line. The pitch should be large enough to accommodate the size of teams you are using and to offer a satisfying game. A good guideline is 30 metres long by 20 metres wide (100 ft x 66 ft) when playing 5v5. Bear in mind that the wider you make the pitch, the easier it will be to score.

The required equipment is simply a rugby ball and two sets of bibs to distinguish the teams.

> **Lesson hints:** *Try to include game play, skill-development tasks and periods of intense activity in every lesson, to allow the children to appreciate the running aspect of these games and to promote skill, insight and physical preparedness.*

Rules

The following two rules apply to all the games in this section:

The touch tackle A player is successfully tackled when an opponent puts both hands on him/her simultaneously, below the waist. S/he must immediately release the ball.

Free-pass restart The usual way of penalizing a player who breaks a rule is to give possession to the other side, with a free-pass restart from the place where the offence was committed.

BASIC RUGBY GAMES

Game 184 describes a basic rugby-type game. Those which follow gradually introduce the special features which characterize rugby in general. The two codes of the league and union games are not differentiated until the green section

Game 184 Basic touch-rugby (novices)

Object: to introduce pupils to a basic rugby-type game without physical contact and with an emphasis on running and passing.

For teams of up to 5v5.

Techniques: running with the ball in the hands; passing backwards; scoring a try; touch tackling.

Scoring: A **try** (five points) is scored by placing the ball over the opponent's goal-line. The hand(s) must be on the ball as it contacts the ground — the ball may not be dropped onto the ground.

Rules:

• Start with the teams in their own halves; the team to make the first pass has a player right on the centre-line, with the rest of its players ranged behind and to the sides of him/her. The opposing team must be at least 7 metres (23 ft) back from the line.

• Start play with a pass from the centre of the pitch — make sure that the passer's team stay behind the ball.

• When the ball goes over a sideline it is passed into play by a member of the team which did not touch the ball last.

• After a try the game restarts from the centre, the team conceding the try making the first pass.

• Players may not pass or knock the ball forwards — all passes must go sideways or backwards (penalty: free-pass restart).

• If a player running with the ball is touch-tackled, s/he must pass as quickly as possible and in any event within three strides (penalty: free-pass restart).

• A player must not hand-off or fend-off an opponent (penalty: free-pass restart).

• The ball may not be kicked (penalty: free-pass restart).

Game 185 Five-metre retreat (novices)

Object: as for Game 184.

For teams of up to 5v5.

Rules: As for Game 184, but with the following changes:

• Having made a successful tackle the defending team must retreat 5 metres (16.5 ft) before the ball is put into play.

• The tackled player must stop, wait for the defenders to retreat, and then pass.

• If the attacking team has not scored a try after six tackles the ball is given to the other team for a free-pass restart.

Game 186 Roll-back restart (novices)

Objects: to introduce pupils to the **roll-back**, where the ball is rolled back to a supporting player using the sole of the boot, as a way of putting the ball into play; to emphasize running forwards with the ball but passing backwards.

For 4v4 or 5v5.

Techniques: roll-back; passing backwards; running with the ball; touch-tackling.

Rules and scoring: as in Game 2 above, except:

• Play is started and restarted by a player from the team with possession performing a roll-back to a team-mate.

• Defending teams may also get the ball by intercepting a pass, and in that case they are allowed to counter-attack immediately.

• If a foul move results in the ball going over the goal-line incorrectly (a 'foul try'), play restarts with a roll-back to the defending team 5 metres (16.5 ft) from the line.

INTRODUCING SCRUMMAGING

In modified versions of Game 186, the roll-back can be replaced by a 'chicken-scratch' scrum (see skill card 26) or a 3v3 uncontested scrum (see skill card 27). In both these scrums, the team that puts the ball in always wins the ball — the opposing team is not allowed to challenge for it.

Make sure that pupils have rehearsed the skills of the scrum and accept the 'uncontested' rule before introducing scrummaging in competitive games.

> Passing backwards: skill card 24
>
> Roll-back: skill card 25
>
> Chicken-scratch scrum: skill card 26
>
> Three-person uncontested scrum: skill card 27

INTRODUCING KICKING TECHNIQUES

Instinctively pupils want to **kick** a rugby ball. If this aspect of play is denied for too long, your pupils will become frustrated. So permit a limited amount of controlled kicking once they have developed a free-flowing game with running and passing.

Game 187 Grubbing on (advanced players)

Object: to introduce the grubber kick.

For 5v5 up to 7v7.

Rules: As for Game 184, but replace the no-kick rule with the following rules:

• The ball may be dropped from the hands and kicked forward, but it must touch the ground within 5 metres (16.5 ft) of the kicker. If it does not, the opposition gains a free-pass restart.

• All players in the attacking team must be behind the ball when it is kicked.

• A loose ball must not be kicked, but must be picked up in the hands.

Game 188 Punt and go (advanced players)

Object: to introduce the skills of kicking from the hands (the **punt**) and catching a high ball safely.

For 4v4 up to 6v6.

Techniques: punting the ball; running with the ball; catching a high ball; passing backwards.

Use a playing area marked out as shown in the diagram. Note the goal areas at each end. Adjust the size of the pitch according to the players' kicking ability and team sizes.

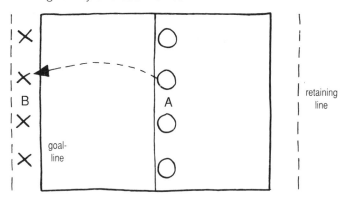

Rules and method of play:

• Team **A** lines up on the centre-line; the team **B** players wait in their goal area.

• To start, one player from team **A** kicks the ball from the centre of the pitch to drop inside **B**'s goal area.

• The players in team **B** try to catch the ball — if they fail, they retrieve it as quickly as possible — and run forward to try to score in team **A**'s goal area.

• Team **A** cannot move forwards until the ball is in the hands of a team **B** player.

• As soon as both teams are moving, play continues as in the normal two-handed touch-rugby game. Both teams attempt to score tries in the opposing goal area.

• After a successful touch-tackle, the ball is given to the opposition and the defenders must retreat 5 metres (16.5 ft).

• No kicking is allowed once the game is in progress.

• After a try is scored, the opposing team kicks off; the players in each team must take turns in doing this.

• If the ball goes over a sideline, the team which did not touch the ball last restarts with a kick-off from their end-line.

Scoring:

One point if the kick-off goes into the opponents' goal area without bouncing first.

One point to the defenders if a kick-off does not drop into the goal area.

One point to the defenders if the kick-off is caught before it touches the ground.

Five points for a try.

Kicking from the hands: skill card 28

Grubber kick: skill card 29

TRY-SCORING GAMES
COMPLEMENTARY SKILL-DEVELOPMENT TASKS

Task 189 *Tag-ball (novices)*

Objects: to help players to move the ball quickly by running and passing; to encourage sudden changes of pace and direction to avoid being tagged; to become alert to the actions of other players.

Work in groups of eight.

Play in any suitably-sized rectangular area.

The pupils are paired, and two pairs (the taggers) each have a ball. The game is tag, in which the pairs with a ball try to tag the others (the runners) by touching them with the ball. Tagging pairs may run with the ball and pass it between them, but the tagger must be **holding the ball** when the tag is made — **the ball must not be thrown at a runner**.

When tagged, runners must stand still until another runner touches them to release them back into play.

Rotate tagging pairs and running pairs frequently so that the pupils experience both roles.

Tag-ball can be made competitive by seeing how many players a pair can tag within a time-limit.

Task 190 *Double dodge (novices)*

Objects: to swerve and evade tackles when running with the ball; to react quickly to an attacker's actions.

Set out two sets of five markers as shown in the illustration.

Work in groups of five. Three of the children each carry a ball, and are the attackers; the other two are defenders.

A single defender stands in each marked zone. The attackers, going one at a time, have to try to get past the defenders without being tagged as they go through the zones. Each attacker starts from a single cone as the one in front gets past the defender.

The defenders may only move sideways and must face forwards all the time. A succesful tag is a one-handed touch below the waist.

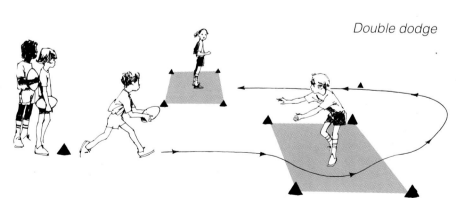

Double dodge

Task 191 Backpass and try (novices)

Objects: to pass backwards accurately to left and right; to practise try-scoring.

For pairs, with one ball per pair.

Use a marked square or rectangle, with a single marker placed as shown.

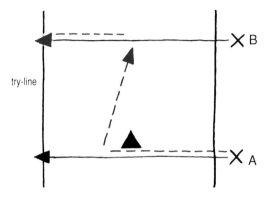

The players run into the area; B must keep parallel with A, but a metre or two (3–6 ft) behind. As A passes the marker, s/he throws the ball to B, who must catch it cleanly and run forward as fast as possible to ground the ball over the line. Player B then returns the ball to A. The pattern is then repeated in the opposite direction, with the pass now being made to the left. Change roles after several turns.

Make sure that the players hold their relative position so that the pass is always a backwards one.

Extending variation: add an extra marker at each end, about 2 metres (6 ft) beyond the try-line. Challenge the player receiving the pass to score a try before the passer can get to the marker beyond the try-line.

Task 192 Bring it back (novices)

Object: to gather up a loose ball and run on to score a try.

For pairs.

Place one marker on a line, and another 12–15 metres (40–50 ft) away.

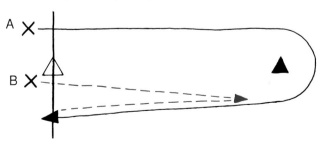

The players start side-by-side, behind the line. Player A runs around the far marker; as s/he starts to return, B rolls the ball forwards for A to run onto, pick up, and score a 'try' with by grounding it over the line by the start marker.

The players then change roles; the practice is continuous.

Extending variations:

"How many tries can your pair score in two minutes?"

Allow more-able players to use the grubber kick to send the ball, instead of rolling it.

Allow B to throw the ball high, for A to catch on the way back.

Task 193 Pick it up (intermediate players)

Object: to pick up a ball coming to the side while running; to give support to the ball-carrier.

For groups of four, with one ball per group.

Set out three markers as shown in the diagram. The idea is for pairs of players to run around the outside of the triangle, passing the ball between them. Once each lap, one of the players pauses at the third marker to roll the ball across the triangle for the inside player in the other pair to pick up. It works like this: player A runs from the first marker, closely supported by B. Player C rolls a ball from the third marker for A to pick up and then pass to B who runs on with A in close support; meanwhile C runs to join D at the start, and B pauses at the third marker to roll the ball for C and D. Look at the diagram; once the players get going it is not as confusing as it sounds!

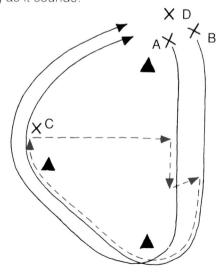

The practice should be continuous. After several turns, reverse direction so that the feed is made from the other side.

Task 194 *Along the line (intermediate players)*

Object: to receive the ball from one side and pass to the other.

For groups of three.

This exercise needs quite a lot of space. The player on the left of the line, **A**, starts by passing to **B** and running **behind** the other players to the end of the line. **B** passes to **C** and s/he too runs to the end of the line, and so on ... Play is continuous until the group runs out of space. When this happens, make the return run with the passes going in the opposite direction.

Make sure that the receivers are always behind the passers.

Task 195 *Hoop kicks (advanced players)*

Object: to kick accurately from the hands to land in a target area.

Work in pairs.

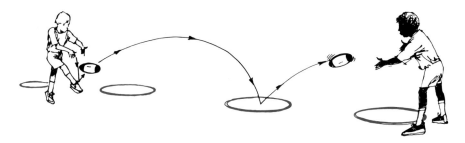

Set out four large hoops as shown in the illustration. The players take turns in trying to kick the ball into one of the distant pair of hoops. The player at the receiving end must let the ball bounce and then retrieve it as quickly as possible. After a

period of practice each kicker must nominate the hoop s/he intends to aim for by calling 'front' or 'back' to his/her partner. Score one for the front hoop and two for the back one.

Extending variation: The receiver stands inside the nominated hoop and tries to catch the ball.

Task 196 *Grub and go (advanced players)*

Object: to retrieve your own grubber kick and turn to make a quick second kick to a target.

Work in pairs, with one ball per pair.

Set out two markers and a target area as shown in the diagram.

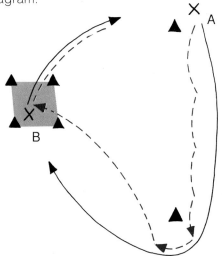

Player **A** grubber-kicks the ball from the first marker to the second. S/he runs after it and retrieves it close to the marker, turns, and immediately punts it to the target area where **B** is waiting. **B** catches it and runs to the first marker to take his/her turn, while **A** runs to the target area. Play is continuous.

"How many safe catches can you make within the target area?"

Task 197 Treble chance (novices)

Object: to learn to create an overlap in attack.

For groups of four.

Use a small marked square or rectangle. Place one marker about 1 metre (3 ft) in from the edge of the area as shown.

Three attackers, one with the ball, start at one corner of the area. The lone defender stands on the far line. The attackers attempt to move the ball around the marker and across the defender's line for a 'try'. They can pass the ball once it has been carried beyond the marker. The defender has to touch-tackle the ball-carrier; s/he must wait until the ball passes the marker before moving forward from the line.

As the attack is made, the support attackers must decide where to place themselves. Do they go one on each side? Or both to the same side? The attack fails if the defender touch-tackles the ball-carrier or forces the ball out of play over either sideline.

After each attempt, successful or not, a different attacker takes his/her turn to start with the ball. The defender changes place with an attacker after a set number of turns.

Task 198 Line attack (intermediate players)

Object: to practise attacking in a line; to use the width of the area to outflank defenders.

For groups of six.

Use pitches of reasonable size — enough width to give the attackers a chance of outflanking the defenders, and enough length for the game to have continuity.

Four attackers attempt to score tries over the two defenders' goal-line; the defenders can stop them by touch-tackling the ball-carrier with both hands. No forward passing!

The attackers start with the ball on their goal-line; the defenders stand 7 metres (23 ft) in front of them. The attackers can pass up and down their line. If touch-tackled, a player must pass. If the ball goes over a sideline, or if it is passed forward, or knocked-on, possession goes to the other team. No kicking is allowed. If the defenders intercept a pass or gather a loose ball, they may counter-attack immediately, and score if they can.

Easier variation: instead of requiring a tackled player to pass, substitute the roll-back. The defenders have to retreat 3 metres (10 ft) until the ball is picked up after the roll-back.

Extending variation: allow each player to score only once; after four tries, change the defenders with two of the attackers.

Task 199 Switch on the pitch (advanced players)

Object: to probe a defence and find a route to goal; for defenders to remain alert and anticipate the onset of an attack.

For groups of eight.

Play on a rectangular pitch marked with a centre-line.

Four players, identified by wearing bibs, are the attackers. They start with a pass from the centre and may attempt to score over either endline.

Two defenders occupy each half of the pitch; they cannot stray out of their halves, and have to try to prevent the attackers from scoring.

The switch

Whenever an attacker has the ball in his/her hands, s/he can turn and reverse the direction of play at will. Play **must** be reversed if the ball-carrier is touch-tackled or if a forward pass is made. Kicking is not permitted.

The attackers attempt to score as many tries as they can in a given time period; then the defenders change over with them and try to beat their score.

Extending variation: You can require the attackers to start play by using either a roll-back or a scrum.

Further practices for rugby games

Refer to the green section for information on New Image Rugby, mini rugby and mini-league.

Remember that some of the practices for goal-throwing games can be adapted for rugby.

LESSON PLAN 6

Invasion games
(try-scoring)

Intention: by the end of this lesson your pupils should know why it is important to pass the ball safely, and should come to realize how quick passing can help them to penetrate or outflank the opposing defence.

Pre-lesson organization: send the pupils to the playing area with one ball between two.

Organization for Task 1: Mark out a grid of squares with sides 8–10 metres (26–33 ft) long. Allocate two markers per square.

Task (What pupils do)	Observations (What to look for)	Points to remember
Warm-up "Run freely in pairs, passing the ball between you without dropping it. Try passing and then running behind your partner to receive a return pass. "Run one behind the other, the ball with the front player. On command, place the ball on the ground and run on — your partner must pick it up and try to tag you before the whistle. Change over."		

Bridging organization: while the remainder of the class go on working, set up a demonstration of the task in a grid square with two pupils. Call the class over to see the demonstration, and then send the pairs to their stations to begin work.

Revision Task 191 Backpass and try (page 114), plus its extending variation.	Does the passer look for the target and aim for it? Does the ball travel straight to the target? Is it far enough ahead for the receiver to accelerate onto? Are the receiver's hands ready? Is the ball caught and then held ready for the next pass?	Make sure passes are made to left and right.

Bridging organization: mark out larger grid squares (about 15 metres [50 ft]). Join pairs of pupils to make groups of four; return one ball and two markers to the basket. Demonstrate the task in one grid square. Send a group to each station to begin work.

Revision Task 197 Treble chance (page 116).	Do the attackers off the ball position well to receive a pass away from the defender? Does the sender pass the ball so that the receiver accelerates onto it? When running with the ball, do they run straight?	

Bridging organization: join fours into twelves; two balls per group. Use double squares and put the markers and spare balls away. Four players in each group wear bibs.

New work
Station the defenders and attackers as shown in the diagram; the first pair of defenders must be at least 7 metres (23 ft) from the attackers. Place a ball immediately in front of each row of attackers. On command, the first four attackers pick up the ball and pass it fast between them while attempting to get past the two defenders; if they are successful, the second pair of defenders runs forward to intercept the attackers and the beaten first pair of defenders goes back to the defensive endline ready for when a new attack begins. The attacking lines take turns to attack.
      X = attacker
      O = defender
	Do the attackers try to stretch the defence by quick passing and fast running? Do any players try to cut behind the running line to outflank the defence? Do attackers make good decisions about when to pass and when to run?
	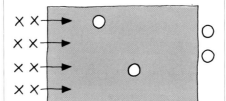
		Rotate the fours through attack and defence.

Closing organization: return the equipment to the side of the area ready to be carried in. Sort the bibs into colours as they are removed.

Cool-down
"Spread out in the area and jog freely; stand still and raise your arms out to your sides — shoulder-high; turn round as far as you can, keeping your feet still; now the other way; repeat several times; stand up tall; walk in."

GOAL-STRIKING GAMES

Unless stated otherwise, all the games detailed here are suitable for learning both hockey and soccer skills. Where there are specific differences or recommendations, the signs **H** for hockey and **S** for soccer are used.

Teams and pitches

It is recommended that competitive goal-striking games are played between equal teams of three to seven players.

The pitch size should be chosen according to the number of players and their size and strength. Here are some basic suggestions:

Team size (without goalkeeper)	Pitch size
3v3	30 x 20 metres (100 x 65 ft)
4v4	30 x 20 metres (100 x 65 ft)
5v5	40 x 25 metres (130 x 80 ft)
6v6	50 x 30 metres (165 x 100 ft)
7v7	60 x 40 metres (200 x 130 ft)

Allow an extra player each side if there are to be goalkeepers. Games may be played without goalkeepers, but use them if you can.

Older, stronger players will need a larger pitch than younger ones, so adjust the size as necessary. If in doubt, always err on the large side, because in games-play space gives time.

In the descriptions of the games, expressions such as 'midfield' and 'attacking and defending thirds' are sometimes used. The diagram shows which areas are being referred to.

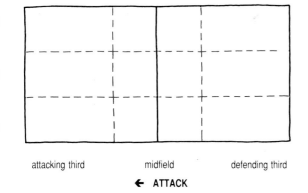

attacking third midfield defending third

← **ATTACK**

When you are setting up several games for a class, remember that it may not be necessary or desirable for all of them to have the same team sizes or to use pitches of the same size.

You can mix different levels of ability within your teams, or try to make each team consist of similar abilities. However, when organizing competitive games, do try to match teams of similar overall ability. If this is difficult, you can make adjustments to help the weaker team, such as making the goal they are attacking larger, or restricting the opposition to two-touch play.

See page 93 for variations in the siting of goals, and page 94 for deciding on team size.

Important safety points

Hockey beginners

A stick is a potentially dangerous implement, so apply the following rules to hockey-type games played by inexperienced youngsters:

• Only the flat side of the stick (i.e. the side facing left when the stick is held out in front of the body) may be used to play the ball.

• The stick must be held close to the ground except when striking the ball.

• In hitting, the stick must not be raised in a manner which is dangerous or intimidating to other players.

Hockey goalkeepers

Because of the hard ball and the use of sticks, goalkeepers should not play in competitive hockey-type games unless they are protected by a full helmet, body-protector, kickers, pads and gloves. Do not let pupils play in goal until they are comfortable in the kit and well practised in the additional skills of goalkeeping. **Never coerce a pupil to play in goal.**

Keep the ball on the ground

Although the rules of both hockey and soccer allow the ball to be sent through the air, this is very undesirable in the early stages of playing hockey, where both sending and controlling skills need to be well established to ensure safety. Lifted strokes in hockey are best left to the over-11 age group.

Body contact

Do not permit body contact in hockey. In soccer it should be discouraged until legal body-contact play has been learned and can be used with control.

119

Umpiring

Be firm. Do not permit dissent from players. Encourage pupils to know the rules and to act as umpires or referees themselves.

Rules

Refer to page 97 for shared rules applying to invasion games generally.

There are two fundamental differences between hockey and soccer:

• In hockey the ball may not be shielded by the body or stick from an opponent who is trying to play it. In soccer the body is used to shield the ball from an opponent.

• In hockey the ball may be played only with the stick. In soccer it may be played with any part of the body except the hands and arms. This does not, of course, apply to goalkeepers, who in both games may play the ball with any part of their body.

To help the games to flow, it is best not to introduce **offside** in either hockey or soccer at this stage.

The following rules apply to all the games in this section:

• When a ball passes over the endline, having last been touched by a defender, the game is re-started by a **corner**. The ball is placed on the endline close to the corner of the pitch and hit (H) or kicked (S) into play by an attacker. All other players must stand away as the corner is taken (usually 3–5 metres [10–16 ft]).

• When a ball passes over the endline having last been touched by an attacker, it is placed on the edge of the penalty box (S)

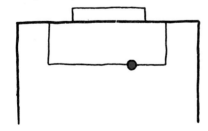

or the striking circle (H)

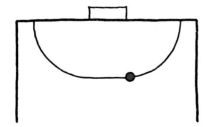

and played by a defender, with all other players 3–5 metres (10–16 ft) away. If the pitches are not fully marked, the ball should be brought back into play with a hit or kick from a point about 5 metres (16 ft) in from where it crossed the endline.

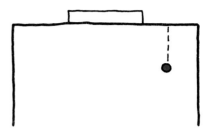

• When the ball goes over a sideline it is thrown (using a two-handed overhead throw) (S) or hit (H) into play from where it crossed the line. All other players should be 3–5 metres (10–16 ft) away.

• In all games a goal is scored when the ball wholly crosses the goal-line between the posts, having been legally propelled there.

Introducing goalkeepers

In both games, if you are introducing goalkeepers for the first time, change the rules so that shots can be made only from outside the areas marked in front of the goals. This gives the novice goalies more time and protection.

Using all the pitch

When learning, two factors lead to crowding and confusion in the excitement of a game:

• the ball — which the majority of pupils chase all over the pitch

• the central goals — which become magnets for the ball, and thus cause play to be confined to a central channel between the goals.

You will need to take steps to spread play so that your pupils have space to think and act, yet don't have their natural enthusiasm dampened. They need to develop the sequence of looking, thinking, choosing and acting, rather than just rushing after the ball.

Refer to page 93 to see how altering the siting of goals can encourage more open play. Game 200, which follows, provides another approach.

Game 200 Outside the markers (intermediate players)

Object: to encourage pupils to use the width of the pitch to open up clear routes to goal.

For 5v5 or 6v6; no goalkeepers.

Play to the rules of a basic invasion game, but use two markers on the pitch; the attacking team must always take the ball outside a marker before making a shot at goal. As the diagrams show, the positions of these markers may be altered from time to time, to produce different patterns of play.

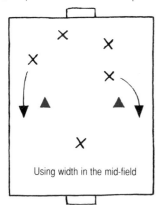

Using width in the mid-field

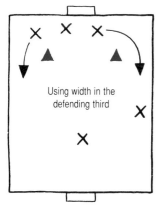

Using width in the defending third

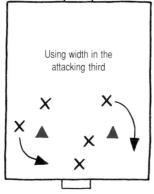

Using width in the attacking third

Supplementary rules:

• The ball must pass between a marker and the sideline before the team in possession can shoot for goal.

• At the start or restart of the game all players must be in their own half of the pitch. One of the attackers starts play with a back-pass from the centre.

• Players may enter the half they are attacking as soon as the ball is played.

• Players may shoot from anywhere once the marker has been passed correctly.

It is best to avoid using a pair of markers at each end: experience suggests that with relatively inexperienced players this causes the game to break down too frequently.

Extending variations:

• widen the goal and add a goalkeeper to each team

• ask each team to nominate a central pivot player whose job it is to distribute the ball to either side.

UNDERSTANDING POSITIONS

When pupils go home and say they have been playing a game, they will usually be asked "Which position did you play?" They need to know and understand where they played and what was expected of them there. So introduce named positions, even though there may only be a few players in a team.

To start with, keep to very basic positions such as forward (striker), half-back (link), full-back and sweeper. Later they may be more precise: left-half, centre-back, right-winger, etc. The introduction of positions helps pupils establish their priorities, both in attack and defence.

PRIORITIES

❝ **When you have the ball:**

• If there is a chance to score, take it!

• If you cannot score, try to pass the ball to a team-mate who can, and then keep supporting him/her.

• If you are too far away to score, try to move the ball towards the goal either by travelling with it or by passing it.

When a team-mate has the ball:

• Get positioned so that you can receive a 'good' pass. This can mean being forward in a scoring position, or being wide to switch the attack, or being able to support from behind when a challenge comes.

When your direct opponent has the ball:

• Stop him/her from shooting.

• Try to get the ball by forcing him/her to make a mistake.

• Get between the ball and the goal.

When other opponents have the ball:

• Mark your direct opponent to stop him/her receiving a pass. ❞

DEVELOPING INSIGHT AND DECISION-MAKING

Once your pupils understand the priorities, they can begin to make their own decisions. Explaining why they chose to do what they did will help them with this. For example, having completed a pass they should be able to answer questions like the following posed by the teacher:

• "Why did you pass rather than shoot?"

• "Why did you pass instead of carrying on with the ball?"

• "Why did you pass to Sharon?"

• "Could you have passed to anyone else?"

During games, occasionally gather a team together to discuss how they are doing. Give them a chance to switch players into different roles if they think it will benefit the team.

In any case, make sure that your pupils try many different positions and roles and so improve their understanding of the whole game. Specialization should come much later.

APPRECIATING TACTICS

Tactics exist as soon as one player competes against an opponent. Pupils need to build up knowledge so that they can apply tactics effectively. Help them to recognize when similar tactical situations recur, so that they consciously benefit from previous experience.

The complementary practices which follow will help you to teach defensive and attacking skills as reciprocal — opposite sides of the same coin. The children will soon learn to think "If I do this, what might she do?" and "If he does that, what should I do?". They will find that to succeed they need to see things from the other person's perspective — an important step towards maturity.

After a while, the pupils will appreciate the tactical thinking and teasing which can be such an enjoyable feature of playing games. It can also lead to an appreciation of the needs of others and respect for those who display special talents.

COMPLEMENTARY SKILL-DEVELOPMENT TASKS

The following skills are covered in the practices that follow:

Attacking

- Travelling with a ball
- Passing and receiving a ball
- Shooting

Defending

- Challenging a player with the ball
- — to win the ball
- — to force an error
- — to stop the player from using the ball
- — to force the player away from goal
- — to steer the player towards another defender
- Marking and intercepting
- Goalkeeping

Although each skill will need to be practised in isolation from time to time in order to refine performance, it is important for your pupils to combine the range of skills and to learn to use them in sequences, e.g. to travel with the ball, leading to a shot at goal; or to pass, run, receive and shoot.

In all the following games and practices, when hockey skills are used it is assumed that each player will have a stick, unless stated otherwise. Only the number of balls required for a task will be indicated.

TACTICS AND PRACTICE

The tasks and modified games which are suggested here will lead your pupils to use their skills in tactical situations. For example, they will find themselves travelling with the ball to take it past an opponent, as well as challenging and tackling players with the ball. They will learn to mark opponents closely, while remaining ready to get free to receive a pass.

In this way pupils learn to recognize the problems posed by games and to understand how the skills they are building can fit in. Tactical ideas can be tried and evaluated, and players can build their own memory banks of causes and effects.

In the later years of primary schooling, your pupils will be ready to develop the understanding which they will need if they are to become intelligent participants and spectators, and they should be encouraged to do so.

TRAVELLING WITH A BALL

Invasion games give pupils lots of opportunities to run with a ball.

Why do players travel with a ball?

- To get nearer to their opponents' goal
- To open up a space through which to send a pass
- To evade an opponent's challenge

When should players travel with a ball?

• When there is space to run into — especially if the space leads to goal

When should players not travel with a ball?

• When a shot or pass would be a better choice

• When there is no free space to run into

• To lose the ball would give too much advantage to the opposition

What must pupils do as they travel with a ball?

• Retain control

• Keep their heads up and look where they are going

• Go straight for their target

• Go fast

• Be able to change pace if necessary

• Be able to stop and start suddenly

• Be able to change direction quickly

Tight control

Only if there is plenty of clear space and no threat from an opponent should the ball be sent well ahead by the runner. S/he must always be able to retrieve the ball before an opponent can challenge or before it goes out of play.

Task 201 Busy dribble (novices)

Object: to travel in a 'busy' area keeping a ball under close control while stopping and changing direction.

Work individually, with one ball each.

The size of the area and the number of players involved will determine how much space they have. Start with plenty of space and gradually re- duce it as control and awareness improve.

On command, all players have to stop the balls and restart in new directions.

> Travelling and stopping (H): skill card 30
>
> Reversed-stick play (H): skill card 31
>
> Travelling and stopping (S): skill card 32

The relay patterns described on page 96 are useful for the introduction of travelling techniques, but keep group numbers small to provide the maximum active time. Relays can be varied as suggested in the following task.

Task 202 Sprint dribble (intermediate players)

Object: to travel as fast as possible without losing control of the ball.

Work in pairs, with one ball per pair.

Place a row of markers about 12 metres (40 ft) from a line. Allow one marker per pair.

The players take turns to dribble the ball around the marker and back. On their return they have to stop it no more than a metre (3 ft) past the line.

After letting the pairs practise in their own time, races can be introduced, either between groups of pairs or involving the whole class.

Variation: Require the players to turn level with a marker rather than around it; they will find that this requires a different technique for fast turning.

Easier variation: Let slower players have a short start advantage — say one metre (3 ft) in front of the line.

Extending variations:

• The player with the ball races a partner without a ball. The latter estimates how far out s/he can place a marker and still beat the ball home. "Which player travelling with the ball has the shortest gap between the markers after several turns?"

• Let a player with a soccer ball race a player with a hockey stick and ball over the same distance; alternatively, see which of them can cover the greater distance and still get home first.

Task 203 Like poles repel (novices)(S)

Object: to travel and turn suddenly, keeping close control of the ball.

Work in pairs.

Two markers are placed 10 metres (33 ft) apart. Each player has a ball, and starts to the right of a marker, facing his/her partner. On command, the players travel towards each other, looking up as they go. When level with the partner's shoulder, they turn away and accelerate back to the start. "Remember to turn **away** from your partner, not towards him/her."

Task 204 Relay laps (intermediate players)

Object: to travel as quickly as possible, both with and without a ball.

Work in groups of six, with one ball per group.

Set out eight markers as shown in the diagram. The distance between the inner and outer squares should be about 3 metres (10 ft). You may need to adjust this as the players gain experience.

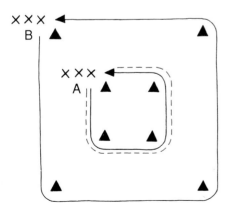

Divide the group into teams **A** and **B** of three players each. On command, team **A** must dribble the ball in relay three times around the inner circuit

while team **B** runs three times around the outside, each player making one circuit. At the end of each lap the **A** player must stop the ball beyond the start marker before the next player sets off; similarly, each **B** runner must complete a full lap before tagging the next off. "Which team of three can complete their circuits first?"

Change roles after every few attempts.

Task 205 Gate dodge (intermediate players)

Object: to change from close control to distant control and vice versa; to develop judgement of the pace of a ball.

Work individually.

Play in any clear space. Set out many pairs of markers to make gates approximately 2 metres (6.5 ft) wide. The gates should be randomly placed, but make sure that they are well separated to avoid crowding.

Each player travels freely in the area, keeping a ball under close control. Whenever an empty gate is encountered, the ball is sent through it while the sender sprints outside the markers before retrieving it. The players have to try to retrieve the ball within 3 metres (10 ft) of the gate.

If a gate is 'busy', players must travel with the ball until they find an empty one.

Extending variations:

• A few 'marauders' may be introduced; these may not tackle a player directly, but must try to capture balls which have passed through a gate before the senders can recover them. A player who loses a ball becomes a marauder. There must always be substantially more gates than marauders, so that a player with the ball can choose an empty gate if faced with the problem of marauders hovering by the gates.

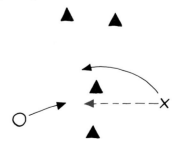

• To introduce the skill of turning, the players have to go through a gate with the ball and then turn as quickly as possible and come back.

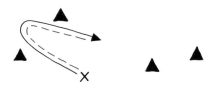

Task 206 Tag-tackle (intermediate players)(S)

Object: to keep control of a ball and move quickly in a confined area; to monitor the movements of another player and respond to them.

For pairs; each player has a ball.

Play in an area about 10 metres (33 ft) square. One player is the tagger, who tries to keep his/her ball under control while trying to touch the opponent. The other acts like an attacker in a full game, trying to avoid being tagged by moving quickly and turning with the ball.

If a ball goes out of the area a tag is awarded to the other player. Change roles after 30 seconds.

"How many times can you tag the 'attacker' in 30 seconds?"

Task 207 Shuttle shield (intermediate players)(S)

Object: to use a turn to avoid an approaching defender.

For groups of three, using one ball per group.

Place two markers about 10 metres (33 ft) apart. Players A and B start by one marker, with C at the other.

The task is a form of shuttle relay. Player A kicks the ball to C and runs after it; C lets the ball run past the marker and controls it while shielding it from A with his/her body. Before A's challenge can succeed, C turns away and kicks the ball to B (who is still at the first marker) and runs after it. The challenge is continued, with the player in possession always first shielding the ball and then passing to the free player at the other marker.

> Turning with a ball (S): skill card 33
>
> Turning with a ball (H): skill card 34

SPEED OF REACTION AND MOVEMENT

Task 208 Mirror touch

Objects: to sprint over short distances; to react quickly to the movements of an opponent.

For pairs.

Place the markers as shown in the diagram; note that the distance between player A's markers is greater than that between player B's.

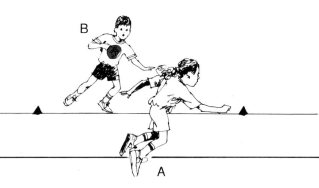

The players stand midway between their markers, facing each other. When A chooses, s/he sprints to touch either of his/her markers. B must react and attempt to touch his/her corresponding marker first. Change over after each three attempts.

Task 209 Race to the pole

Object: to react quickly and sprint over a short distance.

Work in pairs.

Play on grass squares of approximately 10 x 10 metres (33 x 33 ft). Two opposite sides of each square are labelled 'North' and 'South' respectively. The two players lie down side by side, head to toe, in the middle of the square. One player acts as caller to shout "North" or "South". On this command both players get up and race for that line. The first over wins, and the loser acts as caller for the next race. Change partners from time to time.

Variation: This task can also work well if a third player does the calling, but be sure that the roles are changed very frequently so that full involvement is maintained.

TRAVELLING AND SHOOTING

Task 210 Shooting relay (intermediate players)

Object: travelling with the ball and shooting at goal.

For groups of three.

Set out five markers as shown in the illustration. The width of the goal should be adjusted according to the distance and your pupils' ability, but don't make it too easy — the strikers must have to be reasonably accurate to hit the target.

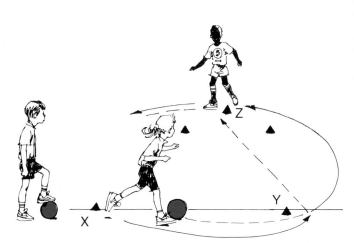

One player takes up a position behind the goal, while the other two stand at marker **X**, each with a ball. One of these starts by dribbling to **Y** and shooting at goal. The player behind the goal tells the shooter if a goal was scored, collects the ball, controls it, and dribbles it around **Z** and on to **X**. Meanwhile the shooter runs forward to get behind the goal, and the third player sets off to dribble and shoot. Play should be continuous.

After each player has completed the circuit several times, move marker **X** so that the players have to travel to their left to shoot.

Safety note: Don't allow players to shoot if another player is between **Y** and the goal.

Task 211 Target choice

Object: to keep tight control of the ball and evade challenges.

For pairs.

Use an area approximately 20 metres x 10 metres (65 x 33 ft), with markers as shown in the illustration.

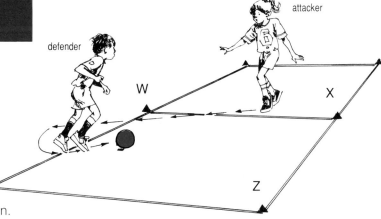

Starting from a position between the four target markers (**W**, **X**, **Y**, and **Z**) the defender passes the ball to the attacker who stands outside the far endline. The attacker traps the ball and dribbles forward to shoot at any one of the target markers. The attacker must keep the ball inside the marked area. The defender may challenge anywhere once the attacker has received the ball. If the attacker passes the line **W–X**, s/he may attack only markers **Y** and **Z** — no turning back is allowed. Change roles after three attempts.

Task 212 *Goal scramble (intermediate players)(S)*

Object: to shoot firmly and accurately under pressure from an opponent.

For groups of three.

Play in a square about 10 metres by 10 metres (33 x 33 ft). Use existing goals or improvise with markers.

To start play, the goalkeeper rolls the ball out from the goal. The two other players compete for it; whoever gets it first becomes the attacker, and the other defends. The attacker tries to score, and the defender tries to pass the ball back safely to the goalkeeper.

Extending variation: add two more players; they now work in pairs, to make the practice 2v2 instead of 1v1.

Soccer goalkeeping: skill card 35

Hockey goalkeeping: skill card 36

TRAVELLING AND PASSING

Task 213 *Island-to-island (advanced players)*

Object: to travel, look up and pass to a free player.

For groups of seven players, with one ball per group. Two players are identified by bibs as defenders.

Mark out two rectangles as shown in the diagram. These are the 'islands'.

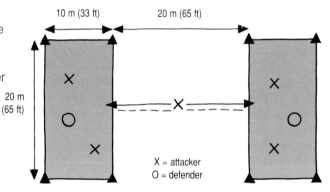

Play starts with one defender and two attackers on one island, and one defender and three attackers (one of whom has the ball) on the other. The attacker with the ball has to break out in order to dribble the ball across to the other island and pass it to one of his/her team-mates, who then plays it back in the opposite direction. The process is repeated. The following rules apply:

• Only one attacker at a time can cross with the ball — the others must stay on their islands.

• Attackers cannot leave an island ahead of the ball.

• Attackers cannot make consecutive runs.

• Defenders have to stay on their islands.

"How many successful runs can the attackers complete in three minutes?"

"Which defender can score most points by winning the ball and playing it off the island?"

Make sure that everybody takes a turn at being a defender.

TACKLING

A good tackle will give the challenger controlled possession of the ball. Sometimes a tackle has to be less controlled, and in an emergency it may be necessary to force the ball out of play or to pressure the player with the ball into making a mistake. However, no tackler should be really satisfied unless s/he comes out with the ball.

Encourage your players always to tackle with the intention of playing the ball: do not allow them to rush wildly into tackles.

Task 214 Tackle tussle (novices)

Object: to chase after a ball, gain possession, and travel with it over a line to score.

For groups of three, with one ball per group.

Use a long narrow rectangle, with a marker towards the centre.

Player **A** starts behind the line, with **C** about a metre in front of it. **B** stands between them, with the ball.

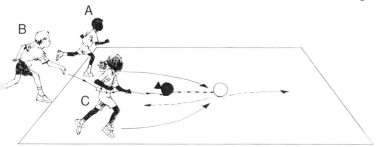

Player **B** sends the ball to roll towards the other end. As soon as it passes the marker, **A** and **C** chase after it; if **A** captures it, s/he has to try to dribble it on across the far line, whereas **C** has to try to dribble it back to the start. The two players may tackle each other but must keep the ball within the area. If it goes out, neither player scores and the practice restarts.

The three players rotate roles after each attempt.

Tackling skills (H): skill card 37

Taking a ball past a defender (H): skill card 38

Taking a ball past a defender (S): skill card 39

Task 215 Tackle turmoil (intermediate players)

Object: to make successful tackles and to keep the ball when in possession.

For groups up to whole-class size. Slightly more than half the players should have a ball.

Play in an area which allows plenty of free movement.

Spread all the players out in the defined area. Those with a ball have to keep dribbling it. Play is simple: "If you haven't got a ball, tackle someone who has. If you lose the ball, tackle someone else — not your successful challenger."

Task 216 Speed dodges (advanced players)

Object: to tackle and evade a tackle.

For groups of four: three players are attackers; one is a defender. Each attacker has a ball.

Place a marker about 12 metres (40 ft) in front of a goal or gate about 8–10 metres (26–33 ft) wide.

The three attackers line up at the marker, while the other player defends the gate. The first attacker dribbles forward, avoiding the defender if possible, on through the gate for a point, and then back to the marker. As soon as one attacker clears the gate, the next one starts off. If the defender wins the ball, s/he rolls it back to the marker.

"Who can get the most points?"

All players take turns at defending.

PASSING

Just as with the other invasion games, the art of passing quickly and accurately plays a vital role in hockey and soccer.

Many of the passing practices suggested on pages 102–107 may be modified to suit hockey or soccer skills, but here are some additional practices specifically designed for these games. In every case, remind players to look for and choose a target before passing — not simply to send and hope! And encourage receivers to help by showing where and when they want the ball.

Task 217 From all directions (novices)(H)

Object: to enable pupils to receive the ball from any direction.

For pairs, with one ball per pair.

Play on a square of about 10 x 10 metres (33 x 33 ft), with a marker at each corner.

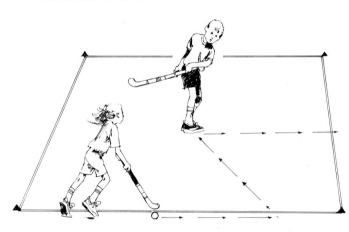

One player waits in the centre of the square; s/he must face in the same direction all the time. The other player travels rapidly around the square, passing the ball to the centre just before s/he passes each marker and receiving a return pass before reaching the next one.

Hockey hint
Encourage your pupils to get used to the idea of keeping the stick 'looking for the ball' by chalking a pair of eyes on the flat striking face. Show them how to twist their shoulders towards the ball to keep the stick in the best position.

Soccer variation: You can use this task for soccer, but allow both players to face each other as necessary. Later it can be extended to let the centre player throw the ball for the outer one to collect on chest or thigh before passing it back. The centre player can also be allowed to handle the return passes, to practise goalkeeping skills.

Always rotate roles frequently.

Task 218 Gate passes (novices)

Object: to find a moving player and pass the ball to him/her through a narrow gap.

For several pairs of players, with one ball per pair.

Play in any large free area. Use markers to set out lots of 2-metre (6.5-ft) gates facing in random directions.

Player **A** sends the ball through a gate to his/her partner **B**, and immediately runs to the far side of another gate to receive a return pass. Encourage **B** to dribble to open up a route for the return pass to reach the gate chosen by **A**. Play continues, with the pairs trying to complete as many passes through different gates as possible.

Extending variation: "Can you time the passage of the ball through the gate to coincide with the arrival of the receiver?" This forces the sender to pass even when s/he may not be ideally positioned to do so.

Task 219 Half-way intercept (intermediate players)(S)

Object: to look up, choose the moment to pass, and pass accurately.

Work in groups of six, with one ball per group.

Set out four markers to form a square 20 x 20 metres (65 x 65 ft). Use two more markers to indicate a half-way line.

Two attackers play in each half. They attempt to score by passing across the half-way line to the other pair of attackers. The defenders, who must

stay on the half-way line, try to intercept the passes. They score if they gain possession of the ball or force the attackers to make a bad pass, sending the ball out of the area. Change roles after a given period of time.

Extending variation: The half-way line is not used. The two defenders run around the area holding a rounders post by the ends between them to form a movable goal. The attackers attempt to score by sending the ball between the defenders (above or below the post). The goal counts even if the ball goes out of the playing area, so there is no reason for the defenders to keep to the sidelines. If the defenders drop the post, or if they kick the ball to stop it going through, the attackers are awarded a point. Change roles after a given period of time.

Sending a ball (H): skill card 40

Sending a ball (S): skill card 41

Receiving a ball (H): skill card 42

Receiving a ball (S): skill card 43

Task 220 Gate run (novices)

Object: to pass accurately and to receive on the run.

Work in pairs, with one ball per pair.

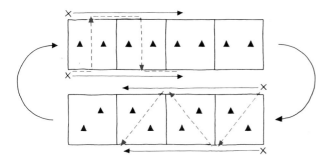

Set up two rows of gates, as shown in the diagram. One row is parallel with the sidelines, to encourage square passes, while the other is in a zig-zag formation, for forward passing. Pairs of pupils travel down the sidelines, passing to each other through the gates and keeping moving as quickly as possible. They are not allowed to pass from inside the lines. The pairs travel down one track and up the other in a continuous practice.

"Can you complete a circuit without missing a gate?"

Provided that care is taken to avoid impeding others, several pairs can work at the same time, overtaking when necessary.

Extending variation: Reduce the size of the gates.

Task 221 Cops and robbers (intermediate players)

Object: to discover lots of different ways of working together to take a ball through defended territory.

For groups up to whole-class size.

Play on a large field.

About a third of the group are 'cops', identified as such by bibs; the remainder are divided up into pairs of 'robbers'. Each pair has a ball — their 'loot'.

The pairs of robbers start at one end of the field and attempt to dribble and pass the balls to each other to reach the far endline without being successfully tackled by the defending cops. If a cop wins the ball, s/he sends it out of play over a sideline; the robbers have to retrieve it before going back to the endline for another attempt.

Game tips:

• After a while the cops will find that they almost always get the best results by retreating close to their own endline; if this becomes a problem, introduce a rule that half of them have to play in the front half of the field.

• Once your pupils are used to the game, introduce the rule that each robber must touch the ball at least twice before the pair can attempt to score. This prevents the stronger players from always going solo.

• Experiment with different numbers of cops and robbers: slightly less than one-third of the group as cops usually gives the best results.

• Make sure that everyone has turns as both cop and robber.

• Teach the pupils that the player off the ball must be ready and positioned to receive a pass when needed, and to be on the alert for interceptions by defenders.

Task 222 Two to one (advanced players)

Object: to solve the problem of how to work the ball past an opponent approaching from a variety of angles.

Work in threes, with one ball per group.

Use a rectangular area approximately 20 metres x 10 metres (65 x 33 ft), divided into two halves. Place three markers, as shown in the illustration.

The first player dribbles from **Y** to **Z**, from where s/he passes back to between **W** and **X**. The first player near **W** immediately runs to intercept the ball and shoot at goal from outside the line. As soon as the shot is taken, another of the attackers at **Y** dribbles forward to start another cycle. The goalkeeper or backstop rolls the balls back to the attackers. Turns are taken as quickly as possible. Passers and shooters change over after several turns each. If the goalkeeper is usually successful, do without a backstop, but otherwise let the backstop change over after one complete round of passing and shooting.

Extending variation: As the attacker at **Z** prepares to pass, a defender runs across from marker **Y** to challenge the shooter.

Safety note: In hockey it is especially important for a running defender to stay on the stick side of the shooter, to avoid running across the shot.

Two attackers start at one end of the area, and have to try to travel with the ball to the far end. The single defender tackles to stop their progress, and tries to get the ball back over the start-line. However, at the start of each run, the defender must be touching one of the markers; s/he cannot move until one of the attackers touches the ball, and must run into the front half of the area (the half entered first by the attackers) before attempting to tackle.

If the ball goes over a sideline during play, it is rolled back in by an attacker and the game continues.

The defender must regularly change the marker from which s/he starts.

Task 223 Back-pass and shoot (intermediate players)

Objects: to pass accurately to an incoming striker, to shoot on the move and to stop shots at goal.

Work in groups of six or eight.

Use a goal and markers **W**, **X**, **Y** and **Z**, set out as shown in the illustration, and two or three balls. One player is the goalkeeper, another the backstop, and the rest — the attackers — divide into two equal groups.

Half of the attackers start at **Y**, the rest to the left of **W**.

Task 224 Advantage attack (intermediate players)

Objects: to give attacking players the time to look for a free player and pass, and for defenders to learn the importance of delaying tactics to enable a team-mate to recover and reinforce the defence.

The pupils work in groups of seven, using one ball per group. Three of the players are defenders, **D1**, **D2** and **D3**, wearing bibs. The other four are attackers, **A1**, **A2**, **A3** and **A4**.

Play on a rectangular area at least 20 metres by 10 metres (65 x 33 ft). Place two markers to form a wide goal, with a further two markers at the other end of the area, as shown in the diagram.

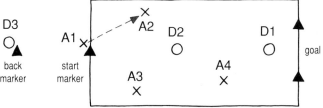

Defender **D3** has to stay behind the back marker. **D1** and **D2** may position anywhere, but must be at least 5 metres (16.5 ft) from the ball at the start of play. All the attackers stay between the start marker and the goal, and attempt to score through the goal by passing and shooting. Play starts with **A1** passing the ball to a team-mate from the start marker. The defenders score if they can send the ball to **D3**, waiting beyond the rear marker.

Extending variation: Allow **A1** either to pass or to dribble at the start, and as soon as the ball is in play, let **D3** run forward from the back marker to join his/her team-mates and assist in defence. The defenders now simply have to send the ball past the rear marker to score.

This variation raises all sorts of questions for the players:

• Where should **D3** go when s/he enters play, and why?

• How can **D1** and **D2** delay the attack to give time for **D3** to join them? Can they keep the ball away from the goal for long enough?

• How can the four attackers position to make it most difficult for the defenders to intercept or tackle?

HEADING IN SOCCER

Heading should be learned using a light, soft ball. The head can be used to intercept passes, send passes, strike at goal or clear the ball out of defence. Initially, let players play balls which are fed by hand at a comfortable height. Later, encourage them to move to head the ball and direct it towards chosen targets, and to jump for high balls.

Several soccer tasks may be adapted for heading instead of kicking — very useful, as heading is an unavoidable part of the regulation game. **Stress the importance of good technique.** Heading should not be unpleasant; do not coerce pupils to head a ball if they are tentative about doing so.

Task 225 Heads only (novices)(S)

Object: to head the ball firmly downwards, with control over direction.

Work in pairs, with one ball per pair.

Mark an area approximately 10 metres long by 4 metres wide (33 x 13 ft).

The players take turns to throw the ball up so that they can head it past their partner. The aim is to get the ball over the partner's endline; the partner is allowed to use his/her hands to prevent this. The ball must not pass the defending player above shoulder height. The practice should be continuous.

Extending variation: Play 2v2 with each goal widened to 8 metres (26 ft). The players take turns to feed the ball for their partner to try to head past the two opponents.

Task 226 Overunda (novices)(S)

Object: to control the height of a header.

Work in pairs, with one ball per pair.

The two players start 5 metres (16.5 ft) apart. One stands with his/her feet apart, and throws the ball for the partner to head back, shouting "over" or "under". To score, the second player must head the ball back above the thrower's head for "over", or through the legs for "under".

Heading: skill card 44

133

MARKING

The weighted games (3v1, 4v2, 4v3, or 5v3) put an emphasis on attacking play. However, they do not encourage disciplined marking. Equal-sided games highlight person-to-person marking early on, and soon the idea of **marking space** is introduced: players position themselves so that they cover a vulnerable area, such as the space in front of goal, and prevent opponents or the ball from moving into it.

Refer to pages 105–108 for marking tasks which can be modifed for hockey and soccer.

The best way of teaching your pupils the art of marking is in small-sided games where each one is paired with a particular opponent. Identify the pairs with bibs carrying the same number, so that they know whom to mark and so that you can easily spot whether they are carrying out their responsibilities.

Help your pupils to see that it is only necessary to mark an opponent when the opposing team has the ball. When their own team is in possession they should try to get away from their marker and be ready to receive a pass or shoot. Encourage them to see this one-on-one marking contest as a game within a game.

Explain that good marking should lead to successful interception – they should learn to anticipate the movement of the ball and get there first!

It is easier to set up a marking practice if the first pass from a dead ball has to go to a specific marked player or group.

Marking tasks are more fun if both defenders and attackers have to achieve an objective, e.g. to score, or to clear the ball out of the area. Here are two tasks which illustrate these principles:

Task 227 Pass in, pass out (novices)

Object: to focus on marking and getting free.

Work in groups of four, with one ball per group. Identify two of the players as defenders, using bibs.

Play in a square of approximately 10 x 10 metres (33 x 33 ft), with a marker at each corner. One side of the square is the goal-line.

One attacker and one defender are inside the square, while the others are just outside it, and away from the goal-line. The outside attacker has to try to pass the ball to his/her partner inside, and then run round to take a return pass when s/he gets behind the goal-line. If the pass is completed, the attackers score a point and reposition to repeat the task. If the inside defender gets the ball, s/he passes to the outside defender, who may position anywhere **except** behind the goal-line. If successful, the defenders get a point. Change roles from time to time.

Task 228 Sharp shots (intermediate players)

Object: to improve marking, passing and shooting.

Work in groups of six, with one ball per group. Three players are attackers, **A1**, **A2** and **A3**; the other three are the defenders, **D1**, **D2** and goalkeeper **GK**.

Set out a large square with a wide goal on a line about 2 metres (6.5 ft) back from one side.

A1 and **A2** play inside the square, marked by **D1** and **D2** respectively. **A3** stays outside the square, along any of the three sides away from the goal; s/he may travel with the ball. The goalkeeper is restricted to the space between the square and the goal.

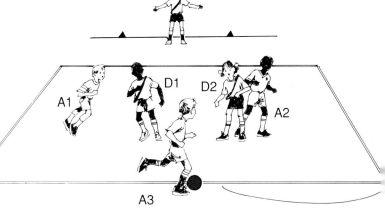

To play, **A3** passes the ball to **A1** or **A2**, who tries to score. **A1** and **A2** may pass to each other before shooting; if under pressure they may pass the ball back out to **A3**, who then feeds it in again. If the defenders clear the ball out of the area, or if the goalkeeper saves the shot, the defenders score a point.

After six plays, defenders and attackers change roles.

"Who scores most points from twelve plays?"

Marking (H): skill card 45

Marking (S): skill card 46

Games-making task 229
Throwing and catching

For this task the pupils should work in groups of four to ten. They make up an invasion game which uses throwing and catching only, or throwing and catching plus one other skill (such as kicking).

"Choose the equipment, and write down the rules which say how the game will start, what happens when the ball goes out of play, and what players can and cannot do while the ball is in play. How do you score goals or points?"

Before attempting this task, the pupils should understand the basic structure of an invasion game. You can check this by noting how they choose and place the goals. Encourage the pupils to try changing the rules to see how this improves or spoils their game.

Games-making task 230
Scoring

"Make up an invasion game in which only certain players are allowed to score. Where may they score from? How big should the pitch be? How many players should make up a team? Can all the players go anywhere in the playing area?"

Games-making task 231
No travel

"Make up an invasion game in which players are not allowed to travel with the ball. Why do you need to think carefully about how the team without the ball may gain possession?"

Answer: If opponents are allowed to grab the ball or knock it out of a player's hands, or tackle when the ball is at the player's feet, this can lead to dangerous physical contact.

Pupils should come to realize the benefits of adding a rule to limit how long a player may keep the ball before releasing or passing it.

Intention: by the end of this lesson your pupils should have begun to learn the basic handling skills for goalkeeping and also improved their skill in shooting low, hard and accurately.

Pre-lesson organization: select a grass area. Provide enough balls for one between two pupils. Place supplies of markers and cones at four locations around the outside of the field. Group pupils into fives, with bibs on two in each group.

Organization for Task 1: as the pupils enter the area they jog freely, and on command go to stand next to a partner to form pairs.

Task (What pupils do)	Observations (What to look for)	Points to remember
Warm-up "Face your partner and mirror these actions together: little bounce-jumps keeping the same rhythm – four bounces, then leap high and stretch arms up. Repeat several times. Run to one side, touch the ground and return to the start. Repeat the other way. Face your partner all the time."	Do the pupils jump high off the ground, bending their knees and thrusting vigorously to get height? Do they swing their arms to get higher? Are they stretching up at the top of the jump? Do they bend their knees before trying to touch the ground?	

Bridging organization: one partner fetches a ball while the other finds a clear space.

Revision "Roll the ball back and forth between you, using both hands. Move about and vary the distance of the passes. Now send the ball 1 or 2 metres (3–6 ft) to the right or left of your partner, so that s/he has to move to collect it."	Do they get feet and body behind the ball before collecting it? Do they pull the ball towards the body to make it secure?	

Bridging organization: "Form up into your original groups of five players and collect three markers per group. Keep one ball and put any others back into the containers." Allocate working areas. Help each group to set out two markers as a goal 6 metres (20 ft) wide and put the third marker opposite the centre of the goal about 25 metres (82 ft) away. This will be the start marker.

New work Soccer 3v2 (three attackers, one defender and one goalkeeper). The game is started and restarted after a score by an attacker passing from the start marker. The defender scores if s/he can hit the start marker (or a larger target may be offered such as a small goal 2 metres [6.5 ft] wide). The goalkeeper can roll or kick the ball out to the defender. No goal is scored if the shot goes above the goalkeeper's head.	Do the attackers look for opportunities to shoot? Can they hit the ball low and hard? Does the goalkeeper get his/her body behind the ball and collect it safely in two hands? Do the defenders look for quick counter-attacks?	Look for pupils who do not get involved in attack, and if necessary introduce the rule that each player must touch the ball at least once before a shot may be made.

Bridging organization: "Return to your pairs. Collect a large cone and put it in a space. Get one ball per pair if you do not have the ball from the previous game."

New work "Stand one on each side of the cone; kick the ball from at least 10 metres (33 ft) away, aiming to hit the cone. Collect your partner's shot with your hands, roll it away, run after it, and shoot. How far away can you be and still hit the marker?"	Check on the handling points given for the previous task, and look for these points when shooting: Is the non-kicking foot placed alongside the ball? Is the head over the ball and still when the kick is made? Is contact made in the middle of the ball with the laced part of the boot?	Be prepared to offer a wider target. Change partners from time to time.

Bridging organization: "Return to the 3v2 game. Two of the attackers change places with the defenders. Put spare cones and balls away."

Revision and new work 3v2 game with pupils focusing on low, hard, accurate shooting. Introduce the goalkeepers to the concept of moving forward from the goal-line to narrow the angle which an attacker has for a shot.	Check on how the ball is struck, as above. Do the players constantly check where they are relative to the goal? Do the goalkeepers move forward to meet the shot?	Widen the goals if you need to challenge the goalkeepers and make scoring easier.

Closing organization: return all equipment to the containers; pupils spread out in the area.

Cool-down

"Jog freely, bob down to touch the ground at the side of your feet on command, touching alternate sides. Stop and sit down. Now lie on your back. Stretch out long and tense your body. Roll onto your left side; now onto your back; and onto your right side. Repeat several times. Lie on your back and close your eyes. Imagine you are at Wembley, saving a penalty for England or scoring the winning goal... Stand up and walk in."

LESSON PLAN 8

Intention: by the end of this lesson pupils should be able to tackle safely while keeping the stick in contact with the ground, and know how to avoid committing the foul of obstruction while tackling or keeping possession.

Pre-lesson organization: set out containers with a stick and ball for each pupil plus a supply of markers and bibs. Later in the lesson the class will be divided into groups of ten and will need fairly large rectangular areas to play in, so pick a suitably marked pitch if possible.

Organization for Task 1: each pupil collects a stick and finds a space in the area.

Task (What pupils do)	Observations (What to look for)	Points to remember
Warm-up "Run freely in the area, and on command sweep your stick along the ground from right to left. Lay your stick on the ground. Run around your stick to the left, but face forward all the time. Now run around it to the right."	Do your pupils bend their knees when sweeping the stick along the ground? Do their feet face forward when running around the stick? Do they take small quick steps?	

Bridging organization: "Form pairs, collecting one ball per pair. Spread out in pairs, side by side along a line, with a reasonable space between each pair."

New work One pupil gently rolls the ball out from the line, and the partner runs out to the right of the rolling ball, collects it with the stick and travels back with it. Change over and repeat several times. Next, one pupil travels out from the line, keeping the ball under close control. The partner chases, takes the ball by sweeping his/her stick in low, and travels back to the line with the first player following. Change over and repeat. Keep the exercise cooperative.	Does the runner bring the stick in along the ground to collect the ball? Are the knees bent? Does s/he pivot to turn and travel back home? Does the tackler face his/her partner as the ball is taken? Do the pupils avoid contact with their partners' sticks and only touch the ball?	Have skill card 38 available for use. Demonstrate how facing your opponent avoids obstruction caused by getting your body in the way to shield the ball.

Bridging organization: bring the class together. Explain the boundaries of the playing area. Supply a few more balls so that rather more than half the class can travel about the area dribbling a ball. Then demonstrate how to go into the area, tackle, get a ball and try to keep it. The remainder of the class follow. Any player whose ball is taken must tackle someone else.

New work Task 215 Tackle turmoil (page 129).	Do the pupils keep their sticks close to the ground and face their opponents when tackling? Do pupils in possession look up and avoid those who are tackling? Do they all keep the balls close to their sticks?	Allow plenty of space, and reduce it as control improves.

Bridging organization: as pupils continue playing, set out sets of five bibs and eight markers. Bring the pupils together and ask them to form a group of ten by each set of bibs. Five pupils per group put on bibs. Send each group to their area to set out wide goals with a shooting area in front of them, and to start play.

Revision Play a basic 5v5 goal-striking game in which the attackers must enter the shooting area before they are allowed to shoot for goal. There are no goalkeepers.	Is tackling controlled and constructive?	Remind the players about not shielding the ball. Remind tacklers to face the opponent as they tackle.

Closing organization: pupils collect bibs together into tidy piles, and put the balls and markers into containers.

Cool-down
"Stand in a space with your stick. Crouch down to reach forward along the ground and place your stick as far away from you as you can; put your hands flat on the ground and jump your feet up to your hands; pick up your stick and repeat. Stand still; hold your stick out in front of you with both hands, toe-up; now turn it toe-down and back again quickly. Repeat ten times. Stand tall and walk in."

NOTES

Striking/fielding Games

INTRODUCTION

The games included in this family are cricket and stoolball, in which scores are built by running between two wickets, and baseball, rounders and softball, where the players run around several posts or bases.

There are many other detailed differences between the games, but the fundamental skills of striking, fielding, catching and running are common to them all. They also share the feature of an 'inning' or 'innings', during which one side bats while the other fields.

OBJECTS OF THE GAMES

When batting: to use skill and insight to achieve the highest score possible

When fielding: to prevent the batting side from achieving their objective

These objects are achieved by:

• striking the ball so that the fielders are deceived or avoided

• running between wickets or around bases so that runs are scored

• delivering the ball to the striker so that s/he is deceived and/or dismissed

• fielding the ball quickly and efficiently so that scoring is minimized

• stopping or catching balls missed by the striker and/or returned by the fielders.

PLAYING AREAS

These games may be played anywhere that there is sufficient space — indoors or outdoors. As with all the other groups of games, you should take the class outside whenever possible.

The essential requirement of any playing area is that the surface should be reasonably smooth and regular. Irregular ground can be a hazard for young players, who will not be able to anticipate the resulting uneven bounces.

In the early stages there is no need for marked pitches, and a playing area may be defined by cones, skittles or multi-purpose markings which are already in place. As long as the pupils are aware of the boundaries of play, the in-play areas and any other markings which relate to the rules, then improvised pitches are acceptable.

Playing-area safety

Children will be running fast and chasing after balls in all these games. Make sure that they play in an area where there is no danger of them running into walls or other obstacles.

EQUIPMENT

At the senior level, all these games require specialist equipment. However, there is no need to spend money on this when introducing children to the basic skills. Any type of bat is acceptable, and wickets and bases can be improvised with only a little ingenuity.

Special balls for junior versions of the games are often available, but tennis balls can usually be substituted.

If your pupils have difficulty connecting bat and ball, try letting them use an oversize ball until their skills develop.

You will find the use of a tee suggested during the early stages of skill-learning in all these games. This is a good way of presenting the ball for beginners to hit. Although special tees are commercially available, you can easily improvise by using cones, plastic bottles or skittles.

Catching gloves or mitts are used in softball and baseball, although a satisfactory introduction to these games can be given without using them. The use of catching gloves should be at the discretion of the school; if the intention is to continue to develop softball or baseball, they will be required at some stage.

Equipment should be such that the children can handle it with ease. Paddle or padder tennis bats are useful in that the large head of the bat gives a greater tolerance for error in the hitting action. However, at some stage children must experience play with the types of bat used in the full games, such as a junior cricket bat, or the most lightweight softball or teeball bat. Again, improvisation is called for to ensure that the skills required to use the equipment do not defeat the objective of the game or task.

BOUNDARY RULES

All the games (with the exception of rounders — see below) have rules concerning the boundary of the field or pitch. If the ball is hit over the boundary, the striker's score is increased. A typical example is in cricket, where a ball passing over the boundary without bouncing scores six runs, while one which bounces or runs over the ground first scores four.

In rounders, boundaries are used normally only at tournament level. In this case one rounder is gained if the ball travels over the boundary, regardless of whether it bounces or not.

THE SKILLS OF THE GAMES

At this stage skill teaching, while always relevant to the game, should involve fun, purpose and maximum activity for **all the class**.

The skills should be introduced within the context of the games. For primary-school children, the term 'game' means a modified and simplified version of the full-scale activity. These versions may be devised by teachers or by the pupils themselves.

By observing pupils' responses to the games, you will be able to select those skills that need development and then work on them separately before re-introducing them in the game context.

All these games involve the following skills:

- striking/hitting
- running
- catching
- throwing
- bowling/pitching
- stopping/keeping

They also demand effective **fielding**, which is a combination of many of the skills in the list above, plus an added sense of how to be in the right place at the right time.

The activities in this section cover skills which are common to all the games in the striking/fielding family. The games from which they originate are included, in brackets, for information only. Few of the activities isolate skills exactly, since, for example, a batting game will inevitably require a bowler and fielders as well. This section does, however, distinguish between those games and tasks in which the emphasis is on skills needed by the batting side and those which concentrate on fielding-side skills.

INSIGHT

As well as developing skill, all the activities which follow will help the pupils to:

- appreciate the intentions and purposes of the games

- understand the scoring system and what is required to win a game

- select and use the skills appropriate to the needs of the situation

- respond quickly to the ever-changing situations which occur in games

- act as a part of a cohesive team, pooling abilities and strengths for the benefit of the team.

PHYSICAL PREPAREDNESS

Active games contribute to the physical well-being and development of the children. Always remember to include the warm-up and cool-down sessions which are a vital part of every games lesson.

KEEP THEM INVOLVED

Games and tasks in which pupils are inactive once they are 'out' should be discouraged. It is vital at this stage that the children's interest is maintained and that they are physically active throughout the lesson.

It is therefore very important that players should gain experience in all positions and should not be allowed to play in one position to the exclusion of all others.

One of the problems in the striking/fielding family of games can be that of ensuring that all the pupils have equal opportunities to contribute to the play. A practical way of overcoming this is to form them into pairs to play restricted versions of the games. In cricket, for example, you can start with a three-pair game in which one pair bats, one pair fields,

and the third pair bowls and keeps wicket. At the end of every over (six balls), the batters change ends, the fielders change sides, and the bowler and wicketkeeper change duties. The pairs rotate positions completely after every second over.

As skills improve, extra pairs can be introduced into this basic plan, until five pairs are involved.

The pairs system works particularly well for cricket and stoolball, but can be easily adapted to the other games.

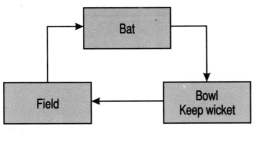

3 pairs

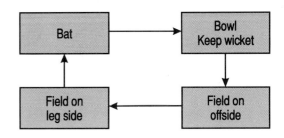

4 pairs

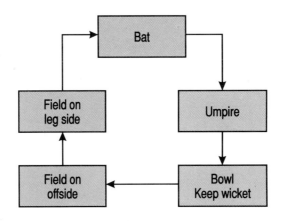

5 pairs

RUNNING GAMES

These games teach an understanding of the importance of running in the scoring of runs or points. They encourage correct contact with base, post or crease, and they help the pupils to develop a good running technique.

Game 232 Beat the runner (softball/baseball)

Object: to develop circular-running skills.

For 4v4.

Arrange four 'bases' (use cones, skittles or baskets) as shown in the illustration. Adjust the distances according to the age and skill of the players.

The fielding-team players take up positions at the bases, with the ball at the home base. The first member of the running team stands by the home base.

The game is a race between the ball and the runners. At a signal, the fielders pass the ball from base to base, in order, while the runner dashes around them.

For the first few attempts, start each runner and the ball together; as skills improve, you can make play continuous, with a fresh runner starting as soon as the previous one returns home. Change running and fielding teams frequently.

Scoring: The runners score a point each time they beat the ball. The fielders score a point each time they beat the runner. For the continuous game, see who can do the most circuits in a given time.

Extending variations:

• The fielders attempt to get the ball around the bases twice during the runner's one lap.

• Each fielder must make contact with his/her base before passing the ball on.

• The runners must touch each base on the way round.

• The runner starts with the ball which s/he rolls anywhere in the field and then starts to run. The nearest fielder retrieves the ball, which must then go round the bases in order.

Game 233 R.A.F. (cricket/stoolball)

Object: to develop **R**unning **A**nd **F**ielding skills.

For 5v5: a fielding team (four fielders plus a wicketkeeper) and a batting team. (Note that the 'batters' do not in fact use bats at all — they simply have to run.)

Play in any convenient area with two marked parallel lines approximately 20 metres (65 ft) apart. Use a cone or skittle as a 'wicket'. One ball per game. The teams line up side by side as shown in the illustration.

The wicketkeeper rolls the ball to the first fielder, who intercepts it and returns it as quickly as possible before going back to rejoin his/her team. As soon as the wicketkeeper rolls the ball, the first batter can start to run. The game is a race to see if the wicketkeeper can touch the ball on the wicket before the batter can tag the wicket to score a 'run'.

After each batter has had two attempts, the teams change roles. Rotate the team positions and make sure that every player has a turn as wicketkeeper.

The winners are the team with the most runs.

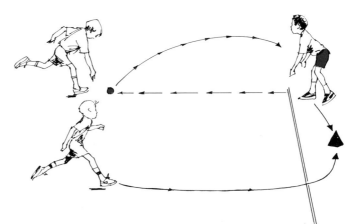

Game 234 Team 'runders' (rounders)

Object: to develop base-running and catching skills.

For two equal teams of any size.

Set out five markers to indicate a rounders field, as shown in the illustration. One team lines up by the home marker; these are the runners. Two more markers are placed nearby, about 10–15 metres (33–50 ft) apart. Half of the second team (the catchers) line up behind each of these markers.

The idea is for the catchers to complete as many catches as possible in the time it takes the runners to complete a set number of laps of their bases.

Each runner may set off only when the previous one reaches first base. The runners are not allowed to overtake each other. The last runner to reach the fourth base shouts "Stop!" as s/he touches it.

The catching team take turns to throw a soft ball to each other, running to the back of their respective lines after each throw. Each successful throw and catch is counted until the last runner calls "Stop!". Count only clean catches made when both thrower and catcher are behind the markers.

The teams then change roles. The winners are the team with the highest total of successful catches.

Easier variation: Allow the ball to bounce once (or more) before being caught.

Extending variation: Individual members of the running team run around the bases separately, the next following as soon as the previous one gets home.

BATTING/STRIKING GAMES

Batting has a natural appeal for children, but the rules of the games limit the opportunities. By giving them plenty of opportunities to practise through games and the skill-development tasks on page 148, they will enjoy mastering the physical demands of batting at the same time as developing judgement of line, length and speed of the ball.

Teaching batting

In all the striking/fielding games the use of tees can be a great help in encouraging young batters. These enable very inexperienced players to make contact without having to judge the speed and flight of an approaching ball. Put the stress on hitting the ball **cleanly** from the tee. See page 140 for further information about tees.

When young children are practising hitting from a tee, arrange them in a row about ten paces from any convenient wall or net. If the balls are aimed at this, a lot of retrieving time and effort will be saved.

The elements of batting

In spite of the detailed differences between the games, the fundamental elements of successful batting or striking are the same throughout:

- the grip on the bat or stick
- the stance
- the stride
- the pick-up or swing
- the contact with the ball
- the follow-through

In softball and baseball there is also a wrist 'snap' on contact.

Cricket is the only striking/fielding game in which the ball is struck after it has bounced on the ground. As a result, most of its techniques and skills differ from those of the other games, but the basic elements are the same.

In all the games, remember that you will need to rearrange the field placings according to whether the batter is right-handed or left-handed.

Batting safety

When any type of bat is being used, great care must be taken to prevent the pupils from getting too close to the batter. This is particularly vital in the case of the danger zone directly behind him/her.

The grip

Diagrams illustrating the correct grips for the different games are shown below:

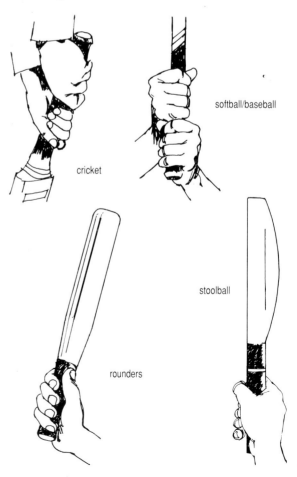

cricket

softball/baseball

rounders

stoolball

BATTING-SIDE GAMES
COMPLEMENTARY SKILL-DEVELOPMENT TASKS

RUNNING: WHY AND WHEN

At primary-school age, children do not require isolated skill training for running. The emphasis should be on understanding **why** they are running and on judging **when** and **when not** to run. They also need to learn how to coordinate their running with the actions of other players so that they give the support needed to score.

RUNNING IN CRICKET

Judging when to run is important in all the games, but never more so than in those which are cricket-based. Cricket players should be taught these rules:

For the first run

• **The striker** should call every ball that s/he hits **ahead** of him/her:

"Yes" means run

"No" means stay

"Wait" means not sure

• **The non-striker** should call every ball that goes **behind** the striker. (The same calls are used.)

Hints to the non-striker: "Walk forward as the bowler runs up, keeping your bat in contact with the crease. Once the bowler has released the ball, you may dare to move further forward, well ahead of the crease — but always be ready to get your bat safely behind the crease again if necessary. This is called 'backing up' the batter.".

For second or subsequent runs

The player who can see the ball most clearly should call. If in doubt, call "Wait".

Get the bat on the ground

The bat is not 'in the crease' unless it is touching the ground — it is not enough for it to be behind the line but in the air. Therefore, children need to be taught to slide the foot of the bat along the ground as they run towards the crease.

RUNNING TASKS

Task 235 Shuttle bats (cricket)

Object: for the bat to make contact with the ground.

For 3v3 or 4v4.

Play on any flat surface with a crease marked near each end. Each player carries a bat. The task is simply for the players to run as fast as possible between the creases, making sure they slide the bat over the crease each time. Each team has a minute.

The team members all start at the same end and take turns to complete double runs. The opposing team act as umpires to check that the bats are in contact as they cross the line.

"How many runs can each team make in one minute?"

Extending variations: The right-handed players have to carry the bat in their left hands and vice versa; the players have to change hands for the return run.

Task 236 Touch base! (baseball/softball)

Object: to develop the skill of base-running.

For several teams of four or five pupils.

Use two rows of squares marked on the ground as illustrated below. The front row are the 'home bases', and the distant row the 'first bases'. The teams line up in front of the home bases, one team to each base.

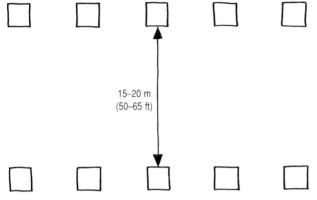

15–20 m
(50–65 ft)

The pupils take turns to sprint from home base to first base, touch the base, yell "touch" and glance to the right. They then jog back to the end of their line ready to run again.

"Use your arms very vigorously, make sure you make contact with the base, and always check to the right so that you can see what is going on around you, just as you would in the actual game."

This task can be turned into a competitive relay game if you wish, but be sure to keep the emphasis on good technique.

If two groups share one set of bases, one group can observe while the other runs. An observer at each base checks for foot contact. On completion of a circuit by one group of four, the observers and the runners change roles.

Extending variations:

• See which team can be back at their starting bases in the shortest time

• See how many accurate circuits can be made in a set time. Any runner who misses a base drops out of that particular circuit. The winners are the team which completes the greatest number of accurate circuits within the time allowed.

Running: skill card 47

Starting from the base or crease: skill card 48

Task 237 Making turns (baseball/softball)

Object: to develop the skill of base-running; to use the feet correctly in making contact with the bases.

For groups of four.

Mark out four bases in a square, as shown in the illustration; chalked squares are ideal. Each of the four pupils starts on a base.

"On the signal, sprint around all the bases, making sure that you contact them on the inside corner as you pass. Try to complete the four bases as quickly as you can, checking that you make good foot contact on each."

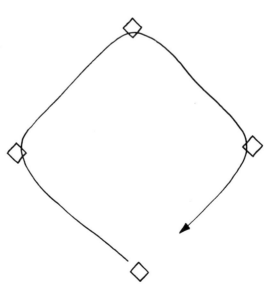

BATTING/STRIKING TASKS

Task 238 Tee strike (all striking games)

Object: to get used to the feeling of striking the ball in a desired direction.

Play in small groups. Use a tee and one or two balls. If the task is to be cricket-based, use a relatively low tee. One player is the batter; the others arrange themselves in a fan shape, about 10–12 paces in front of the batter.

The batter attempts to hit the ball directly to each of the other players in turn. Rotate places after every five strikes.

Extending variation: Mark three target lines on the ground. The batter attempts to score 'runs' by hitting the ball over the lines: 1 run for the nearest line, 4 runs for the middle, 6 runs for the furthest. The fielders can move freely to try to stop the ball from reaching the lines.

Task 239 Feed and strike (rounders)

Object: to make good strikes.

For groups of up to ten players.

Mark out four bases in a square, using markers such as skittles or cones. The distances between them should be adjusted according to the skill of the children and the type of ball being used.

The players take turns to bowl, to bat, to act as backstop and to field. The bowler can throw from any safe distance — the aim is to deliver the ball, without a bounce, so that the batter can hit it easily. Each batter is bowled six balls.

There is no running between the bases; instead, the batter is given points according to how far the ball is hit:

- inside the bases: 1 point

- beyond the bases: 2 points

- over a designated boundary: 3 points

After every six balls the players rotate positions. All the players should be given the opportunity to play in all the positions, provided that the bowlers are capable of delivering good 'easy' balls.

Batting in:

cricket: skill card 53

stoolball: skill card 54

rounders: skill card 55

softball/baseball: skill card 56

FIELDING-SIDE GAMES

Objects

The objects of all the fielding games are:

• to teach the essential fielding skills of catching, intercepting and throwing

• to develop an appreciation of the characteristics of the ball in flight

• to encourage cooperation between fielders.

GENERAL FIELDING GAMES

Game 240 Defend the line (cricket/stoolball)

For 6v6.

Mark two parallel lines, about 5 metres (16.5 ft) apart and 10 metres (33 ft) long. Start with one ball.

Each team spreads out just in front of one of the lines, facing the other team. The object is to roll the ball across the opposing line to score a point. Once the game has started with a player from team **A** rolling the ball towards team **B**'s line, any player in team **B** can intercept it to defend his/her own line, and send it back to attempt to score across **A**'s line.

At no time can the players go more than one pace forward of their lines. The ball must always be rolled — no throwing!

The winners are the team with the most points at the end of a given time.

The lengths of the lines and the distance between them can be adjusted to suit the abilities of the children.

Extending variations:

• As the teams become more proficient, extra balls may be added.

• Allow the teams to pass the ball before sending it across to the other side.

Game 241 Variations of Beat the runner (page 143) (rounders, baseball/softball)

For groups of four.

Play **Beat the runner**, but put more emphasis on the throwing/catching aspects. Introduce restrictions which will encourage more accurate throwing, such as not allowing the catchers to move their feet, or not allowing any bounces.

CONTINUOUS GAMES

Game 242 Non-stop rounders

For groups of five.

Set out two hoops and a cone or skittle for each group, and arrange the players as shown in the illustration. Use a tennis ball or air-flow ball.

The batter receives five balls bowled underarm with no bounce. To score s/he has to run around the cone and back before the ball is fielded and returned to the bowler. After every fifth ball, the teams move around one place clockwise. The winner is the player with the most runs after a given number of batting turns.

The batters always receive their five balls — they are never 'out', even if caught cleanly or apparently run out.

Game 243 Non-stop cricket

For groups of about seven players.

This game is basically the same as *Continuous cricket*, described on page 205 of the green section. The difference is that in this game the individuals' scores are counted, rather than team scores. Each time a batter is out, the players all move one place clockwise, so that every player takes a turn at batting, bowling and fielding.

If batters are tending to stay 'in' for too long, you may decide to limit the number of balls any batter can receive — try six or eight to start with.

These games have the overall objective of helping pupils to learn to deliver the ball to the striker within the rules of the game, and to teach the importance of the bowler–backstop combination.

bowler

Game 244 Target bowl (cricket)

Object: to develop the sense of length and line when bowling.

For groups of three.

Set up a wide 'wicket' (a small chair may be used) for each group. Mark a target area in front of the wicket, as shown in the diagram. The positioning of this will need to be adjusted relative to the size of the wicket and the resilience of the ball used — do not use balls with excessive bounce.

The players take turns to deliver twelve balls (two 'overs') at the wicket. The ball must be bowled overarm, and should bounce in the target area. The bowler may bowl over or round the wicket. The wicketkeeper attempts to field every ball cleanly, while the third player, the scorer, notes whether the ball bounces within the target area.

Rotate players after every twelve balls, so that everyone gets to play in each position.

Each group attempts to build a higher score than other groups.

X wicket

1.5 m (5 ft)

TARGET

X scorer

5 m (16 ft)

Scoring:

• Each delivery which hits both the target area and the wicket: 2 points

• Each delivery which bounces within the target area: 1 point

• Each ball which the wicketkeeper catches cleanly after it has bounced within the target area: 1 point

INTERCEPTING

The overall objectives of these tasks are:

• to help children understand **why** players need to be able to stop or intercept the ball

• to teach them **how** to intercept

• to help them to appreciate what other factors are involved.

Task 245 *Stop and throw*

Object: to develop stopping and throwing as one complete movement.

Initially, pupils work in pairs.

The players take up positions 10–15 paces apart. Each pair has a ball, which they roll to one another, each time having to stop it and return it with the minimum delay.

After a few attempts, show the children how to form the 'long barrier', with the lead foot sideways and the hands cupped to receive the ball (see skill card 50).

Extending variations:

• As above, but the ball has to be rolled towards a marker which is a metre or so (about 3 ft) to one side of the receiver, who cannot move until the ball has left the sender's hands. Change the position of the marker frequently, so that the players get used to moving sideways in both directions.

• Play the same task, but with three or four pupils, so that the ball will come from different angles.

Task 246 *Catch-roll-catch*

Object: to develop agility in picking up the ball and throwing it.

For groups of three, using one ball per group.

The pupils stand in a triangle, about 10–12 paces apart.

The players send the ball around the triangle by alternately throwing it and rolling it. If it is caught, then it has to be rolled to the next player; if it is picked up, then it must be thrown, and so on. Reverse direction from time to time.

MAKING A GOOD RETURN

Efficient fielding depends on the player knowing **why** a throw is being made, **where** to throw the ball, and then using the best technique to throw it.

The ball is thrown in order to:

• try to run out the striker or a runner

• return the ball to the wicketkeeper or other team member in order to prevent further running between wickets or bases.

The ball can be thrown to:

• the striker's wicket

• another base or wicket

• any other fielder

A good throw requires:

• the correct grip

• sight of the target

• a good stance

• a good aim and judgement of distance

• speed of arm and body

• use of the appropriate technique

Task 247 Target bounce

Object: to develop aiming skills.

Work in pairs, using one ball per pair.

Mark a rectangular target area on the ground, about 1 metre wide by 3 metres long (3 x 10 ft) to start with.

The players stand either side of the target area, about 15–20 paces apart, and throw the ball to one another via a single bounce.

"Using an overarm action, throw the ball down to bounce in the target."

You can introduce an element of competition in various ways:

"See who can be the first pair to score ten hits on the target."

"Which player can score the most hits in ten throws?"

Extending variations:

• Make the targets smaller.

• Make the children stand further apart — behind lines or in hoops — so that more accuracy is needed.

CHASING AND RETRIEVING

Inevitably, fielding will sometimes mean running after a ball which has passed by, so skill at chasing and retrieving is important.

What does chasing and retrieving involve? Pupils have to:

• watch the path of the ball to judge line and speed

• turn and run after the ball

• collect the ball, turn and throw.

This all demands judgement, speed of movement, agility and mobility.

Task 248 Run and fetch

Object: to collect and return a ball which has passed the fielder.

For two players, A and B, using one ball.

Player A stands 2 or 3 metres (7–10 ft) in front of B, who has the ball. Both players face in the same direction. A indicates which is his/her throwing arm, and B then rolls the ball strongly past that side of A, who chases after it.

A then has to retrieve the ball while it is still moving, half-turn, and throw it back to B.

"Reach down ahead of the ball and try to let it roll into your hand. Don't be too hurried — make sure that you have the ball safely before turning to throw."

Change roles after every five attempts.

Extending variation: place a cone or other target about 5 metres (16 ft) away from the start position. The chaser has to collect the ball and aim it at the target.

"In five tries, how many times can you hit the target?"

Intercepting: skill card 49

Stopping and returning: skill card 50

Chasing and returning: skill card 51

Fielding high catches: skill card 52

BOWLING AND PITCHING

As with batting, there is a major difference between cricket and the other games within this family. Cricket uses overarm bowling, and the ball strikes the ground before being played by the batter. However, if the children are not ready for overarm bowling then underarm should be used.

One of the major requirements of bowling in any game is **accuracy** and the following skill-development tasks reflect this need.

Task 249 Target bowl (cricket)

Object: to develop accuracy in overarm delivery.

For groups of up to ten.

This task is a modification of Game 244 **Target bowl** on page 150. Make the target on the pitch smaller — say, 3 metres long and 1 metre wide (10 x 3 ft).

The players take turns to bowl six balls, overarm. They score one point for bouncing the ball in the target area, and another if they then hit the wicket.

"Out of a six-ball over, how many points can you score? Try to beat your record."

Task 250 Target gallery (rounders)

Object: to develop accuracy in underarm delivery.

For groups of any size.

This is a useful task to have as part of a 'circuit'.

This task requires a wall or net, with a parallel line about 7 metres (23 ft) away from it.

Mark a series of targets on the wall. If possible, make these of different shapes and sizes, and ranging in height between 0.5 metre and 1.5 metres (1.5–5 ft). If a net is used, hoops can be hung on it as targets.

The children bowl balls at the targets, using an underarm action.

"Out of ten balls, how many different targets can you hit?"

Task 251 Slow-pitch bucket (baseball/softball/rounders)

Object: to develop accurate slow pitching.

For pairs.

Mark two parallel lines about 8–10 metres (26–33 ft) apart. Place a bucket or basket behind one of the lines. Use one ball and one cane.

One player stands in front of the line by the bucket, holding the cane horizontally. The other player stands behind the far line and pitches the ball to go past the cane and into the bucket. Players have ten attempts to get the ball into the bucket — it can go over the cane or under it, but the pitcher must call "over" or "under" as s/he makes each delivery. The height of the cane is varied between deliveries, but it must not be altered during a delivery.

The partners change over after every ten balls.

"Out of ten attempts, how many did you get in?"

Task 252 Hoop ball (rounders)

Object: to develop bowling skills; also fielding and cooperation.

For groups of four, using one ball, one hoop and a cone or skittle per group.

The bowler and the 'batter' should be about 8 metres (26 ft) apart; mark two boxes on the ground for them, or simply use two lines. The cone is placed at 'first base' position, and a fielder stands by it. The remaining player is the backstop

To play, the batter holds the hoop out to one side of his/her body above waist-height. The bowler attempts to bowl the ball through the hoop to the

153

backstop. If s/he succeeds, the batter drops the hoop and runs to first base. The backstop must field the ball and throw it to first base to beat the batter.

The batter can alter the height of the hoop between balls, but must not move it during a delivery.

From first base, the ball must be returned to the bowler via the backstop.

After every five balls the players rotate places. Continue the task until all the players have been in all the positions several times.

Bowling and pitching on the move

In the full versions of all the games in this family, the whole body of the bowler or pitcher is moving when the delivery is made. Once your pupils have begun to develop a basic feel for direction and length, they should be encouraged to deliver the ball on the move.

These actions should be incorporated within the games and tasks when the children are ready.

Bowling or pitching in:

cricket: skill card 57

stoolball: skill card 58

rounders: skill card 59

softball: skill card 60

baseball: skill card 61

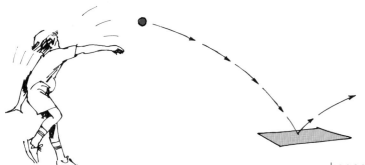

The position directly behind the batter is a very important one in all the striking/fielding games, yet very often the skills involved are never taught: the children are expected somehow to adapt automatically to this highly specific position. The following tasks will ensure that all your pupils experience the basic work necessary to play safely and effectively behind the bat.

Task 253 Wicket bounce (cricket)

Object: to introduce the movement and catching action involved in wicketkeeping.

For pairs, using one ball.

Mark a target area on the ground — the exact size is not critical.

The pupils take up positions on either side of the target. One of them bounces the ball overarm into the target, to be caught by his/her partner, who has to start from a wicketkeeping crouch. The 'keeper must attempt to take each ball cleanly and roll it back to the 'bowler' as quickly as possible.

"Out of ten balls, how many can you catch cleanly?"

Encourage the bowler to take up the 'long barrier' position (see skill card 50) to receive the return from the wicketkeeper.

The players change roles after every ten balls.

Extending variations:

• "Bounce the ball to one side of the wicketkeeper, or to the other, so that s/he has to 'read' the bounce to collect it."

• Introduce wickets, or wicket-substitutes such as cones; require the wicket-keeper to make a stumping action each time s/he catches the ball.

• Introduce a third player — a 'shadow batter' — who plays a stroke at each delivery, but aims to miss the ball each time. This provides a distraction for the wicketkeeper, and makes the practice more realistic.

Task 254 Wicket whizz

Object: to improve accuracy in throwing, catching and wicketkeeping.

For groups of four to six, using one ball and a wicket per group.

One player is the wicketkeeper; the others act as fielders, and spread out randomly, several metres apart, as shown in the illustration.

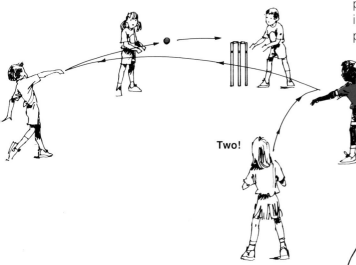

Two!

Play starts with a fielder throwing the ball to one of the others and simultaneously calling out a number. This indicates how many other fielders have to touch the ball before it can be thrown at the wicket. The fielders pass it on, with as little delay as possible, until finally it is aimed at the wicket and the wicketkeeper fields it. S/he then passes it back out to any fielder for play to start again.

The ball cannot be thrown back to the previous player, and there should be a top limit to the number that can be called — usually four or five. The wicketkeepers must be encouraged to send the ball back to different players as often as possible.

After every six attempts, all the players rotate one position clockwise.

Keeping wicket (cricket/stoolball): skill card 62

Backstop (rounders/baseball/softball): skill card 63

Task 255 Surprise shots (rounders)

Object: to simulate the actions needed by a backstop to cover a variety of shots.

For pairs.

Both players face in the same direction; one, with the ball, stands 2–4 metres (6.5–13 ft) in front of the other, who acts as the backstop. The front player throws the ball backwards, giving as little indication of the exact speed and direction as possible: the ball can be tossed from under the arm, over the shoulder, around the side of the body — even from between the legs. The backstop has to collect the ball as quickly and efficiently as possible.

"See if you can fool the backstop with a good ball."

After five balls the players change places.

Task 256 Rounders one-two-three (rounders/softball)

Object: to understand how the roles of bowler, backstop and first-base fielder link together.

For groups of three.

Set out the markers as shown for **mini-rounders** on page 210 of the green section.

The bowler bowls to the backstop, who collects the ball and throws it as quickly as possible to first base. The first-base fielder collects the ball and returns it underarm to the bowler. Keep the action moving at a good speed.

Rotate roles after every five balls.

Games-making task 257
Different course

In conventional striking/fielding games players run between two markers (wickets) or around four markers (bases or posts).

"Can you set out a different running course — for example, with three markers? How will the batter hit — off a tee, a ball bowled by a friendly bowler, or a ball bowled by an opponent? Which kinds of bat and ball make the game work well? What is the best number of players to have in each team? How do you score?"

Games-making task 258
Catch it!

"Make up a game which will give the fielders lots of chances to catch the batters' hits. How will your game be scored? What happens when a fielder catches a ball hit by the batter? How can the batting team build up a score?

"Do you know what an innings means? When will your batters and bowlers change over?"

LESSON PLAN 9

Intention: by the end of this lesson pupils should appreciate the importance of accurate throwing and catching while fielding.

Pre-lesson organization: have a supply of tennis balls (enough for one per pupil) in three or four containers. Space these out to avoid crowding during distribution.

Organization for Task 1: identify the partners for the first task. All the children then go into the playing area and jog freely.

Task (What pupils do)	Observations (What to look for)	Points to remember
Warm-up "Jog around the area. On the command 'left', bend down and touch the ground with the left hand. On the command 'right', repeat with the right hand. On the command 'both' touch the ground with both hands."	Are all the group moving at a steady jogging pace, with no rushing and pushing? Are they selecting the correct hand? Can they touch the ground on the move, or do they have to stop?	Be aware of pupils who have problems with jogging or with selecting the correct hand.

Bridging organization: "Form up into your pairs. One of each pair collects a ball from the nearest container."

Revision **Close catches:** Pupils stand opposite each other about 5 metres (16 ft) apart, and throw/catch so that the ball arrives at about waist height. Later, the throws should be varied, arriving at the front and to either side of the players. **Lofted catches:** Partners move to 10 metres (33 ft) apart. Now the ball is thrown high into the air for the partner to catch.	**For all catches:** head still; eyes on the ball; catcher ready to move if necessary. **For close catches:** hands in the 'downward cradle' position, with fingers at right angles to the flight of the ball. Knees and hips slightly bent. **For high catches:** hands level with eyes; fingers spread and relaxed. Hands and arms give to break the flight of the ball. The ball should be gathered into the chest. Watch if the hands are too rigid so that the ball is dropped. Does catching on the left cause more problems than on the right? Is the feed accurate?	Use skill card 52 if necessary.

Bridging organization: keeping the balls, the pairs join up to become teams of four; two teams per game. If using a playing area marked out as a grid, each game will occupy three grid-squares arranged in a line.

New work Competitive game: tennis catch. In each game the four balls are in play all the time. Opposing teams each take up a grid-square, leaving a vacant square between them. **Objective:** to lob each of the balls, underarm, high into the air, to land in the opponents' court. The opposing team must try to catch each ball before it touches the ground within their court. **Scoring:** each time a ball lands in an occupied square, the team sending it scores a point. Move the teams so that they all play against each other.	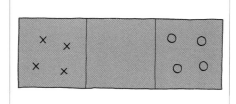	

Closing organization: check the scores of the teams and comment as necessary, providing feedback and support to the group. Players return the balls to the containers.

Cool-down

"Jog gently around the area. Stop, space out, and reach both your arms up in the air above your head. Slowly return your arms to your sides. Stand as tall as you can. Walk in and change."

NOTES

NOTES

NOTES

Introduction to Mini-games

This green section contains information provided by national governing bodies about their mini-games. These have been designed especially for children of primary-school age. They provide satisfying but challenging games in which each player has a high level of involvement. As far as possible they represent the essential characteristics of the full regulation games which pupils may study in Key Stages 3 and 4.

The mini-games are listed in the same categories as the formal games in the blue section (see family tree on page 63).

INTRODUCTION TO MINI-GAMES

Rules

Having experienced formal games, and had opportunities to make their own games, pupils should now be familiar with the significance of rules. Up to now, teachers and pupils have used rules flexibly to shape a game, reduce or increase its demands, and make it accessible to all pupils. However, the rules of mini-games are not generally flexible in this way, for they are laid down by the governing bodies. It is an important development for pupils to learn to discipline their play within the boundaries of a stricter code.

Playing to a recognised code of rules has two additional major benefits:

• Pupils in different classes and other schools will all be playing the same game, so that fair competition becomes possible within a school and between schools.

• It provides opportunities for pupils to serve as officials: to umpire and referee games, and where appropriate to keep score.

Notwithstanding the above comments, some governing bodies specifically state that the rules of their mini-game may be adapted to some extent for beginners. This will normally apply to practices rather than to competitions.

Contents of each mini-sport

The sports are generally divided up as follows, although not every one has all these sub-divisions:

• Introduction

• Equipment

• Playing the mini-game (or games — some sports have more than one)

• The rules

• Practices — if a mini-game introduces skills not previously covered in the yellow and blue sections, then additional information has been provided on how to teach these skills.

• Resources — courses, equipment, booklets, books and videos. We have not included any prices, as these soon become out-of-date.

• Suitable national governing body awards

• Governing-body information.

Net and Wall Mini-games

SHORT TENNIS

Younger children can enjoy short tennis, which uses a small court, plastic rackets and a foam ball but introduces all the skills of the full game.

EQUIPMENT

The court

The short-tennis court is 44 x 20 ft (13.4 x 6.10 m). This is exactly the same as a full-size badminton court, which is often used. In this case you use the outside perimeter lines and an imaginary continuation of the centre service line.

The table below gives guidelines for the minimum space around the court. When a foam ball is used you can get away with more restricted boundaries, but when the livelier outdoor ball is used the competition boundaries become the minimum practical distances.

	General play	Competition
Runback	6 ft (1.8 m)	8 ft 6 in (2.6 m)
Siderun	5 ft (1.5 m)	7 ft (2.1 m)
Siderun between courts	6 ft (1.8 m)	9 ft (2.7 m)
Unrestricted height over court	13 ft (4.0 m)	17 ft (5.2 m)

If you are using a badminton court and the sides or baselines are particularly close to a wall, you can gain more space by using the inner sidelines or the base 'tramlines' as the court limits.

The net should be 2 ft 7 in (80 cm) high at the centre and 2 ft 9 in (85 cm) at the posts. A suitably lowered badminton net is often used.

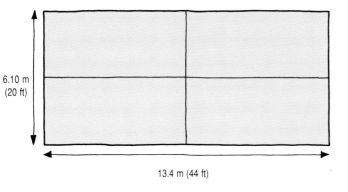

6.10 m (20 ft)

13.4 m (44 ft)

PLAYING SHORT TENNIS

Short tennis is played in exactly the same way as full lawn tennis. The rules given below are the basic ones, but if appropriate you can introduce other rules from the full game.

Introduce the following simple tactics, of which the first two are especially fundamental!

• Hit the ball over the net

• Hit the ball into the court

• Hit the ball where the opponent is not (into space)

• Hit the ball to the opponent's weakness

• Hit the ball forcefully

THE RULES

Scoring

Scoring is on a simple numerical system: love (for 0), 1, 2, 3 and so on. The winner is normally the first to reach 11 points, although you can play to other limits, such as 9 or even 7 points, to suit individual circumstances.

If the score reaches 10–10, the match continues until one player has a lead of 2 points (e.g. 13–11).

If desired, the full tennis scoring system can be introduced at a suitable stage.

Service

1 The service is delivered from behind the baseline, alternate points from the right and left sides.

2 The service may be delivered overarm or underarm, but the ball must not bounce before it is hit.

3 The ball must fall within the diagonal half of the opponent's court. If it doesn't do so, the server is allowed to make a second attempt, but if this also fails the server loses the point.

4 If the ball touches the top of the net on its way into the opponent's court, the service is replayed.

5 The ball must be allowed to bounce before the receiver hits it. If the receiver strikes the ball before it bounces, s/he loses the point.

6 The service alternates between players after every two points.

Play

1 Except when receiving service, players may strike the ball either before or after it bounces.

2 If the ball hits the floor outside the court area, or hits the ceiling, walls or any other obstruction, the player who played that shot loses the point.

3 Players change ends every eight points.

Doubles

The rules are exactly the same for doubles as for singles, except that the players serve in rotation. If the teams are A and B, the service order runs as follows: A1, B1, A2, B2, A1 ... As in singles, each player serves two points before the service moves on to the other team.

RESOURCES

Short Tennis Leaders Course

If you wish to develop your skills in teaching short tennis, this course is for you. It covers the basic principles of teaching short tennis, and a Certificate of Attendance is awarded. Contact the LTA Trust Coaching Department for information on courses in your region.

Books and booklets

Coaching Children and Young People in Tennis, International Tennis Federation

On Handling a Ball with a Racket in the Game of Tennis, Quebec Tennis Federation

Short Tennis Leaders Handbook, LTA Trust

Short Tennis Practices, Charles Applewhaite

Tennis Handbook for Teachers, LTA Trust

The Tennis Teachers Guide, Eve Kraft

United States Tennis Association Schools Program Tennis Curriculum, USTA

All the above books, and many others, are available from the LTA Trust: contact them for an up-to-date price list.

AWARDS AND COMPETITIONS

GOVERNING-BODY INFORMATION

The LTA/Coca Cola Tennis Award Scheme

The LTA Tennis Award Scheme, sponsored by Coca Cola, is designed to encourage school-children throughout the United Kingdom to enjoy taking part in short tennis and tennis.

The Scheme aims to promote an interest in tennis during those early years when racket skills can develop easily without the pressure of competition.

There are six awards, increasing in difficulty as the level of skill progresses. Each award consists of six skill tests. A player will normally complete one award before moving on to the next.

The starter pack includes three full-colour wall posters illustrating the awards and skill tests, class progress charts, individual progress charts, order forms for resources, and a 24-page handbook for teachers covering organisation, administration, teaching points and objectives, assessment, and how to incorporate the Scheme into a teaching programme.

For more details, contact the LTA Trust Coaching Department.

The Tretorn Starter Competitions

The Tretorn scheme is designed to give the beginner ample opportunities to enjoy playing in competitions. The age range is from 8 to 18, usually subdivided into 10 and under, 12 and under, and so on.

The emphasis is on **enjoyment** and **activity**. Each player plays at the right level, and is involved in as much tennis as possible.

For more details, contact the LTA Trust Coaching Department.

British Schools Lawn Tennis Association

Keep up to date with developments in school tennis (including short tennis) by joining the British Schools Lawn Tennis Association (BSLTA).

The numerous benefits of membership include:

• Access to competitions, both locally and nationally

• Coaching clinics for children

• INSET courses for teachers

• Availability of up-to-the-minute resources

• Fun days and starter tournaments

• The opportunity to take part in the Wimbledon ticket ballot

• The *Schools Tennis Bulletin*, published three times a year, to let you know the latest developments in school tennis at primary and secondary level.

For further details, contact the LTA Trust Parks and Schools Department.

Lawn Tennis Association

All departments may be contacted at the following address:

The LTA Trust
The Queen's Club
West Kensington
London
W14 9EG

Tel: 071-385 4233
Fax: 071-381 6507

TABLE TENNIS

There is no regulation game of mini-table-tennis as such, but young players can have a satisfying game by playing according to the simplified rules described here.

It's a good idea to encourage other children to act as umpires once they have enough knowledge of the game.

EQUIPMENT

Most players will use a full regulation table (2.74 m x 1.525 m x 0.76 m; 9 ft x 5 ft x 30 in), but it is permissible to use other tables of a similar specification. The regulation height of the top of the net above the playing surface should be 152.5 mm (6 in), but again this can be varied to help players who are having difficulty.

The racket can be of any size, shape or weight provided that the blade is flat and rigid. Standard table-tennis balls should be used.

PLAYING SIMPLIFIED TABLE TENNIS

Table tennis is already in principle a simple game. The idea is to hit the ball into your opponent's half of the table in such a way that it cannot be re-turned into your half.

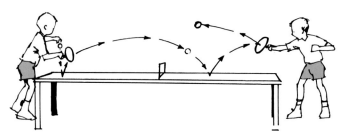

THE RULES

Service

In table tennis you serve by throwing the ball into the air and hitting it, observing the following rules (which may be relaxed at first if necessary):

• The ball initially rests on the palm of the free hand, which must be stationary, open and flat, with the fingers together and the thumb free.

• The free hand must be above the level of the playing surface and behind the server's end-line all the time it is in contact with the ball.

• The server throws the ball vertically upwards, without imparting spin to it. It must rise at least 160 mm (6.3 in) after leaving the palm.

• The server strikes the ball with the racket as the ball is dropping (not while it is still rising). It must be behind the end-line but in front of the server's body.

• From the start of the serve (when the ball is resting on the stationary free hand) until the ball is struck, the whole of the racket must be above the level of the playing surface.

• Once the ball has been struck, the rules are slightly different for singles and doubles. In singles, the ball must first touch the server's court and then pass over the net and touch the receiver's court. In doubles, it must be the **right-hand** court in each case — in other words, the ball is always served diagonally from the right-hand court.

After a point is scored, the rally ends and another service is taken. The right to serve changes after every five points.

Let

In service, if the ball touches the net but still goes over to the opponent's side of the table, a **let** is called and the point is replayed.

The rally is also a let if a disturbance outside the players' control causes either of them to fail to make a good service or return.

Rallying

Once the ball has been served, the two players continue to hit it back and forth over the net. It must bounce once on the receiver's side of the table before it is hit, and it then has to pass over the net and touch the opponent's court.

In doubles play, the server serves, the receiver returns, the server's partner returns, the receiver's partner returns, and thereafter each player in turn in that sequence plays the ball.

Scoring

Unless a let has been called, a player scores a point if his/her opponent makes one of the following errors:

• fails to make a good service

• fails to make a good return

• volleys the ball (i.e. hits it before it has bounced on his/her side of the table)

• plays the ball after it has bounced twice on his/her side of the table

• strikes the ball twice successively

• touches the playing surface with his/her free hand

• touches the net with any part of the body or anything worn or carried

• moves the table with any part of the body or anything worn or carried

• plays out of sequence in doubles

The game is won by the side that first scores 21 points, provided that the margin of victory is at least 2 points. If the score reaches 20-all, the game continues with alternate service, and is won by the side that first scores 2 points more than their opponent(s).

A match normally consists of the best of three games.

RESOURCES

The following coaching and teaching aids are available from the English Table Tennis Association:

Laws of the Game (free booklet)

Take up Table Tennis, Donald Parker (England Team Manager)

How to Coach Table Tennis, David Hewitt

ETTA Coaching Manual

Learning to Play the Game (video)

Advanced Stroke Play (video)

AWARDS

Details of the Dunlop Skills Award Scheme are available free from the ETTA. This scheme consists of a series of objective practical tests, suitable for beginners onwards. Badges and certificates are awarded to successful players at each level: Rookie, Improver, Player, Matchplayer and Masters. The first three levels can be assessed by teachers or student teachers, among others.

GOVERNING-BODY INFORMATION

Enquiries of any nature concerning table tennis are welcome and encouraged. Contact:

The English Table Tennis Association
Queensbury House
Havelock Road
Hastings
East Sussex
TN34 1HF

Tel: 0424 722525

SHORT BADMINTON

Short badminton is a version of badminton specially adapted for young children. The court is smaller, with a lower net, and the rackets are shortened and lighter in weight; however, standard shuttles are used. Short badminton helps the children learn the basic skills and strokes easily and naturally, and they readily transfer to the adult game as they learn and grow taller.

EQUIPMENT

The court

The full doubles badminton court is 44 x 20 ft (13.4 x 6.10 m), whereas the short-badminton court is 36 x 17 ft (11.0 x 5.18 m) for doubles and 36 x 15 ft (11.0 x 4.57 m) for singles.

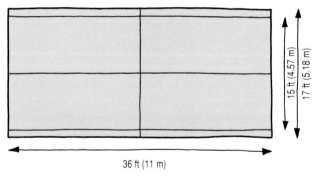

15 ft (4.57 m) 17 ft (5.18 m)

36 ft (11 m)

For recreational play you can use most of the long half of a full court to make a playing area of 36 x 10 ft (11.0 x 3.05 m).

The net should be lower than the full height of 5 ft (1.52 m) at the centre and 5 ft 1 in (1.55 m) at the posts. The recommended height varies according to the age of the players:

Age	Height at centre	Height at posts
Under 8	3 ft 11 in (1.19 m)	4 ft (1.22 m)
8 to 11	4 ft 2 in (1.27 m)	4 ft 3 in (1.29 m)

Rackets

The short-badminton racket is about 2 inches (5 cm) shorter than the full racket. Some manufacturers now make specially designed shorter rackets for children.

Clothing

Shorts and a T-shirt are ideal for playing in. A sweater or tracksuit is useful for keeping warm between games.

Lightweight trainers are suitable, but the ideal is to wear special badminton shoes with good cushioning and a sole which provides adequate friction.

PLAYING SHORT BADMINTON

Short badminton is played the same way as badminton, with slight adaptations.

THE RULES

When short badminton is played strictly, the full Laws of Badminton apply except for the following variations.

Scoring

A match consists of either one game of 11 points, or the best of three games of 9 points each. Unlike the full game, you gain a point whenever you win a rally, whether or not it was your serve.

Serving

The rules are basically the same for singles and doubles. Here they are given for a singles game, with the doubles rule in *italics*.

1 You continue to serve while you [*your team*] are winning points. When you lose a point, the serve goes to the other player [*team*].

2 The serving player serves to the opponent's service court diagonally opposite. If his/her score is even, s/he serves from the right service court; if odd, from the left service court.

3 *In doubles, each receiving team player receives in the service court s/he was in when the team was previously serving.*

GETTING STARTED

Here are some simple practices for beginners:

Individual practices

1 Count how many times you can keep hitting the shuttle up in the air.

2 See how far you can hit the shuttle with an underarm stroke.

3 Place a hoop or box on the ground about 10 feet (3 metres) away from you, and try to hit the shuttle into it. Count how many times you succeed out of five attempts.

Rally practices with a partner

These practices introduce the basic skills of the game. Start each rally by hitting the shuttle upwards with an underarm stroke.

1 Rally with your partner and count your best score.

2 Rally, hitting the shuttle high above your partner's head.

3 Rally, hitting the shuttle gently to each other.

4 Rally: one partner hits the shuttle quickly downwards, and the other hits it upwards.

5 Rally, trying to hit the shuttle away from each other, to the back, front and sides of the court.

6 Make up similar practices of your own.

Practice game

Five lives

Each player starts with five lives; you lose a life if you don't hit the shuttle back over the net. You take it in turns to serve, no matter who wins the rally, and you must serve into the court diagonally opposite. Whoever loses all his/her lives has lost the game.

RESOURCES

The *Short Badminton Handbook* is available from the Badminton Association of England Coaching Department. It gives much more information about the game, skill practices, detailed coaching points, and practical hints on introducing short badminton.

AWARDS AND COURSES

Contact the BAE Coaching Department or the English Schools Badminton Association for information on:

• coaching award courses for leaders, teachers, instructors and coaches

• personal performance courses for players of all abilities.

GOVERNING-BODY INFORMATION

Contact the BAE at:

Coaching Department
Badminton Association of England Ltd
National Badminton Centre
Bradwell Road
Loughton Lodge
Milton Keynes
MK8 9LA

Tel: 0908 568822

The English Schools Badminton Association is at the same address and telephone number. It runs competitions and award schemes, and publishes a magazine, *ESBA Post*.

MINIVOLLEY

Minivolley is an exciting game, specifically designed for 9- to 13-year-olds, which the English Volleyball Association is promoting throughout primary and middle schools.

Minivolley is played between two teams of three players, which gives each player twice as much ball contact as a full 6v6 volleyball game. This helps the players learn skills more quickly, and gives them a greater sense of involvement in their team and in the game.

The minivolley court is slightly smaller than a badminton court. This requires the ball to be sent over the net in a controlled fashion, and the basic skills of service, dig and volley become all-important. The rallies are often long and exciting.

EQUIPMENT

The standard minivolley court is 9 m x 6 m (29.5 ft x 20 ft), as shown in the diagram. (This means that minivolley courts will fit across a full-size volleyball court.) If these dimensions are impractical, existing markings can be used to produce courts in the range 9–12 m (29.5–40 ft) long and 4.5–6 m (15–20 ft) wide.

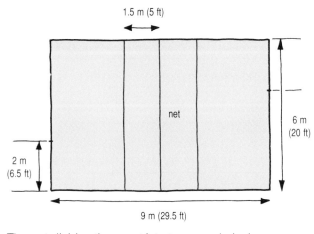

1.5 m (5 ft)

net

6 m (20 ft)

2 m (6.5 ft)

9 m (29.5 ft)

The net divides the court into two equal playing areas. Its height is 2.10 m ± 100 mm (6 ft 10.7 in ± 4 in).

For practice any suitable light, soft ball can be used; foam balls are ideal in the early stages. An EVA-approved minivolley ball should be used for matches.

PLAYING MINIVOLLEY

As in full volleyball, two teams play the ball over the net. Each team aims to make the ball touch their opponents' playing area, or to play the ball in such a way that their opponents cannot return it. Naturally, they have to try equally hard not to let the ball touch their own playing area.

THE RULES

The teams

Each team consists of three players and three substitutes. The coach, as team organiser, can call time-outs and arrange substitutions (see below). Only the coach may communicate with the referee.

Scoring

If the serving team wins the rally, they win a point and continue serving. If the non-serving team wins the rally, they win the right to serve — this is called side-out. A team can score a point only when serving.

A team wins the set when it has scored 15 points, provided that it has a lead of at least two points. Otherwise play continues until one team has a lead of two points.

The match is won by the team that first wins two sets, so matches consist of either two sets (2–0) or three sets (2–1).

Position of players

Each half of the court is divided into two zones (front and back). At the time of service the players are positioned as shown in the diagram at the top of page 171.

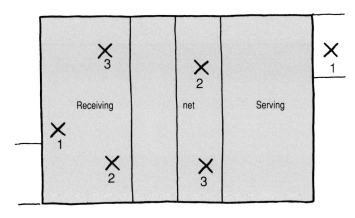

Player **1** is the server, and also plays as a defender, being designated a back-court player. Player **2** usually plays as the setter*. Player **3** normally plays as the attacker, but can also have a defensive role.

The setter plays the ball high and parallel to the net, so that a team-mate can play an attacking shot across the net. This shot is called the set, and is preferably executed using the volley skill.

Whenever a team wins back the service, the players in that team rotate one position clockwise, as shown in the diagram.

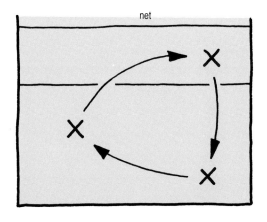

During rallies, the back-court player can only play the ball over the net from within the attack-line area if it is below the height of the net at the moment of contact.

Choice of court or service

A coin is spun to decide the choice of courts or service for the first set. The second set is started by the team which did not serve at the start of the first set. The third set starts in the same way as the first.

Teams must change ends at the start of the second and third sets, and also in the third set as soon as one team has scored 8 points. This change does not affect the score or the players' rotational position on court.

The service

The service is the act of putting the ball into play. It is always done by the back-court player, who must stand in the 2-metre (6.5-ft) service area with both feet behind the baseline.

The ball must be hit with one hand only, and must travel over the net without touching it, being aimed so as to land inside the opponents' court.

Hitting the ball during play

After the service, the ball can be hit with one or both hands, or with any part of the body above the waist. It must not be slapped, caught or held. If both hands or arms are used, they must both hit the ball at the same time.

Each team is allowed to make contact with the ball up to three times before sending it over the net. The exception is that when a player blocking at the net contacts the ball, this does not count as a touch, and the team can have a further three contacts before they have to play the ball over the net.

The ball may not be contacted by the same player twice consecutively, except after a block, which (as we have seen) does not count as a touch.

Play at the net

When the ball touches the net, it remains in play, except for the service.

The players are not allowed to touch the net with any part of the body. If a player's foot is completely in the opponents' court, that is also a fault, but the foot can go partly over the centre line without penalty.

Control of the match

The match is controlled by the referee. S/he blows a whistle for play to start, and in the same way halts play to signal the end of the rally when a fault occurs. The referee makes sure that the rules of the game are not broken, and that the match is played in a sporting spirit. In minivolley, as in volleyball, the players should always show a spirit of fair play and cooperation.

Time-outs and substitutions

Each team may take two time-outs of 30 seconds each per set, in order to take advice and instructions. In addition, up to three substitutions may be made in each set.

Only the coach may request time-outs and substitutions, and then only when the ball is dead (not in play).

A substituted player can return to the game in the same set, but only in place of the player who first replaced him or her, and provided that the allowed number of substitutions has not been exceeded.

PRACTICES

Here is a suggested series of practices in six stages, leading up to standard minivolley. The players should be reasonably competent at each stage before moving on to the next.

Phase 1

Game development

Catching and throwing games over a net 3 m (10 ft) high: 1v1, 2v2, 3v3

Skills

• Catching and throwing skills

• Moving underneath and behind the path of the ball

• Encourage passing

Phase 2

Game development

1v1 games on small courts (6 m x 2 m; 20 ft x 6.5 ft) with a net 3 m (10 ft) high

Skills

• Introduce the volley

Phase 3

Game development

2v2 games on wider courts (6 m x 4 m; 20 ft x 13 ft) with a net 3 m (10 ft) high

Skills

• Volleying through angles — i.e. being able to receive the ball from one direction and play it in another direction

Phase 4

Game development

Games on intermediate-size courts (8 m x 4 m; 26 ft x 13 ft) with a net 2.5 m (8 ft) high:

• 2v2 game using the dig pass

• 3v3 game using volleys only

Skills

• Introduce the dig pass

• Continue work to improve the volley

Phase 5

Game development

Various 3v3 games on a standard minivolley court (9 m x 6 m; 29.5 ft x 20 ft) with a net 2.10 m (6 ft 10.7 in) high:

• Volleys only

• Volley, dig, and volley service

• All skills: volley, dig, and underarm service

Skills

• Continue work to improve volley and dig

• Introduce the underarm service

Phase 6

Game development

3v3 games on the standard minivolley court and net (as Phase 5), using the full rules and all skills. This is minivolley!

Skills

• Continue work to improve serve and dig; introduce the 'set' (see page 171) at this stage

• Introduce attacking shots: the 'tap smash' and the 'dump'

• Introduce the block to counter the smash

RESOURCES

Courses

To help you give minivolley a try, the EVA runs Minivolley Teachers Award Courses throughout the country. If you are interested in learning more about the game and how to teach it to children, write to the EVA for details of forthcoming courses in your area.

The resources listed below can be obtained from the EVA Volleyshop at the EVA address. Send for the Volleyshop Collection Catalogue for further information on equipment, publications and clothing.

Equipment

The following trainer balls are suitable for use in primary schools:

Trial Supersoft (pink) Ref: TL01

Trial Minivolley (yellow) Ref: TL02

These may be purchased from the EVA.

Publications

Minivolley (EVA)

Volleyball Teachers Guide

Introducing Volleyball (video)

AWARDS

The recently launched Volleyball Skills Award Scheme is ideally designed to help you develop minivolley.

The scheme consists of four stages: Preliminary, Bronze, Silver and Gold. The first two stages are particularly aimed at youngsters playing minivolley, and can be assessed during 3v3, 4v4 or 6v6 games.

Each award can be assessed by a qualified teacher, by a club leader, or by the holder of an EVA Teachers Award or of an EVA coaching badge.

Further details, and entry forms, are available from the EVA.

GOVERNING-BODY INFORMATION

For all information about minivolley and full volleyball, contact:

English Volleyball Association
27 South Road
West Bridgford
Nottingham
NG2 7AG

Tel: 0602 816324

MINI-SQUASH

Mini-squash is a form of squash modified for young players. Its aim is to allow beginners to enjoy playing squash in competition.

EQUIPMENT

For obvious practical reasons, mini-squash is normally played on a standard squash court. Play can also take place in a sports hall or even against any suitable wall. In New Zealand and Germany a specially constructed micro-court is sometimes used.

The rackets and ball are modified so that players can quickly start to enjoy good rallying, as there will be no problems due to the ball going deep into the corners of the court.

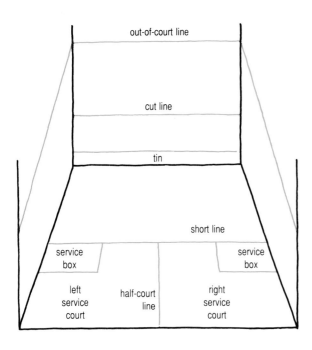

A short, lightweight aluminium racket has been developed for the game. If this recommended racket is not available, a lightweight junior squash racket or a short-tennis racket may be used.

The recommended ball for mini-squash is a foam plastic ball similar to a short-tennis ball which may be used instead if the mini-squash ball is not available.

PLAYING MINI-SQUASH

Mini-squash is played in exactly the same way as squash, and the rules for rallying are identical. However, the service rules are somewhat relaxed, and the scoring system is different.

THE RULES

Service

1 As in squash, the players spin a racket to decide who serves first.

2 The player winning the spin has two serves, one from each side; s/he may start at either side. The second player then has two serves, one from each side, and the service alternates in this way throughout the game.

3 During the service, the server must have part of one foot in contact with the floor in the service box. If this is found to cause difficulty, the server may be allowed to stand in front of the short line.

4 To make the serve, the server throws the ball into the air and hits it before it reaches the floor. A player who finds this difficult may be allowed to bounce the ball on the floor or off the wall first before hitting it.

5 The service must go directly to the front wall above the cut line, and must return anywhere in the opposite half of the court (beyond the half-court line or an imaginary extension of it).

6 Two attempts to serve are allowed. If neither is good, the server loses a point. A player who has difficulty with serving may be allowed a greater number of attempts.

Rallying

The rules for rallying are the same as in squash, with the players hitting the ball alternately either on the volley or after one bounce.

1 The rally is lost if the ball:

— hits the tin

— is hit onto the floor before it reaches the front wall

— goes out (on or above the out-of-court line)

— is missed completely

— is struck twice

— bounces more than once before it is played

2 If the ball hits either player, or the players obstruct each other, a 'let' is called and the point is replayed, with the serve being made from the same box.

Scoring

The player who wins each rally gains a point, whether or not s/he served. The first player to 15 points wins the game.

If time allows, a match of more than one game may be played. In the second and subsequent games the winner of the previous game serves first.

Matches can be decided in any of several ways. The match winner may be:

1 The first player to win a set number of games, usually from 2 to 5.

2 The player who wins more games out of a fixed number of games, such as the 'best of three games'.

3 The player who scores more points over a fixed time of play.

RESOURCES

A booklet entitled *The Rules of Mini-Squash* is obtainable from the SRA.

SRA JUNIOR SKILLS AWARDS

These awards are designed to encourage young learners by testing their ability in the basic skills of squash and their understanding of rules and tactics. A pack is available which provides all the information needed; please contact the Squash Rackets Association for details.

There are four awards: Red Star, Bronze Star, Silver Star and Gold Star. The Red Star award is suitable for a beginner who has received about six hours of coaching. At this level there are no defined targets of length or width, so there can be a great deal of flexibility in the assessment. Players progress through the awards, reaching the Gold Star level when they are at good junior-team standard.

Throughout the awards, pass marks have been kept consistent. For example, in any skill at any level, a player normally needs a score of 4 out of 6 to pass.

The tester can be any qualified leader, teacher or coach in charge of a junior group. There is no need for the whole of an award to be taken at one time, so the skill tests can be included in coaching sessions. There is no limit on the number of attempts which can be made at each skill test, nor is there any time limit.

Those skill tests which require feeding or cooperative rallies may be carried out with the coach or another player.

A group record sheet is available for the coach to keep track of the skill tests that have been completed, and individual record cards can be given to the players to encourage them to practise the skills. These record sheets and cards may be photocopied from the masters supplied.

In addition to the skill tests, the award pack includes a questionnaire to test knowledge of the rules.

Players who successfully complete an award will be sent a free certificate, and may purchase an attractive badge.

GOVERNING-BODY INFORMATION

Further details may be obtained from:

The Squash Rackets Association
West Point
33/34 Warple Way
Acton
London
W3 0RQ

Tel: 081-746 1616
Fax: 081-746 0580

NOTES

Invasion Mini-games

GOAL-THROWING GAMES

MINI-BASKETBALL

Mini-basketball is a team game for boys and girls under the age of 12. It is based on full basketball, but uses smaller equipment. All children are encouraged to play, whatever their level of talent, and unlike in basketball every member of the team must play.

The aim of the game is simple: each team strives to throw the ball into their opponents' basket. The ball is played with the hands only, and can be passed, thrown or dribbled in any direction.

EQUIPMENT

Mini-basketball is played on a court the same size as the standard basketball court. The basket is 2.60 m (8 ft 6 in) high rather than 3.05 m (10 ft).

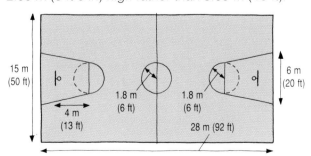

The ball is smaller and more manageable than a full-size one: 450–500 g (16–17.5 oz) in weight, with a circumference of 680–730 mm (27–29 in).

PLAYING MINI-BASKETBALL

Each team consists of ten players, but only five can be on court at any one time. The substitution rule ensures that everyone in the team takes part in the game.

The game is divided into four periods of ten minutes each. The teams change ends halfway through the game, after the second period.

To allow for substitutions, there are intervals between the periods. The half-time interval is ten minutes, and the other two intervals are each two minutes. The game clock continues all the time, unlike in full basketball, and is stopped only on the referee's instruction and during the intervals.

A coach can ask for play to be suspended for one minute — this is called a **time-out**, and can be used to discuss tactics, to make substitutions (both coaches can do this), or just to give the players a brief rest. Only one time-out per team is allowed, and this can only be taken in the fourth period.

THE RULES

Scoring

A successful shot into the opponents' basket scores two points, or one point if it was a free throw. After a team scores, the game is restarted from the end-line by the opposing team.

At the end of the game, the team with the most points is the winner. If both teams scored the same number of points, the game is a draw.

Substitutions

Each member of each team must play at least one 10-minute period, and by the end of the third period, every member of the team must have played for at least one period, but not more than two. In the first three periods substitutions have to be made during the intervals. Further substitutions may be made by the coaches during time-outs in the fourth period.

Progression rules

1 Travelling

You are not allowed to 'travel' while carrying the ball. This means that you can only take one step while holding the ball, and must get rid of it before taking a second step (except for the pivot; see below).

If you receive the ball while running, you are allowed to use a 'two-count rhythm' of two steps to come to a stop or pass the ball. The same applies to the completion of a dribble.

2 Pivot

A player who receives the ball when standing still, or who stops correctly after catching it, is allowed to **pivot**. This means moving one foot in any direction while the other remains in contact with the ground.

3 Dribbling

You *are* allowed to move with the ball, but only by **dribbling**: repeatedly bouncing the ball on the floor with one hand.

You are not allowed to:

• Dribble with both hands at the same time

• Start dribbling again after the ball has come to rest in your hands

• Allow the ball to rest in one hand while dribbling.

Penalty: If any of the progression rules are broken, the referee blows the whistle, and possession is given to the opposing team. The ball is put into play from the sideline nearest the place on court where the violation occurred.

Fouls

The basic rule is **no contact**. Whether attacking or defending, all players should make every effort to avoid contact with their opponents.

1 Personal foul

You are not allowed to stretch out your arms or legs to impede another player, or to bump into a player or to get in his/her way.

Penalty: The opposing team takes a throw-in from the sideline.

2 Shooting foul

No one is allowed to touch a player while s/he is in the act of shooting, or to interfere with the act in any way.

Penalty: Two free throws are awarded to the player who has been fouled.

3 Intentional foul

This is a personal foul committed by a player who **deliberately** makes contact with an opponent in order to prevent him/her from playing normally.

Penalty: Two free throws are awarded to the player who has been fouled. In the case of a blatantly unsporting foul, the offender can be disqualified, in which case s/he must leave the court and may not play again during that game. The disqualified player is replaced on court by a substitute.

Jump ball

A jump ball is one of the ways of starting or re-starting play. The referee throws the ball into the air between two opposing players, in one of the circles. Each player stays in the half of the circle nearest his/her own basket. They both jump for the ball and try to tap it to a team-mate; each is allowed to tap the ball twice.

A jump ball takes place in the following circumstances:

• At the beginning of every period, in the centre circle

• During play, when two opponents hold the ball at the same time ('held ball')

• When the ball lodges in the basket supports

• When the ball goes out-of-bounds (see below) and this is caused by two opposing players, or the referee is uncertain which team sent the ball out-of-bounds.

Except at the beginning of each period, the jump ball is held in the free-throw circle that is nearest the spot where the incident took place.

Out-of-bounds

The ball is out-of-bounds when:

• It touches the floor (or any object or person) outside the court or on the boundary lines. (It is the **inside** of the lines that define the playing area.)

• It touches a player who is outside the court or on the boundary lines.

• It hits the basket support or the back of the backboard.

The player who touched the ball last is held responsible for causing it to go out-of-bounds, and the ball is awarded to the opposing team for a throw-in.

Free throws

The free-shooter stands behind the free-throw line (4 m [13 ft] from the backboard) and receives the ball from the referee. S/he must shoot at the basket within five seconds. The other players can stand in the spaces marked along the zone lines — two defenders in the spaces nearest the basket, and two attackers in the other spaces. They can enter the restricted area only after the ball has left the free-shooter's hand.

If the shooter succeeds but breaks the line before the ball touches the ring, no point is scored, and the other team gains possession of the ball for a throw-in from the sideline.

If another attacking player breaks the line early, the point counts if the shot goes in, but if it is missed the defending team gains possession for a throw-in from the sideline.

If a defender breaks the line, the point again counts if the shot goes in, but if it is missed the shooter is allowed another attempt.

Three-second rule

No player is allowed to remain in the opposing team's restricted area for longer than three seconds when his/her team has possession of the ball. This rule should be enforced strictly, especially when a player deliberately stays inside the restricted area in order to receive the ball.

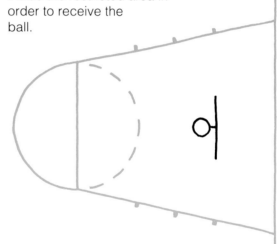

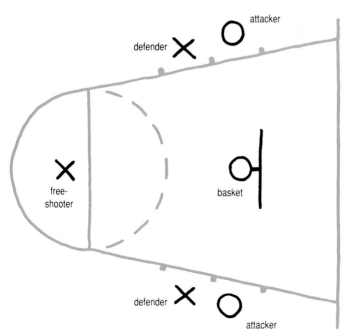

RESOURCES

The following publications, which include information relevant to mini-basketball, are published by and available from the EBBA:

Basketball Curriculum Guide, ed. B. E. Coleman

Basketball Skills (video)

Coaching Basketball (booklet), B. E. Coleman

The Rules of Basketball (including the FIBA Rules, Mini-basketball Rules and Official Wheelchair Basketball Rules)

The following specific mini-basketball publications are published by and available from the EMBBA:

Mini-Basketball — The Rules

Mini-Basketball Officiating Award:
1 A guide for teachers and coaches
2 A guide for children

Mums and Dads — We Welcome Your Support
A parents' guide

AWARDS

The English Basket Ball Association provides a player proficiency scheme called the Champion USA Basketball Award Scheme. This includes mini-basketball. New awards specifically for mini-basketball are in preparation.

GOVERNING-BODY INFORMATION

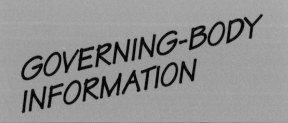

English Basket Ball Association

English Basket Ball Association (EBBA)
48 Bradford Road
Stanningley
Leeds LS28 6DF

Tel: 0532 361166

The EBBA is the governing body for basketball in England. It ensures uniformity of rules and equipment, organizes the national teams, and provides national and regional competitions for players of all ages.

English Schools Basket Ball Association

English Schools Basket Ball Association (ESBBA)
c/o Mr N. Waldron
Hon. General Secretary
44 Northleat Avenue
Paignton
Devon
TQ3 3UG

Tel: 0803 523183 (home); 0803 842289 (school)

The ESBBA is the governing body of school basketball in England. It is affiliated to the EBBA, and provides international, national and regional competitions for school players.

English Mini Basket Ball Association

English Mini Basket Ball Association (EMBBA)
c/o Mr K. G. Charles MBE
Hon. General Secretary
The Greneway School
Garden Walk
Royston
Hertfordshire
SG8 7JF

Tel: 0223 207213 (home); 0763 243650 (school)
Fax: 0763 241499

The EMBBA, which is affiliated to the EBBA, is largely concerned with the development of mini-basketball, and organising festivals, demonstrations of the game, conferences, coaching days, and regional and national competitions. It also publishes a range of material (see above).

MINI-HANDBALL

Handball uses the varied skills of running, jumping, throwing and catching. It is easy to introduce — particularly in its simplified form, mini-handball — and beginners can be on the court and playing within a few minutes. The rules are very straightforward.

Because it uses a small ball and a relatively large goal, handball is designed to allow the players to achieve successes from lesson one. It allows everyone to participate, irrespective of physical stature or height, and anyone can score, for there are no positional restrictions. Teams can consist of both boys and girls together.

The game is fast and dynamic, characterised by attack and defence, lots of shooting and not much midfield play. The aim of mini-handball is simple: to score goals!

EQUIPMENT

The mini-handball court is as shown in the diagram. In the early stages you can use a netball court or a five-a-side football court, with netball posts or crash mats for goals.

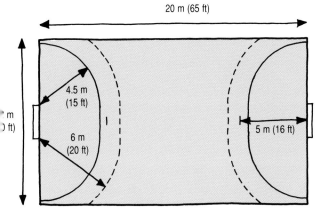

20 m (65 ft)

4.5 m (15 ft)

6 m (20 ft)

5 m (16 ft)

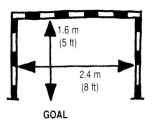

1.6 m (5 ft)

2.4 m (8 ft)

GOAL

Mini-handball uses a ball of circumference 47–49 cm (18.5–19.3 in). This is about 15 cm (6 in) in diameter — an easy size to catch and throw. Such balls are available from the BHA.

PLAYING MINI-HANDBALL

A game of mini-handball is divided into two halves, normally of 10 minutes each, although they may be shortened. The half-time break can be of any convenient duration.

The teams

Each team consists of a maximum of eight players (seven plus goalkeeper), of whom no more than five (four plus goalkeeper) are allowed on court at the same time. The other three are substitutes: they can enter the game at any time and as often as desired, provided that the player to be substituted has left the court before the substitute enters it.

Players are allowed to enter and leave the court only via the halfway line.

Starting the game

The two teams toss a coin, and the winner has the choice of possession (i.e. attacking first) or end. The attacking team lines up on the halfway line, while the defenders take up positions to defend their goal. When the referee blows the whistle, the attackers move forward towards the opposing goal, passing as they advance. When they get the chance, they try to score by throwing the ball into the goal.

Defending

The defenders try to capture the ball, using various tactics:

• harassing the player with the ball to prevent a pass being made, or at least to cause the pass to be a bad one

• harassing attackers without the ball to prevent them from receiving it

• trying to intercept a pass

• blocking shots at goal.

As soon as the defending team have gained possession of the ball, they start to attack in their turn.

After a goal, the game is restarted from the halfway line by the team which conceded the goal.

THE RULES

Scoring

The winning team is simply the one that has scored the most goals at the end of the game.

Playing the ball

There are three things you **can** do:

✓ hold the ball for up to three seconds

✓ take up to three steps while holding the ball

✓ dribble the ball by bouncing it repeatedly against the floor with one hand;

and there are three things you **must not** do:

✗ touch the ball more than once, unless it has in the meantime touched the floor, another player, a goalpost or the crossbar (but fumbles are not penalised)

✗ touch the ball with any part of your leg below the knee

✗ dive for the ball when it is lying on the floor.

Dealing with opponents

You are not allowed to:

• strike or snatch the ball from an opponent

• throw the ball intentionally to strike an opponent

• obstruct an opponent with your arms, hands or legs

• hold, trip, push, run into, jump at, or throw yourself in front of, an opponent

Goalkeeper

Only the goalkeeper is allowed inside the goal area. He or she may defend the goal with any part of the body and can move with the ball within the goal area without any restrictions — but must not waste time! The goalkeeper must not leave the goal area with the ball after it has been brought under control.

Any defensive action by the goalkeeper must not endanger an opponent.

Throws

A **throw-in** is taken when the ball crosses the sideline, by a player from the team that did not touch the ball last.

When the ball goes out of play across the goal-line, having last touched a defender, play is restarted by means of a **corner throw**, taken by any member of the attacking team.

A **free throw** is awarded to the opposing team when a player infringes any of the rules already mentioned.

A **penalty throw** is awarded in various circumstances:

• When a defender breaks one of the rules and so deprives an opponent of a clear chance of scoring a goal, no matter where on court this happens

• When a court player intentionally enters his/her own goal area for defensive purposes

• When a player passes the ball to the goalkeeper within his/her goal area

The penalty throw is taken from the 5-metre line, in front of the centre of the goal, by the player who has been fouled.

PRACTICES

Teachers can devise their own special rules to encourage maximum participation and to increase the children's sense of achievement. As the players become more practised, the regular mini-handball rules are brought in.

The following special rules are recommended:

1 All court players must have touched the ball before a shot at goal is allowed. This gives all the players the sense that they are actively involved in the game.

2 Award plenty of penalty throws to begin with. This means that more players will get the chance of a shot at goal, and of scoring. At the same time players will soon discover that fouls do not pay, and this should lead to cleaner handball.

3 After a goal, let the goalkeeper put the ball straight back into play. This rule saves time, as the ball does not have to go back to the halfway line, and so makes many more fast counter-attacks possible.

RESOURCES

The following publications are available from the British Handball Association:

Mini-handball: a complete guide including rules and exercises for the class and for individuals

The Rules of Mini-handball (illustrated)

Teaching Handball: a 45-page illustrated manual full of ideas for teaching the full sport; ideal for teachers

ABC Coaching Manual (including some 70 photographs and 60 diagrams)

3-2-1 Handball Defence: an illustrated manual outlining the principles of defensive systems

AWARDS

The NatWest Target Gold Award Scheme

'Target Gold' is the British Handball Association's proficiency award scheme, sponsored by National Westminster Bank plc. The aim is for as many children as possible to take part and to succeed, so raising the general standard of play both locally and nationally.

There are six awards in all: Grade 1, Grade 2, Grade 3, Bronze, Silver and Gold. Successful participants receive a badge denoting the grade, a certificate, and a booklet in which to enter their record of achievement.

The successful completion of each award is entirely at the discretion of the teacher, who does not need to be a qualified BHA coach. Supervising the tests has been made administratively as simple as possible.

A school that wishes to take part must register as a member of the 'Target Gold' Scheme. Registered member schools receive a comprehensive pack, including wall-charts, *The Rules of Mini-handball*, *Teaching Handball* and *A Guide to Handball*. Membership of the Scheme automatically includes associate membership of the British Handball Association, so schools are kept abreast of the latest news and developments within the sport.

GOVERNING-BODY INFORMATION

Further details may be obtained from:

British Handball Association
60 Church Street
Radcliffe
Manchester
M26 8SQ

Tel/fax: 061-724 9656

POP-LACROSSE

Pop-lacrosse is an invasion game played by two teams of five or six players. Exciting, fast and free-flowing, it is a simplified alternative to traditional field lacrosse which can be enjoyed by players of any age and ability, including those with disabilities. Teams may be all-male, all-female or mixed.

Pop-lacrosse is the ideal introduction to lacrosse for beginners. It incorporates the basic skills and strategies of lacrosse, but uses a more flexible set of rules which can be adapted to suit the number of players and the equipment and playing area that they have available. The rules given here are the version modified for under-11s; older players use a slightly different set which can be obtained from the governing bodies.

EQUIPMENT

Any lacrosse stick may be used; special beginners' sticks are available for younger players. For competition a pop-lacrosse stick must be used.

The ball should be either a standard lacrosse ball or — for use with beginners' sticks or in competition — the specially designed soft plastic ball for pop-lacrosse.

Pop-lacrosse goal-rings are ideal, but you can use improvised goals such as hoops, buckets or even chairs. (If a chair is used, the ball hits the seat or back to score, or you can use a chair seat between two chairs.) Allow space to play behind the goal. In competition, each goal must be a 4 x 4 ft (1.2 x 1.2 m) square cage with net (street-hockey type).

The above equipment can be bought or hired from:

T. S. Hattersley & Son Ltd, 63 Weymouth Road, Eccles, Lancashire M30 8NN.

Tel: 061-789 1374 Fax: 061-787 8632

The playing area is not strictly defined: it can be indoors or outdoors, and on any surface. An area the size of a netball court is generally suitable. The boundaries must be easily identifiable, the centre point must be marked, and there should be a designated goal area about 5 m (16 ft) around each goal.

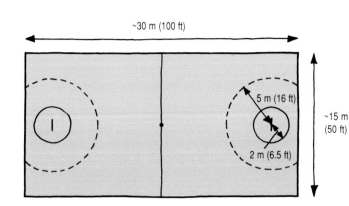

PLAYING POP-LACROSSE

The object of the game is to score goals by throwing the ball, using a lacrosse stick, into the opposing team's goal. The winners are the team that has scored the most goals at the end of the agreed playing time, which is divided into two halves. The ball is propelled down the field of play from stick to stick.

The game is controlled by an umpire.

Players

There are eight players in a squad, five of whom are playing at any one time. Substitutions may be made at half-time or after injury. There is no goalkeeper in the under-11 game.

Starting and stopping play

The umpire starts and stops play by blowing a whistle. There is no 'stand' in pop-lacrosse (unlike women's field lacrosse) and therefore repositioning is allowed.

The under-11 game is started and restarted with alternate centre passes.

THE RULES

Boundaries

Indoors, the walls form the boundary, and pupils should play the rebound whenever possible.

If the playing area is outdoors, there is no strict boundary, but the umpire decides what area is in bounds. Play should be as continuous as possible, but when the ball does go out of bounds or becomes trapped, the nearest player gets possession. This player then comes in 1 metre (3.3 ft) from the boundary, the other players stand 1 metre clear, and the game restarts. If two players are the same distance from the ball, a throw is taken (see below).

Throw

A throw is taken if two players are the same distance from an out-of-bounds ball or if two fouls are committed at the same time.

The players stand 1 metre (3.3 ft) inside the boundary and 1 metre apart. If the throw is for simultaneous fouls the players must face the centre of the playing area.

The umpire blows the whistle as s/he tosses the ball vertically to about shoulder height between the two players, who can then move to take it.

Scoring

A goal is scored when the ball goes over the goal-line into the goal, having last touched an attacker's stick. If the ball goes into the goal off the attacker's body, it does not score.

An own-goal is scored if the ball goes into the goal off the stick or body of a defender.

In the under-11 game, no player may enter the goal crease, and stationary defending of the goal is not allowed. This encourages person-to-person marking, and discourages blocking tactics.

Fouls

The following actions are prohibited, and count as fouls:

- Contact (stick or body)
- Intentionally sending the ball off the body
- Dangerous propelling or following through
- Entering the goal crease
- Trapping or guarding the ball
- Possessing the ball for longer than four seconds

The rules are there to protect players and to keep the game as continuous as possible. Therefore the umpire should not blow the whistle for an unintentional foul which does not give any advantage to the offender or his/her team. In general, the whistle should be used sparingly, although unsafe play must always be penalized.

Penalties

When the whistle is blown for a foul, play stops and a **free position** is awarded to the other team. It is taken where the foul occurred, unless this was inside the 5-metre arc, in which case the free position is taken on the arc. The offender is placed 3 metres (10 ft) behind the player who has been awarded possession; all other players have to be at least 3 metres away. When the whistle is blown, play restarts.

RESOURCES

Leaflets giving the full rules of pop-lacrosse and lacrosse can be obtained from the AEWLA or the ELU.

Equipment can be bought or hired from T. S. Hattersley & Son Ltd (see above).

GOVERNING-BODY INFORMATION

Enquiries should be addressed to either of the national governing bodies:

All-England Women's Lacrosse Association (AEWLA)
4 Western Court
Bromley Street
Digbeth
Birmingham B9 4AN
Tel: 021-773 4422

English Lacrosse Union (ELU)
Ryecroft Mills, Smith Street
Ashton-under-Lyne OL7 0DB
Tel: 061-339 7508

MINI-NETBALL

One of the things that sets netball apart from many other ball games is that each player has a specific positional role which is restricted to a specific area of the court. For adults this is part of the game's appeal, in that each player works to develop the particular skills needed to fulfil her/his responsibilities within the team.

In primary schools, however, the aim is to look not for specialization but for the development of a wide range of movement and ball skills coupled with a basic understanding of team play and cooperation. Teachers will also want to provide their young pupils (boys and girls) with a positive, enjoyable first experience of netball, creating the perfect environment in which to practise their new skills.

For this reason, the two mini-games described here are designed to create an open and flowing form of netball with the minimum of intervention from the teacher. Rotating the positions allows all the children to experience play in different parts of the court. It also means that they all have the chance to develop their shooting skills — a vital part of netball.

Having enjoyed these mini-games, the children will soon want to progress to the seven-a-side game described in *Netball Rules for Young Players* (see below). This then leads naturally into full adult netball.

Unless otherwise stated, the information given below applies to both forms of mini-netball.

EQUIPMENT

The ball used should be a size-four netball or football.

The height of the goal-posts should normally be 3.05 m (10 ft) as in adult netball, but this can be varied to any height between 2.43 m (8 ft) and the full height, according to the players' age and ability.

The teams should be identified by wearing different bibs or bands.

Playing area

The playing area can be indoors or outdoors; playground or grass. The dimensions recommended here are given as parts of a full netball court (30.5 x 15.25 m; 100 x 50 ft), but any court or area of similar size can be used.

Both mini-games are played like adult netball, but with the exceptions described here.

You should do all you can to encourage open and uninterrupted play. *The rules are flexible, and may be adapted to suit the skill and fitness of the children in your group. This applies particularly to footwork, where a player may be allowed a certain amount of shuffling to gain her/his balance — as long as s/he is not gaining ground down the court.*

Person-to-person marking should always be encouraged rather than zoning or two-on-one marking.

General rules

• Players may hold the ball for up to five seconds (rather than three). *This is to accommodate slower reactions and difficulty in making decisions.*

• In defence, the covering position — stretching out the arms to cover the player with the ball — is not permitted. The player holding the ball must be allowed to throw or shoot unimpeded, although a jump to intercept a pass or shot may be made from a distance of 1 metre (3.3 ft). *This allows throwing and shooting skills to be developed more confidently.*

MINI-NETBALL 1

This game is played in one-third of a netball court, divided by a halfway line.

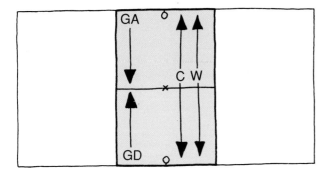

The teams

Mini-netball 1 is a four-a-side game. Two players — Centre (C) and Wing (W) — are allowed anywhere on court, while the other two — Goal Attack (GA) and Goal Defence (GD) — are allowed only in their own half. All the players except GD are allowed to shoot.

The sets of two players change places and bibs at half-time, so that C and W become GA and GD, and vice versa.

Start of play

Each half is started by a toss-up between the two Centres, taken on the mid-point of the halfway line. The C who wins the toss-up is awarded the first centre pass, and the game then starts when the umpire's whistle blows.

At the centre pass

The C always takes the centre pass from the mid-point of the halfway line. The GA and GD may be anywhere in their half of the court, and the Ws should be together in the attacking half of the court. When the whistle blows, all players should be at least 2 m (6.5 ft) from the C with the ball, except the opposing C, who must be at least 1 m (3.3 ft) away.

Scoring

A goal is scored when the ball is propelled completely through the ring from top to bottom by one of the players (GA, W, C) who is allowed to shoot. They may do so from any point in their attacking half of the court. At least three passes must have been taken from the centre pass before a shot at goal is allowed.

When a goal is scored, the non-scoring team is awarded the centre pass to restart the game.

MINI-NETBALL 2

This game is played on two-thirds of a standard netball court, with two shooting circles marked as shown.

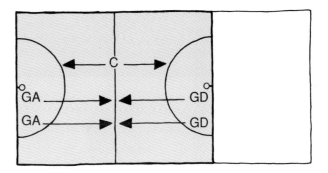

The teams

Mini-netball 2 is a five-a-side game. The Centre (C) is allowed anywhere on court except in the shooting circles, while the other four players — two Goal Attacks (GA) and two Goal Defences (GD) — are allowed only in their own half (including their circle). Only the GAs are allowed to shoot.

The players rotate two positions at half-time (see diagram).

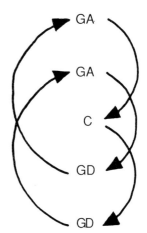

Start of play

Each half is started by a toss-up between the two Centres, taken on the mid-point of the halfway line. The C who wins the toss-up is awarded the first centre pass, and the game then starts when the umpire's whistle blows.

At the centre pass

The C always takes the centre pass from the mid-point of the halfway line; the GAs and GDs may be anywhere in their half of the court. When the whistle blows, all players should be at least 2 m (6.5 ft) from the C with the ball, except the opposing C, who must be at least 1 m (3.3 ft) away.

Scoring

A goal is scored when the ball is propelled completely through the ring from top to bottom by one of the players (GAs) who is allowed to shoot, and this must be done from within their shooting circle.

When a goal is scored, the non-scoring team is awarded the centre pass to restart the game.

RESOURCES

The publication *Netball Rules for Young Players* is recommended for everyone working with under-11s. Published jointly by the AENA and the ESNA, it describes in simplified form the essential rules of netball in this age-group, and gives advice for umpires.

For details of this and other publications, including the *Official Netball Rules*, please contact the AENA. Full details of the AENA official mini-game, similar to the two games described here, are available as from September 1992.

AWARDS

For full information about the award schemes listed below, please contact the governing body indicated in brackets.

Award schemes for teachers

- Coaching the Young Player (ESNA)
- Preliminary Coaching Award (AENA)
- 'C' Award for Umpiring (AENA)
- Netball Leaders' Award (AENA)

Award schemes for children

- Shooting Award (AENA)
- Skills Award (AENA)

GOVERNING-BODY INFORMATION

All England Netball Association
Netball House
9 Paynes Park
Hitchin
Hertfordshire
SG5 1EH

Tel: 0462 442344

English Schools Netball Association
c/o Miss J. Bracey, ESNA Secretary
76 Macklands Way
Rainham
Kent
ME8 7PF

Tel: 0634 376826

MINI-LEAGUE

Mini-league is the mini version of rugby league football, designed to introduce the game to young children and to ensure that all the players enjoy it. The game is scaled down to help them understand the rules and tactics, and the teams are reduced in numbers so that everyone is fully involved in the action. *All this encourages the development of game-awareness and the ability to make decisions.*

Mini-league is suitable for boys, girls or mixed play.

Both in training and in competition, your chief aim should be to help each young player develop the basic skills of the game. The rules are specifically designed to encourage them to:

- run with the ball
- pass the ball along the line
- be alert and anticipate the movement of the ball

For further information, please contact the Rugby League National Development Scheme (see page 192).

Ethical considerations

Right from the start, it is important for everyone involved — the players, parents, spectators, and you the teacher — to follow the rugby league Code of Ethics. The children must play fairly and according to the rules, and criticism of the players or the match officials should not be tolerated.

EQUIPMENT

A size three rugby ball is recommended, but a size four is acceptable.

The recommended size of the pitch is 50 x 40 m (165 x 130 ft), but mini-league can be played in any suitable area. Often two games are played at the same time, one in each half of a full-size pitch, but in this case two considerations are important:

- For safety, the goal-posts must be outside the playing area.

- Make sure the playing area is wide enough: an area that is too narrow is too easily defended, while a wider area creates more space for the attacking team to run into.

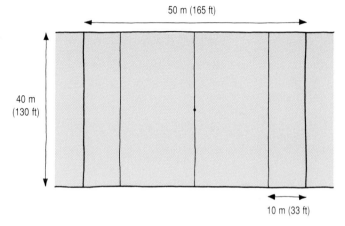

PLAYING MINI-LEAGUE

The game is a simplified version of rugby league, played according to the rules given below. The playing time is divided into four equal quarters of 7–10 minutes' duration, with 2-minute breaks in between.

THE RULES

The teams

The maximum number of players per team is eight, with up to four reserves. Any number of substitutions may be made, provided that each child plays for at least half the game.

Strictly speaking, mini-league is to be played only by children who are under 10 on 1 September in the current calendar year. This rule is enforced for official mini-league competitions, but can be relaxed for practice and informal competition.

Tackling and tries

• The normal six-tackle rule applies — i.e. if one side makes six successive tackles, the referee orders a scrum.

• A try is scored by grounding the ball in the normal way. If the try is scored after only one or two passes in a single tackle-period, it is worth four points; however, if it is scored after three or more passes in a single tackle-period, it is worth six points.

• After each tackle, all the defenders have to retreat 5 metres (16 ft) away — i.e. there are no markers. The tackled player must restart play by a correct play-the-ball backwards (towards his/her own goal). The ball must then be picked up by another member of the team.

• If the player who is acting as half-back is tackled while in possession of the ball, a hand-over is awarded.

Kicking

The chief difference from adult rugby league is that in mini-league **no kicking is allowed**.

• The team that wins the toss starts the game with a tap at the centre spot — i.e. the player with the ball touches it with his/her foot, and then the game commences.

• After one team has scored a try, the other team restarts the game in the same way, with a tap at the centre spot.

• There are no kicks at goal.

• A player who kicks the ball in the field of play is penalized: his/her team loses possession of the ball, and the opposing team restarts play with a tap at the point where the kick took place.

• If a kick takes place in the goal area, or the ball goes dead, the non-offending team restarts play with a tap at the centre of the 10-metre line.

Other offences

Apart from the penalties for kicking described above, all other infringements of the rules result in a hand-over and a play-the-ball.

The scrum

An uncontested scrum takes place when the ball goes out of play over the touchline.

Each side of the scrum consists of three players, who must be correctly bound together to form the front row. (There is no other row.) The scrum-half of the non-offending team puts the ball in from the side of the scrum (his/her own players are on the right), and must then immediately go behind his/her own hooker ready to receive the ball. The other scrum-half must also stand behind his/her own hooker. The hooker of the team with the put-in must be the first to strike for the ball, after which the props may assist. All the forwards forming the scrum must stay bound until the ball has emerged from the rear of the scrum.

If a scrum is inappropriate for the age or skill of the players, a hand-over may be used instead.

TACKLING

Tackling is a vital ingredient of rugby, and the RFL advise that it should be introduced at an early age. It is, however, crucially important that the techniques of tackling are taught accurately and safely.

Side tackle

The side tackle is the easiest to do, and so should be introduced first.

Coaching points

• The tackler should tackle with determination.

• S/he should keep his/her eyes fixed on the target — the thigh.

• The tackler's head should be behind the player with the ball at all times.

• The shoulder should make contact and drive powerfully into the target.

• The arms should encircle the thighs and grip them tight (see illustration).

• The tackler should hold the ball-carrier until s/he is well and truly tackled and on the ground.

• The tackler should end up on top of the ball-carrier.

Rear tackle

The coaching points are exactly the same as for the side tackle.

Front tackle

Tackling head-on (from the front) is vital to team play. There are two types of front tackle: **passive**, when the tackler uses the ball-carrier's body weight, and the **blockbuster**, when the tackler forcefully knocks the ball-carrier backwards.

Coaching points for the passive front tackle

• The tackler should keep his/her eyes fixed on the target — the thigh.

• The tackler's head and neck should be positioned to the side of the ball-carrier.

• S/he should use the ball-carrier's own weight and momentum in making the tackle.

• The tackler should block the thighs of the ball-carrier with his/her shoulder.

• The tackler's arms should powerfully encircle the ball-carrier's legs and grip them tightly.

• The ball-carrier should be rolled onto his/her side.

• The tackler should end up on top of the tackled player.

Coaching points for the blockbuster

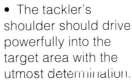

• The tackler should keep his/her eyes fixed on the target — the waist — and quickly move forward into position.

• The tackler's shoulder should drive powerfully into the target area with the utmost determination.

• The tackler's head should be to the side of the ball-carrier.

• The tackler's arms should powerfully encircle the ball-carrier below the centre of gravity (i.e. below the buttocks) and grip tightly.

• S/he drives powerfully with the legs, and pulls and lifts with the arms and shoulder, thus driving the ball-carrier upwards and then backwards.

• The tackler should end up on top of the ball-carrier, with the shoulder buried in the target area.

• Timing is the key to success.

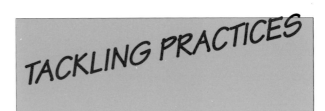

TACKLING PRACTICES

Introductory practices in pairs

Progress through the different tackles in order, and check all the coaching points.

• Tackler kneeling, ball-carrier stationary
• Tackler kneeling, ball-carrier walking
• Tackler crouching, ball-carrier walking
• Tackler standing, ball-carrier walking
• Tackler standing, ball-carrier jogging

Consecutive tackle drill in pairs

Players **A** and **B** face each other 2 metres (6.5 ft) apart. **A** tackles **B**. Both stand up again quickly, and the practice continues with **A** trying to make as many tackles as possible in a given time (perhaps 30 seconds).

After sufficient rest the players exchange roles and repeat the drill.

Confidence and timing practice in pairs

Again, players **A** and **B** face each other 2 metres (6.5 ft) apart. On a command from the teacher, **A** runs backwards, **B** chases **A** and executes a determined tackle, making contact on the thighs, head to the side.

After sufficient rest the players exchange roles and repeat the drill.

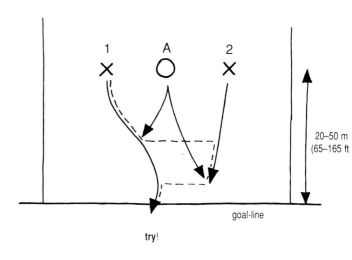

20–50 m
(65–165 ft)

goal-line

try!

Technique drill (relay)

The players form two lines at right angles; those in one line are the tacklers, the others are the ones to be tackled. 1 moves forward; 2 judges his/her run, comes in and tackles 1 at **T**. After the tackle, 1 runs behind 10 and 2 runs behind 9. The other players repeat the process in succession.

The tackles should be practised from both right and left, and each group should take turns at tackling and being tackled.

This drill can be used, with some variation, for all methods of tackling.

Consecutive tackling (relay)

T, the tackler, faces a line of five attackers. On the teacher's command, 1 runs forward to be tackled by **T**. As soon as the tackle has been completed, **T** gets up again and 2 runs forward to be tackled. The relay continues.

The tempo can be increased as the players become more proficient.

Defence from the rear (one on two)

The defending player **A** starts in line with the attacking players 1 and 2. 1 starts to run with the ball, while **A** attempts to defend against 1 and 2 to prevent them from scoring a try.

RESOURCES

Mini-league (booklet)
Mini-league (video)
Rugby League — Skill and Small-sided Games (video)
Rugby League Coaching Manual

The publications listed above are available from the Rugby Football League.

AWARDS

At the time of writing, the RFL award scheme is in course of preparation.

GOVERNING-BODY INFORMATION

The Rugby Football League
180 Chapeltown Road
Leeds
LS7 4HT

Tel: 0532 624637
Fax: 0532 623386

The Rugby League National Development Scheme
West Yorkshire House
4 New North Parade
Huddersfield
HD1 5JP

Tel: 0484 544131

RUGBY UNION

The game of rugby contains many of the elements enjoyed by children of all ages — running, dodging to beat an opponent, passing the ball skilfully to a team-mate, and of course scoring. As a team game, it incorporates the elements of cooperation, reliance on others and support for others, which are also of value outside the context of the game.

In the adult game, other more physically demanding elements become important, such as physical contact and the tackle, and the starting-points after stoppages become more complex as the scrum and the line-out are introduced.

In order to develop those elements of the game which are most relevant to younger children as they mature, and which bring them the greatest enjoyment, the Rugby Football Union has developed two separate forms of the game through which it can be introduced to youngsters:

* New Image Rugby

* The continuum of Junior Rugby

EQUIPMENT

The recommended size of the pitch depends on the age, ability and number of the participants; it should be large enough to allow the skills of running and handling to predominate. For a 12-a-side game of players aged 10, the size should be about 30 metres long by 20–25 metres wide (100 ft x 65–80 ft), reducing proportionally as the age and number of players decrease. The pitch can be marked out with cones.

At age 7–8 the recommended ball is size 3, increasing to size 4 at age 9–10.

NEW IMAGE RUGBY

Because New Image Rugby is essentially a non-contact game, it is the most appropriate form of rugby for the primary-school environment. Teams can be of any size, but the game tends to work best with teams of between nine and twelve players.

There is no tackling in New Image Rugby. Instead of tackling the player with the ball, the defender touches him/her on each side of the hips with both hands simultaneously; the player with the ball must then pass it at once. This light touch is the only form of contact allowed.

The game starts with a free pass from the centre spot. At every free pass the passer's team must be behind the ball, and their opponents must be at least 7 metres (23 ft) away. The ball cannot be passed forwards. The team with the ball run and pass the ball (sideways or backwards) to score a try by placing the ball firmly behind their opponents' try-line. A try scores 5 points.

Kicking is not allowed: if a player does kick the ball, the opponents are awarded the ball for a free-pass restart.

The set-piece restarts of rugby are incorporated into New Image: the **set scrum** occurs when the ball is passed forward, or when it is dropped to the ground; the **line-out** takes place when the ball goes off the pitch. Both these are **uncontested**: the team putting the ball in must regain it without opposition, and normal play then resumes.

The scrum and line-out are made up as follows: in 11- and 12-a-side there are two rows, with three players in the front row and two in the second row; in 7-a-side up to 10-a-side there is only one row, consisting of three players.

If the scrum or line-out prove too difficult, the 'chicken scratch' restart (see skill card 26) can be used instead.

JUNIOR RUGBY

Junior Rugby is made up of a series of games forming a continuum from Start Rugby for children aged 6 and 7 through to full 15-a-side rugby union for 12-year-olds and upwards. The characteristic elements of rugby are introduced progressively as the games develop. By the age of 12 the young players will have advanced through these carefully planned stages to understand and to play the full game as effectively and skilfully as their abilities allow. None of these games uses the hand-off.

As a means of introducing children to rugby, Junior Rugby is generally most appropriately used in rugby clubs.

Start Rugby

As a non-contact game, Start Rugby is fairly similar to New Image Rugby. It is played with small numbers in the team, and a two-handed touch on the hips is used instead of the tackle. A size-three ball should be used.

The game starts with a free pass from the centre spot. At every free pass the passer's team must be behind the ball, and their opponents must be at least 7 metres (23 ft) away.

Unlike New Image, there is no scrum and no line-out.

Age 6 (under 7)

• There should be no more than five players per team.

• The children may pass anywhere until comfortable with passing, then sideways and backwards only.

• Encourage them to carry the ball in both hands.

Age 7 (under 8)

• There should be no more than seven players per team.

• At this stage the players should pass backwards only.

• Towards the end of the season (February to April), move to introduce the idea of set-piece positions:

— the 'chicken scratch' restart, as illustrated in the video The Coaching Guide to Mini-Rugby

— the uncontested scrum, with a three-player front row; the opposing backs should be 7 metres (23 ft) behind the scrum, except for the scrum-half, who stands behind the hindmost foot of the scrum

— all players should experience play as both forwards and backs.

• During this end-season period the children should preferably play limited interclub matches, the non-contact principle being strictly adhered to.

Mini-rugby

Mini-rugby is the introduction to the contact game. It is designed for players aged 8 to 10. For details, see the publications and video listed under **Resources**.

Mini-rugby is a nine-a-side game, with three forwards and six backs. 8-year-olds should use a size-three ball, while the 9- and 10-year-olds should use a size-four. A suggested use of a rugby field for mini-rugby is shown in the diagram.

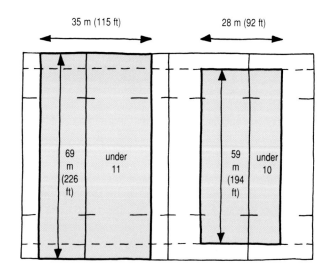

Age 8 (under 9)

• Tackling is now introduced (see the video Confidence in Contact).

• The uncontested scrum, with a three-player front row, continues to be used; the opposing backs should be 7 metres (23 ft) behind the scrum, except for the scrum-half, who stands behind the hindmost foot of the scrum. Introduce the offside line.

• No kicking is allowed as yet.

• A free pass is used to start the game at the 'kick-off' and to restart after an infringement and when the ball goes into touch. The starter cannot run with the ball, and the opponents must be 7 metres (23 ft) away on a line parallel to the goal-line.

Age 9 (under 10)

This is the same as for age 8, with the following changes:

• Continue to teach tackling.

• The scrum is now contested: all opposing backs, including the scrum-half **not** putting the ball into the scrum, should be behind the hindmost foot of the scrum.

• The contested line-out is now used to restart the game when the ball goes into touch. The line-out should consist of two players on each side, 2–7 metres (6.5–23 ft) from the touch-line. A third player throws in; a quick throw-in is not allowed. All backs should be 7 metres (23 ft) back from the line of touch except the scrum-half.

• With the exceptions given here, the laws of the game now apply.

Age 10 (under 11)

• The scrum is as before.

• The line-out is also as before, except that a quick throw-in is now allowed.

• Controlled kicking is now allowed (i.e. no fly-kicking). Kicking is used at kick-off, at penalties and free kicks (a tap can also be used), and wherever the laws allow in open play.

Midi-rugby

This intermediate game is for children aged 11 (under-12s). It is played with 12-a-side teams, five forwards and seven backs.

• The front row of the scrum is still three forwards, but now with two second-row locks binding around the hip. The scrum-half restriction remains.

• The line-out now consists of four players on each side, and a fifth player throws in 2–10 metres (6.5–33 ft) from the touch-line. The offside line is 10 metres (33 ft) from the line of touch.

• The recommended pitch size is across a full-size pitch, 2 metres (6.5 ft) from the goal-line to 5 metres (16.5 ft) from the halfway line.

Starting the full game

From age 12 (under 13) the full 15-a-side game may be played, using all the laws. The hand-off is now legal. A size-four ball is recommended up to and including age 13 (under 14).

PRACTICES

The RFU has produced a range of skill practice materials, the most appropriate for children aged 6–11 being *Start Rugby coaching cards* and *Skills Practices for All*. These can be obtained from the RFU Shop at Twickenham or from the RFU Resource Centre (see below for addresses).

RESOURCES

The following may be obtained from the RFU Shop at Twickenham:

New Image Rugby (video and leaflet)

Mini-rugby (leaflet)

The coaching guide to mini-rugby including midi-rugby (video)

Confidence in contact (video)

Mini-rugby — the real thing (book)

Mini-rugby — the cartoon coaching book

Start Rugby coaching cards (pack of 40)

Rugby coaching cards — a guide for teachers and coaches

Instant rugby — a five-minute guide to the laws

AWARDS

The RFU has a series of proficiency awards for young players: the Bronze Award, Silver Award and Gold Award. They assess the basic skills of the game. Full information can be obtained from the RFU Resource Centre.

There is also a range of courses and coaching awards available. At the junior level, the most relevant courses for coaches and teachers are 'Start Rugby' and the Preliminary Award. These courses are most frequently organized by the 36 RFU Youth Development Officers based throughout Great Britain, whose addresses can be obtained from the RFU Resource Centre.

GOVERNING-BODY INFORMATION

Rugby Football Union
Whitton Road
Twickenham
Middlesex
TW1 1DZ

Tel: 081-892 8161

Full details of New Image Rugby and Junior Rugby can be obtained from:

RFU Resource Centre
Nortonthorpe Mills
Scissett
Huddersfield
HD8 9LA

Tel: 0484-865950

MINI-HOCKEY

Mini-hockey is a simplified version of hockey, ideal for introducing young players to the game. It is played with fewer players on a smaller pitch, which makes for an exciting game in which everyone is fully involved. The description given here is for under-11s; the full rules give some variations for the 11–13 age-group.

EQUIPMENT

Mini-hockey is played with a relatively soft, light ball (4 oz; 110 g) if available.

The stick is of a standard regulation type, but its length and weight should be suitable for the age-group playing.

Any suitable clothing can be worn, but anything that might be dangerous to other players is not allowed.

In the interests of safety, goalkeepers must wear full goalkeeping equipment. A helmet or face mask, body protection, gloves, pads and kickers are essential.

The pitch

The pitch, or 'ground', is smaller than a full-size hockey pitch, and is laid out as in the diagram. The goals are full size (12 x 7 ft; 3.65 x 2.13 m), as are the shooting circles.

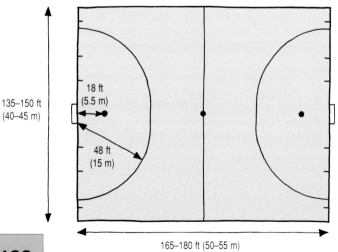

135–150 ft (40–45 m)

18 ft (5.5 m)

48 ft (15 m)

165–180 ft (50–55 m)

PLAYING MINI-HOCKEY

The aim of mini-hockey is the same as that of the full game: to move the ball up the pitch and into your opponents' goal using the flat side of the hockey sticks alone. Only the goalkeepers can use their hands and feet to play the ball.

The game consists of two halves of not more than 10 minutes each, with an interval of not more than five minutes. The game is controlled by one or two umpires.

There are two teams of seven players each, and up to three substitutions are allowed in each half.

The captains toss for the choice of ends or possession of the ball, and the game is then started by a pass-back from the centre spot. It is restarted in the same way after a goal.

THE RULES

Scoring

A goal is scored when the ball passes completely over the back-line into the goal, having been touched by an attacker's stick. The ball must be within the circle when it is struck.

Offside

There is **no** offside rule in mini-hockey — this is one of the most significant differences from the full game.

Fair play

Only the face (flat side) of the stick may be used. The ball must not be intentionally stopped by any part of the body, except in the case of a goalkeeper.

The ball must not be played in a dangerous way. Indeed, any rough or dangerous play is prohibited, as is any behaviour which, in the umpire's opinion, amounts to misconduct.

If any of these fair-play rules is broken, a **free hit** is awarded; details are given in *Rules of the Game of Mini-hockey*. Persistent offenders are sent off.

Ball outside the field of play

• When the ball passes over the sideline, it is put back into play by an opponent of the player who last touched it.

• When the ball is sent over the back-line by an attacker and no goal is scored, the game is restarted by a hit taken level with the top of the circle and opposite the place where the ball crossed the back-line.

• When the ball is sent unintentionally over the back-line by a defender (and no goal is scored), the game is restarted by a **long corner** — a hit taken by the attacking team from a spot on the back-line within 3 yards (2.74 m) of the nearest corner flag.

• When the ball is played intentionally over the back-line by a defender (and no goal is scored), a **penalty corner** is awarded to the attacking team. Details are given in *Rules of the Game of Mini-hockey*.

Penalty corner

A penalty corner is awarded to the attacking team if a defender:

• unintentionally commits a foul inside the circle

• intentionally commits a foul outside the circle but within his/her own (defending) half of the pitch

• intentionally plays the ball over his/her own back-line.

Penalty strokes

A penalty stroke is awarded to the attacking team if:

• a defender intentionally commits a foul inside the circle

• a goal would probably have been scored, if a defender had not unintentionally committed a foul inside the circle.

The penalty stroke is taken from the penalty spot; details are given in *Rules of the Game of Mini-hockey*.

RESOURCES

The following publications are available from the All-England Women's Hockey Association Coaching Office or from the Hockey Association Coaching Office:

Rules of the Game of Mini-hockey (also entitled *Mini-hockey for Boys and Girls*)

Know the Game. Hockey

Rules of the Game of Hockey

Rules of the Game of Indoor Hockey

Play the Game: Hockey, Carl Ward

Hockey: the Skills of the Game, John Cadman

Indoor Hockey, Slocombe and Ward

How to Coach Hockey, John Law

Umpiring poster (with cartoon characters)

Play Hockey — Slazenger Style (video)

HOCKEY STIX AWARDS

The Hockey Stix Awards have been specially designed to help young hockey players improve their skills and prepare for their future game. The awards give them the challenge and motivation to practise and make progress. The technical and physical ability of the players is tested, and their accuracy and speed are taken into account. These tests also give the young players the opportunity to check their progress by comparing their performance against a table of standard scores.

The Hockey Stix Awards scheme is designed for boys and girls in the under-10, under-12, under-14 and under-16 age-groups. The under-10s and under-12s will normally be playing mini-hockey.

A package including full details of the tests, and score sheets, is available from the Hockey Association. On returning their completed score sheets (plus a small fee) the candidates receive an award certificate and a badge.

The six skill tests are:

• Open-stick dribble

• Dribbling and lifting over a flat stick

• Dribbling — moving the ball to the left and right

- Passing — left to right using the reverse-stick position and right to left using the open-stick position

- Beating a player to the right and passing to a target

- Shooting and goal-scoring

Although designed to meet the requirements of modern hockey played on artificial turf, the Awards can be carried out on any surface, indoor or outdoor.

Generally speaking, it is recommended that testing should take place outside lesson time, although practices for the tests may well be carried out during school hours — and of course curriculum work will complement the tests. The tests should **not** be seen as a method of teaching or coaching, nor as a means to instant success, but as a valuable form of assessment.

The Hockey Association

The Hockey Association
Coaching Office
6 St John's
Worcester
WR2 5AH

Tel: 0905 426009

All-England Women's Hockey Association

All-England Women's Hockey Association
Coaching Office
2nd Floor
10 Parsonage Street
Dursley
Gloucestershire
GL11 4EA

Tel: 0453 548096

MINI-SOCCER

Mini-soccer is a simplified version of association football, designed to introduce the game to young players aged 5 to 13. The full eleven-a-side game is over-competitive for this age-group, and is inappropriate in other respects also. However, mini-soccer has the same basic purpose and structure: the children feel that they are playing 'real' soccer, and in an especially enjoyable form.

Like other mini-games, mini-soccer fulfils the needs of youngsters to play in a team, to play to rules, to play to win, and to discover the essence of soccer.

EQUIPMENT

The playing area should be between 60 x 40 yd (55 x 37 m) and 30 x 20 yd (27 x 18 m). The recommended sizes are shown in the table:

Age	Size of pitch
9–10 (U10–U11)	60 x 40 yd (55 x 37 m)
5–8 (U6–U9)	40 x 30 yd (37 x 27 m)

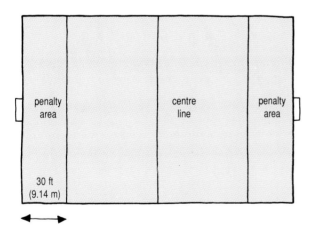

The penalty area extends 10 yards (9.14 m) from the goal-line across the full width of the playing area, regardless of the pitch size. The penalty area can be marked by cones on the touchlines and also by one or two markers across the playing area.

The goal size should be 12 x 6 ft (3.66 x 1.83 m).

The ball used should be no larger than size four; size three is recommended for children aged 5–6.

PLAYING MINI-SOCCER

Mini-soccer is played in the same way as full soccer, and all the laws apply except for the variations given here. The game is started by a kick-off from the centre of the pitch, and restarted in the same way after a goal.

The referee is the sole arbiter, and is the only person entitled to interpret the rules. He or she should also be seen as a kind of supervisor and game leader. The referee is expected to keep out of the playing area as far as possible.

THE RULES

Age-ranges

Strictly speaking, mini-soccer is for boys and girls aged 5 (U6) to 10 (U11) as at midnight on the 31 August immediately preceding the season in question. Mixed football is allowed for the under-11 age-groups (i.e. those aged 5 to 10).

Offside

There is no **offside** rule in mini-soccer for the 5–10s.

Team size and substitutes

The recommended team sizes (including goal-keepers) are shown in the table:

Age	Size of teams
9–10 (U10–U11)	6v6
7–8 (U8–U9)	5v5
5–6 (U6–U7)	4v4

Any number of substitutes may be used, and the substitutions may be made at any time with the referee's permission. Players may re-enter the game. All the substitutes must have a period of play, and as far as possible all the players should play for an equal period of time.

Duration of game

Each game should last for a maximum of 20 minutes, and games of 10 minutes are recommended, especially for younger players. Half-time need not be taken.

Restarting play

- **Throw-ins** are taken in the normal way, but the referee should exercise reasonable latitude.

- When a **corner kick** or **free kick** is taken, the opposition must be 3 yards (2.74 m) away. All free kicks are direct.

- A **goal kick** is taken from a front corner of the penalty area, with the opposition 3 yards (2.74 m) away. The ball must be kicked out of the area. In the 5–8 age-ranges only, the goalkeeper may kick the ball out of his/her hands.

- **Penalties** are taken from the edge of the penalty area, opposite the centre of the goal.

Goalkeepers

The goalkeeper can handle the ball within the penalty area, and there is no limit to the number of steps s/he may take when holding the ball. Goalkeepers can also kick the ball when it is on the ground anywhere, but may then be challenged.

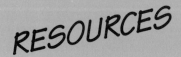

RESOURCES

Instructional courses

The Football Association Coaching and Education Scheme organizes a comprehensive service of instructional courses throughout the year:

- The **FA Preliminary Award**: a 26-hour examinable course, requiring some experience of regular football participation (at any level) and the ability to demonstrate techniques

- The **FA Football Leaders Course**: a 12-hour non-examinable course for junior team managers and those involved in the recreation and leisure industry

- The **FA Teaching Certificate Course**: a 12-hour non-examinable course for teachers and trainee teachers.

For further details of the above courses, please contact the Football Association at the address on page 201.

- The **FA Treatment of Injury Course**: a non-examinable course to meet the needs of amateur, youth and school clubs. For details, please contact:

Mr Alan Hodson
The FA International Sports Medicine Institute
Lilleshall Hall National Sports Centre
Nr Newport
Shropshire
TF10 9AT

Tel: 0952 605828

Publications

Books

Soccer Star Book

Winning Formula

Soccer Tactics and Skills

Referee's Chart

Mini-soccer

Coaching and Teaching Footballers with Disabilities and Learning Difficulties

Videos

Soccer Star Video

Winning Formula:
 1 Direct Play
 2 Scoring, the Finishing Touch
 3 Winning the Advantage
 4 Defending to Win
 5 Goalkeeping

Soccer Tactics and Skills:
 1 Attacking the Attacking Third of the Field (parts 1 and 2)
 2 Passing and Support
 3 Creating Space (parts 1 and 2)
 4 Defending (parts 1 and 2)
 5 Defending from Free Kicks and Corners plus *Attacking from Free Kicks and Corners*
 6 Shooting (parts 1 and 2)
 7 Goalkeeping (parts 1 and 2)

For details of special offers, prices and availability, please contact the Football Association (Publications) at the address on page 201.

AWARDS

The Coca-Cola Football Association Soccer Star Scheme was launched in 1988 after extensive research. Unique as a soccer education programme, it has been developed to help boys and girls aged 6 to 16 to enjoy and improve their football. The Scheme reinforces good sporting attitudes and behaviour.

The Soccer Star Scheme offers the following benefits to teachers:

• The Scheme is open to all teachers, irrespective of their previous football experience and teaching or coaching qualifications.

• All participating teachers receive a free starter pack with posters and books, including the 64-page instructional *Soccer Star Book*, compiled by the Football Association. To obtain your starter pack, write to the FA at the address below.

• The Scheme consists of six tests which assess the young players' ability in the most important soccer techniques. The tests are valid, relevant and easy to administer; they require a minimum of equipment and facilities.

• The free *Soccer Star Book* outlines the tests and also provides simple practices suitable as class activities.

• When the tests are completed, all the teacher has to do is return the scores to the FA — no need to spend hours over complicated result tables.

• The teacher then receives a computerized printout, suitable for display on a notice-board, showing the award each child has obtained. If the same class completes the Scheme on more than one occasion, the printout graphically outlines the progress of the class over the past three attempts.

• Each child receives a cloth badge, a certificate, a bannerette, a personalized letter from the England Team Manager, and a computerized graph outlining his/her current strengths and weaknesses and the results of the previous tests.

• The Scheme provides an ideal way to profile the soccer development of all your pupils, whatever level of skill they have reached.

In addition, the FA has recently launched the Preliminary Soccer Star Scheme for children with sensory or physical disabilities or with learning difficulties. It is based on the Soccer Star Scheme, and can easily be integrated with it.

GOVERNING-BODY INFORMATION

For further details of mini-soccer, contact:

The Football Association
9 Wyllyotts Place
Potters Bar
Hertfordshire
EN6 2JD

Tel: 0707 50057

NOTES

Striking/fielding Mini-games

STOOLBALL

Unlike the other games in this green section, stoolball is not a mini version of an adult game, but a game in its own right — an ancient sport which was one of the ancestors of modern cricket. The name 'stoolball' derives from the fact that originally stools were used as wickets. Today stoolball is played mostly in the south-east of England by ladies' and mixed teams, but it is also popular in primary schools.

Stoolball is a useful introduction to cricket, and has the great advantage that the pitch does not need to be especially well maintained.

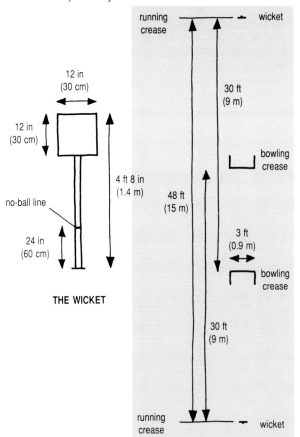

THE WICKET

EQUIPMENT

The stoolball pitch is laid out as shown in the diagram (below left). The boundary must be agreed, and preferably marked out, before the game begins. The wickets are usually constructed of wood, and must be maintained in a splinter-free condition.

The solid, leather-covered ball is slightly smaller than a rounders ball, and a special bat shaped like a frying-pan is used to strike it. The bat is no more than 8 in (200 mm) in diameter and no more than 18 in (460 mm) in length.

PLAYING STOOLBALL

Stoolball is played very like cricket. Matches are played between two teams of eleven players or fewer. During lessons, it is best to use smaller teams and to organize more than one game so that everyone is fully involved.

The match consists of two innings. One team bats while the other bowls and fields. An innings is completed when ten batters are out, and the fielding team then take their turn to bat for the second innings. For lessons it may be more appropriate to have a time-limit on each innings, or for each batter to face a given number of balls. The winning team is the one with the most runs at the end of the match, when both teams have completed their innings.

THE RULES

Bowling

An over consists of eight legitimate balls bowled to a wicket. When the ball is back in the bowler's hands after eight balls, the over is completed, and the next over is bowled from the other end. Bowlers are not allowed to bowl consecutive overs.

The ball must be bowled **underarm**, not thrown or jerked; the delivery is a full toss to the wicket. The bowler must have both feet behind the bowling crease when the ball is bowled.

Wicketkeeper

The wicketkeeper has to remain behind the wicket until the ball delivered by the bowler touches the bat or the batter, or passes or strikes the wicket, or the striking batter attempts to run, or a 'no ball' is called.

Scoring runs

After a hit, or when the ball is in play, a run is scored each time the batters cross over from wicket to wicket and touch the wicket with their bat or hand. Touching the wicket is an important feature of stoolball: the batter must do this at the start of his/her innings, after each run, and after each attempted run.

If the batter is caught out or run out (see below) the unfinished run does not count.

If the umpire signals a 'no ball' or a 'wide', a run is added to the score and an extra ball is bowled. A 'no ball' is a ball that is not bowled with a smooth underarm action, or which hits the ground before reaching the wicket, or which reaches the wicket below the no-ball line. A 'wide' is a ball bowled so high or wide of the wicket that it is considered to be an unfair delivery.

If the ball hits or crosses the boundary, four runs are scored if it touched the ground first, otherwise six runs. If the fielders throw the ball over the boundary, the score is four runs plus the number of runs completed so far.

Out

A batter is **out** if s/he

• is caught out

• is bowled out:
 — the ball touches the wicket directly
 — or the ball touches the wicket indirectly off the bat or body
 — or any part of the batter's body stops the ball hitting the wicket

• is run out:
 — a fielder throws the ball and it hits the wicket before the wicket has been touched by the batter's bat or hand

• hits the ball twice (unless this is accidental)

RESOURCES

The following publications are available from the NSA Sales Office (see below):

The Rules of Stoolball

Stoolball score books

Stoolball coaching leaflets

GOVERNING-BODY INFORMATION

Mrs Delia Saunders
Chairperson
National Stoolball Association
3 Bramber Way
Burgess Hill
West Sussex
RH15 8JU

Tel: 0444 241644

Mr Mick Cawley
NSA Sales Office
18 Victory Road
Horsham
West Sussex
RH12 2JF

Tel: 0403 51195

CRICKET

The National Cricket Association has devised a series of five mini-games to introduce young players to the skills of cricket. The rules given here are suggestions, and can be varied if appropriate.

For another game related to cricket, see Stoolball (page 203).

EQUIPMENT

The size and weight of the bats used should be appropriate to the height and strength of the pupils. A rough guide is that the top of the bat handle should be about 4 in (100 mm) below the hip joint when the bat is standing vertically next to the leg.

At first it is best to use a tennis ball, progressing to a team-cricket ball and then to a proper but lightweight cricket ball weighing 4–4.75 oz (115–135 g). If a cricket ball is used, the batters and wicketkeepers must wear protective pads and gloves. Boys should be encouraged to wear a box. If the bowling is fast (not usual in this age-group) helmets might be advisable as an additional precaution.

Any suitable stumps and bails can be used. Expensive equipment does not have to be purchased — pieces of wood or old chairs are perfectly satisfactory.

CONTINUOUS (OR NON-STOP) CRICKET

This game is for any number of players.

Lay out the playing area as shown in the diagram. Organize a batting team and a fielding team; place the batting team in order, choose a bowler, and spread out the remaining fielders.

Suggested rules

• The bowler bowls underarm, and bowls again as soon as the ball is returned to him/her by the fielders.

• Every time the batter hits the ball, s/he runs around the appropriate marker and back to the wicket, scoring one run for doing so without being out.

• The batter is out if:

— the bowler hits the wicket with the ball;

— the batter hits the wicket;

— the ball is caught from a hit.

• If the batter is out, s/he is replaced at once by the next batter.

• The teams change over when the first batting team is all out.

• When both teams have batted, the team that has scored the most runs is the winner.

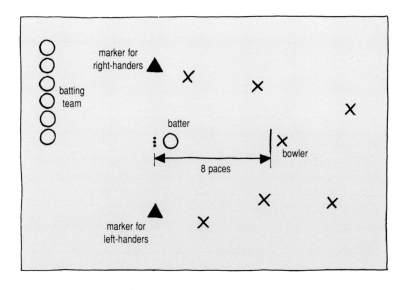

STRIKING/FIELDING MINI-GAMES

SINGLE-WICKET CRICKET

This is a game for any number of players; it can last for as long or as short a time as you wish. It requires two sets of stumps, a bat and a ball.

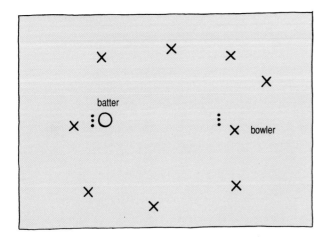

Lay out the pitch as shown in the diagram; the dimensions should suit the age of the children. Number off the children: no. 1 is the first batter, and no. 2 the first bowler. Place the fielders, not too close to the batter.

Decide how many overs each batter will play.

Suggested rules

• Each over consists of six balls bowled.

• The first bowler (no. 2) bowls the first over. Then no. 3 bowls the next over, and no. 2 returns to the field. After each over the next available player comes in to bowl.

• Each batter starts off with 50 runs; whenever s/he is out s/he loses one run. The batters have infinite lives.

• The batter is out if bowled, caught or run out.

• The batter returns to the batting end after each run.

• After the agreed number of overs, no. 2 bats and no. 1 takes his/her place in the field. Each player in order comes in to bat in this way until all the children have had a turn at batting.

• The players keep their own scores at batting and at bowling. The batter with the highest score is the batting champion; the bowler who took the most wickets is the bowling champion.

PAIRS CRICKET

Pairs cricket is a game for ten or twelve children. It takes 30–40 minutes to play, and requires two sets of stumps, two bats and a ball.

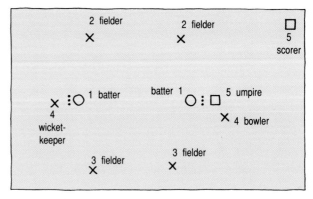

Lay out the pitch as shown in the diagram, with 16 paces between the wickets for under-11s. Divide the group into pairs and number off the pairs.

Suggested rules

• Initially, each pair does the activity shown in the table:

Pair	Activity
1	batting
2	fielding on leg side
3	fielding on off side
4	one bowls, the other is wicketkeeper (they change roles after each over)
5	one umpires, the other keeps score
(6	fielding)

• Each batting pair starts off with 100 runs. Batters have infinite lives, but each time one is out six runs are deducted from the pair's score.

• Pair 1 bat for an agreed number of overs, and their score is recorded.

• All the pairs then change to their next activity, i.e. pair 2 bat, pair 3 field on the leg side, and so on (see the table above).

• Play continues in this way until all the pairs have batted. The winning pair is the one with the highest score.

MINI-CRICKET

Mini-cricket is a game for twelve children, two teams of six. It takes about 35 minutes to play.

You need two sets of stumps, two bats, a ball, and six fielding discs or markers.

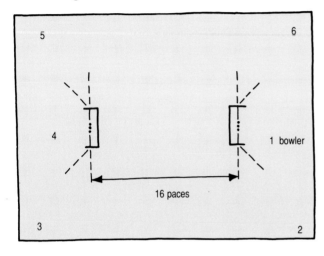

The playing area is set out as shown in the diagram. Fielding discs 1 and 4 are moved to the best positions for the bowler's run-up and for the wicketkeeper. Each member of the fielding team takes up position on one of the six discs.

Mini-cricket is especially suitable for indoor play. In this case the wall behind the bowler counts as a boundary; if it is hit four runs are scored.

The batting team organizes itself into three pairs.

Suggested rules

• The batting team starts with a score of 100 runs (this is to prevent a team ending up with a low or even negative score).

• The bowling must be **overarm**. It takes place from the same end throughout the game.

• There are six balls per over. At the end of each over, the batters change ends, and the fielding team (including bowler and wicketkeeper) all move round one place clockwise.

• The first batting pair bat for two overs. At the end of the two overs they retire, and are replaced by the second pair, who after two more overs are replaced in turn by the third pair.

• Each fielder must be in contact with his or her disc until the bowler starts to run up to bowl.

• The batters must run every time one of them hits the ball. They may also run for byes. Runs are scored in the usual way.

• Every time a wicket falls the batters change ends, except after a run-out.

• When a batter is 'out', three runs are deducted from the batting team's total score. However, all the batters have unlimited lives, so they do not retire when out.

• When the first team have all batted, the other team goes in to bat for their full six overs, and the team with the highest score wins.

NCA TEAM CRICKET

Team cricket is a game for sixteen children, eight a side. Its characteristic features are:

• It rewards the team playing the most enterprising cricket.

• The game can easily be controlled by one person — a major advantage if it is played at school, where often only one teacher will be available to supervise.

• It involves all the players in all three major skills.

• A complete game, with a definite result, can be played within an hour, or 90 minutes if sixteen overs are played per side.

• There is no need to keep individual scores or to analyse the bowling — another significant benefit when there is only one supervising adult.

The pitch is laid out with 16 paces between the wickets, or 19 paces if a 4.75-oz (135-g) cricket ball is used. The method of play is similar to mini-cricket, but without the discs or markers.

Suggested rules

• The batting team starts with 200 runs.

• Each pair of batters bats for three overs before retiring; this number of overs can be adjusted to suit the time available.

• Whenever a batter is out, the batters change ends, and six runs are deducted from the score.

• On the fielding side, each player except the wicketkeeper must bowl in turn. Nobody may bowl more than three overs.

• No fielder (except the wicketkeeper) is allowed to be nearer the wicket than 11 yards (10 m) when the ball is delivered, except behind the wicket on the off side. The 11-yard distance is measured from the middle stump.

• When the first team have all batted, the other team goes in to bat for their full twelve (or sixteen) overs, and the team with the highest score wins.

RESOURCES

Except where otherwise indicated, the resources listed here are available from the National Cricket Association.

Videos

This Game of Cricket
Covers the complete range of cricket skills in five sections

Umpiring with Dickie Bird
An introduction to the laws of the game

A Year in the Life of a Cricket Square
How to look after the turf

Let's Play Cricket

Available from Dudley AV Unit, Saltwells EDC, Bowling Green Road, Netherton, Dudley, West Midlands DY2 9LY:

16mm films

First Things First (for hire)
Shows teachers how to introduce and organize cricket in the primary school

Test Cricket
An introduction to the Proficiency Awards (see below)

Books

Test Cricket in Clubs and Schools
A concise guide to introducing cricket skills and testing them for the Proficiency Awards

Primary Cricket and *Youth Cricket*, Dr P. W. Sutcliffe

Available from J. Abrahams, National Coach North, National Cricket Association, Lancashire County Cricket Ground, Old Trafford, Manchester M16 0PX

Wallcharts

A set of eight wallcharts is available: three on batting, three on bowling, and one each on fielding and wicketkeeping.

Equipment

All games of cricket described in this section may be played with small-size or modified cricket equipment as appropriate. Kwik Cricket equipment is ideal: being made of plastic, it is light and durable. Sets of Kwik Cricket equipment are available, together with an accompanying video, from Kwik Cricket, The Cricket Council, Lord's Cricket Ground, London NW8 8QZ Tel: 071-289 2419

AWARDS

The National Cricket Association has two schemes designed to encourage children to practise cricket skills.

The Milk in Action Kwik Cricket Skills Award

This award should be within the reach of the majority of primary-school children. It consists of simple tests of five basic skills — catching, throwing, bowling, and two batting strokes. The pass rate is 50 per cent; successful candidates are awarded a free certificate and may purchase a low-cost cloth badge if they wish.

Enquiries should be addressed to Mr D. Clarke at the NCA's London address (see below).

The NCA Proficiency Award Scheme

This award scheme, supported by NatWest Bank, has three levels, of which the first level (Bronze, or First Test) is suitable for top juniors with some ability. At this level children are tested on their ability to perform three batting tests, one bowling test and three fielding tests, and to answer ten simple questions on cricket. On payment of a fee, successful candidates receive a certificate, a cloth badge and an enamel lapel badge.

Teachers can run and examine these tests themselves. Entry forms and mark sheets are supplied free of charge. Further information, and an inexpensive explanatory booklet, *Test Cricket in Clubs and Schools*, are available from Bob Carter, National Coach/Coach Education, at the NCA's Edgbaston address (see page 209).

GOVERNING-BODY INFORMATION

The National Cricket Association can be contacted at the following addresses:

National Cricket Association
Lord's Cricket Ground
London
NW8 8QZ

Tel: 071-289 6098

National Cricket Association
County Ground
Edgbaston
Birmingham
B5 7QX

Tel: 021-440 1748

MINI-ROUNDERS

The regulation mini-game is described below, and this is followed by three simpler games which may be used for initial practice and beyond.

EQUIPMENT

The National Rounders Association's full recommendations on equipment are found in *Rules of the Game and Hints to Umpires*. In brief, the basic requirements are:

• four wooden posts, sheathed in plastic, about 1.2 metres (4 ft) tall

• four smooth heavy rubber bases in which the posts are supported

• wooden or metal rounders bats (at least four per team); younger players can use flat bats rather than round ones. The maximum size of the official round bats is 460 mm (18 in) in length and 170 mm (6.7 in) in circumference at the thickest part.

• leather rounders balls if possible (about 180 mm [7 in] in circumference)

Many teachers prefer not to use leather rounders balls with younger players. The 'Incrediball' rounders ball, though slightly too large, is a soft version which behaves and handles more like a rounders ball than a tennis ball or other alternatives.

PLAYING MINI-ROUNDERS

The pitch

The standard rounders pitch may be used, which has the advantage that the distance between bowler and batter does not change when pupils graduate to the full game. Alternatively the pitch may be marked out as in the diagram at the top of the next column.

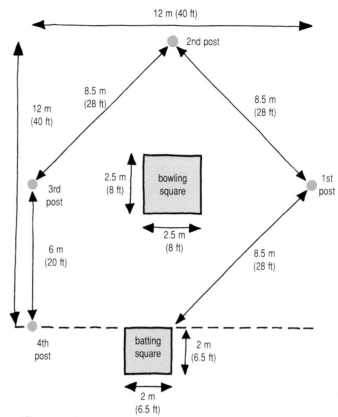

The rules

• Each team normally has six players, but teams of up to nine players may be used if this suits the class size.

• The game consists of one innings per team; the winning team is the one that scores the most rounders.

• Teams must decide the batting order in advance and keep to it throughout an innings.

• When the bowler delivers a good ball*, the batter **must run** (unless s/he is the last in the innings), whether s/he has hit it, attempted to hit it, or let it pass. The batter may run on a no-ball if s/he chooses to.

*A 'good ball' is one that arrives on the hitting side of the batter, within reach, and between the top of the head and the knee.

• The last batter has the choice of three good balls — that is, s/he does **not** have to run on the first two unless s/he chooses to.

• The ball must be bowled underarm.

• If the batter hits the ball into the backward area, s/he may run no further than first post until the ball is again in the forward area.

• The batter may stop at any post on the way round; while stopped at a post the batter must stay in contact with it (with bat or hand). A batter completing a rounder must touch the fourth post.

• When further balls (good or bad) are bowled, previous batters stopped at posts may run on to the next post.

• You cannot have more than one batter at a post, so a previous batter has to run on if the next batter runs to the post s/he is stopped at.

• The batters must run around the **outside** of the posts.

• If a batter stops at a post, but then chooses to continue (for example, because a fielder has missed the ball), s/he is not penalized and can score as normal.

• A batter is put out by being caught, or by being stumped at the post s/he is running to.

• After each six good balls have been bowled, the fielders all rotate one place around the field.

• A batter scores by reaching fourth post without being put out. The score is 3 rounders if fourth post is reached without stopping; if the batter has stopped at one or more of the other posts the score is 1 rounder.

• The umpire awards a rounder to the batting team if:

— the bowler delivers two consecutive no-balls

— the batter reaches fourth post without stopping but without having hit the ball

— there is obstruction by the fielding team.

• If there is no batter waiting to bat, the team may be put out by pitching the ball into the batting square.

PRACTICE GAMES

Four-circle rounders

This game is played on a conventional rounders pitch, but with circles (hoops) in place of the posts.

Teams score points rather than rounders, a point being scored for each circle reached by the current batter. Each member of the first team bats once, and then the other team bats. The team gaining the most points is the winner.

The other rules are the same as for normal rounders, except that two consecutive no-balls to the same batter gives away one point. Batters may be put out in the usual ways, with 'stumping' the circle replacing stumping the post.

You may add additional rules to suit your own situation.

Diamond rounders

This is a 4v4 game which is ideal for practising hitting, fielding, catching and throwing. You will need four bats, three cones or skittles, two large hoops, and one ball chosen to suit the players.

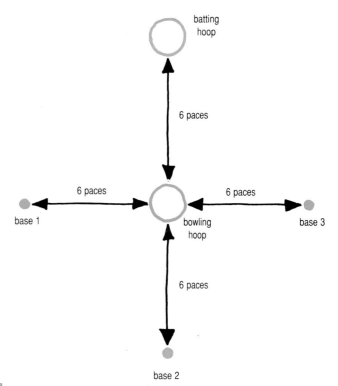

The diagram shows the suggested pitch layout. Distances may be altered to suit the age and ability of the players, but if you are practising for conventional rounders the distance from bowler to batter should be 7.5 m (24.6 ft).

The batter must hit the ball and reach base 3 before the bowler, standing in the bowling hoop, receives the ball from the fielders. Doing this scores 1 point. The batter can stop at any base.

The batters cannot be stumped, caught, or put out in any way. This has the advantage that no player has to sit and watch the remainder of an innings after getting out first ball.

Each batter receives three good balls in turn. When every member of the first team has batted, the teams change over. At the end of the game, the winning team is the one with the most points.

ONE-POST ROUNDERS

This is a 4v4 or 5v5 game using only one post. It can easily be used in games lessons with a number of groups.

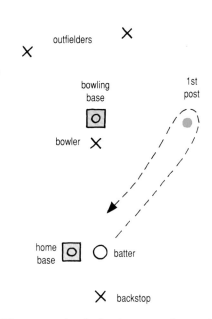

Lay out the pitch as shown in the diagram. The dimensions can vary with the age and abilities of the players. The fielders are organized as shown, with the backstop also acting as home-base player.

The game is similar to normal rounders, except that when the batter reaches first post s/he either stops there or runs anticlockwise around it and tries to return to home base, thus scoring a rounder. If the batter stops at first post, s/he must return to home base after the next good ball.

A batter may be put out by being caught, stumped at first post or home base, or run out at first post — that is, if s/he is waiting at first post and is joined by the next batter, the first batter is out.

All the normal rounders rules may be applied if desired.

One-post rounders has many advantages:

• High scores are easily obtained.

• There is a quick turnround, and each batter has many turns to bat.

• The batters are encouraged to hit out.

• All the fielders are constantly involved.

• The backstop is encouraged to take every ball efficiently, so as to get the batter out — this is good preparation for backstopping in the full game.

RESOURCES

National Rounders Association publications include:

Rules of the Game and Hints to Umpires

Rounders Practices

Coaching the Game of Rounders

Set of four posters (bowling, batting, fielding and backstopping)

These may be obtained from: Miss F. Banks, 110 Broadmead Road, Woodford Green, Essex IG8 7EH. Tel: 081-504 6552.

At present there are no publications specifically on mini-rounders.

AWARDS

The present NRA award scheme is aimed at young players aged 9–16. There are three levels: bronze, silver and gold. Certificates and cloth badges are available at each level.

The tests cover every aspect of the game, and encourage young players to improve all their skills. The organization and testing is left to individual schools and teachers, although *Teachers' Guides* and result sheets are available on request.

Full details and all materials are available from: Mr D. Dorrell, 79 Fernside Road, Poole, Dorset BH15 2JL.

A second, more basic, award scheme will be introduced in 1993. Aimed at young players aged 7–14, it will concentrate on the fundamental skills of rounders. This new award scheme will be even easier to administer, as the youngsters will be able to test each other and to keep their own records of achievement.

GOVERNING-BODY INFORMATION

National Rounders Association
3 Denehurst Avenue
Nottingham NG8 5DA

Tel: 0602 785514

The NRA Affiliations Secretary, Mr T. Woolhouse, may be contacted at:

26 Folds Crescent, Sheffield S8 0EQ.

TEEBALL

Teeball is a modified version of baseball/softball designed to introduce young players to the game in an enjoyable way, and to help them to progress up to the full adult games.

BASIC SOFTBALL/BASEBALL RULES

As softball and baseball are less well known in the United Kingdom than some other games, their basic rules are described here before introducing the teeball variations.

Softball, baseball and teeball are played on a fan-shaped field ('fair territory') bounded by 'foul territory'. There is a diamond-shaped infield with four bases.

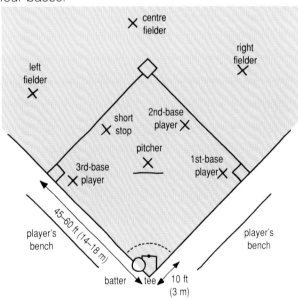

Two teams of nine or ten a side take turns to bat and field through seven or nine innings.

Each batter starts at the home plate. The pitcher pitches the ball to the batter, who must hit into 'fair territory' in order to advance; having done so, s/he runs to first base, and if possible continues anti-clockwise to second, third or even back to home base. Then the next batter comes in, and so the game continues.

A batter who reaches first base safely becomes a runner, and can run to the next whenever it is safe to do so. If s/he does this as soon as the pitcher makes a delivery, rather than waiting for a fair hit, it is called 'stealing a base'; this is not permitted in slow-pitch softball (one variety of softball). You cannot have two runners on the same base, so a player may be forced to leave his/her base to make room for another; if one runner passes another, the overtaker is out.

Runners must touch all bases in the correct order.

A batter can be 'struck out' by failing to hit three good pitches, caught out, or 'forced out' by failing to beat the throw to first base by the fielding side. A runner can likewise be forced out, or while running between bases 'tagged out' by a fielder's hand (or glove) holding the ball.

Each time a batter or runner safely completes a circuit of the bases and arrives back at home base, one run is scored. Regardless of whether the player scores a run or is put out, s/he resumes his/her regular place in the batting order. Whenever three batting-team players are out, their half-inning* is over, and it is the fielders' turn to bat.

*Inning *is commonly used in baseball and softball instead of* innings.

The teams alternate like this through seven or nine innings. At the start of each inning the first player to bat is the next in the batting order after the last batter of the previous inning.

The winning team is the one that has scored more runs at the end of the match.

TEEBALL EQUIPMENT

A list of suppliers of suitable equipment can be obtained from the National Softball Federation or from the British Baseball Federation Administration Secretary (addresses on page 215).

The **bat** is a small, lightweight softball/baseball bat, made of wood or aluminium, with 10–15 in (25–38 cm) of safety grip on the handle. Holding the bat on the thin part of the grip furthest from the end improves control. The length of the bat normally varies from 28 to 34 inches (71–86 cm) according to age.

Various kinds of **ball** can be used: usually a tennis ball, a proper rubber tee ball (larger than a tennis ball but smaller than a softball/baseball ball), or a larger, softer ball. For elementary teeball a hollow rubber ball is best. As the pupils progress, a harder rubber ball can be introduced as a step towards the softball/baseball ball.

The very youngest children, playing with a tennis ball or similar, do not need **gloves**. However, gloves should be introduced at the earliest opportunity, especially as the ball used becomes harder. Make sure the gloves you choose for the children have a pocket — the part between the thumb and finger space — which is big enough to hold the ball but not so big that the players cannot wrap their fingers around the ball. The catcher and the first-base player may wear mitts.

In softball/baseball the catcher must wear a helmet, a mask, a body-protector and leg-guards. These are not mandatory in teeball. If possible, each batter/runner should wear a helmet.

Four **bases** should be used, or three bases plus a home plate. These should be reasonably well secured if used outdoors, and non-slip if used indoors. The bases are 15 inches (38 cm) square, and the home plate is similar but five-sided. The pitcher's plate is 24 x 6 in (61 x 15 cm), and is made of wood or rubber.

A simple **tee** can be made out of suitable materials. It is better if the height is adjustable to allow your pupils a relaxed swing, but old large traffic cones of various heights can be used. The tee should have no sharp edges or protuberances. It must be lightweight, for two reasons: so that it can be removed easily after a successful hit; and so that it is not dangerous if pupils collide with it.

The tee can be positioned so that its stem is over the middle of the front edge of the home plate. Alternatively it can be placed so that it does not impede access to the home plate and can be safely left in position after the ball is hit — preferably in front of the home plate within the infield diamond.

PLAYING TEEBALL

Pitching accurately and consistently is the most difficult skill in the adult games. Teeball avoids the need for pitching: instead the batter hits the ball off a simple tee. It thus concentrates on improving batting and fielding skills within the game. (If you find you have a good pitcher, give him or her separate training using targets and a catcher.)

Despite the use of a tee, there is still a 'pitcher' in the pitching position. This player is the only one allowed within the infield diamond. S/he does not actually pitch the ball, and is not allowed to move until the ball is hit.

The pitching position may be varied. It is usually on an imaginary line drawn through first and third bases, but in teeball it should be not less than 46 ft (14 m) from the home plate, for safety's sake.

The batter takes up a stance with the feet next to the home plate — to the side of it, not in front or behind. S/he tries to hit the ball from the tee into fair territory. A flat swing produces the ideal line of drive. If the hit is successful — i.e. the ball is sent on its way to fair territory — the batter **must run**. Whenever necessary, the umpire should remove the tee after the batter has made a successful hit.

The game can proceed in exactly the same way as softball/baseball, or further variations can be made as suggested below. 'Stealing' is prohibited: runners may move off base only after the ball has been hit into fair territory.

However you play, always put the safety of your players first. This includes warm-ups.

SUGGESTED RULE VARIATIONS

Variations are usually introduced to allow for the age, experience and ability of the pupils, and in some cases to accommodate the game indoors.

• Outdoors, the distance between bases should start at about 46 ft (14 m) for six-year-old players, and progress upwards to about 60 ft (18 m) for nine- or ten-year-olds. Indoor distances are usually much less.

• **Foul territory**: In addition to the standard foul territory, a roughly semi-circular area (with a radius of about 10 ft [3 m]) may be drawn in front of the home plate and declared foul, so that the ball must travel beyond this. If the batter hits the tee, the ball should drop off into foul territory, so that no batters or runners may advance.

• Indoors, space restrictions make the proper area for foul territory impractical, so most of the available area — apart from that immediately behind the home plate — is usually deemed fair.

• **Strikes** are called when the batter swings and misses, or when s/he hits the tee and the ball falls off. Use your judgement, and vary the number of swings allowed to hit the ball. Also, the number of strikes before the batter is out (normally three) can be reduced to speed the game up. In 'One-hit teeball' pupils are allowed only one swing, which needs a high level of batting skill; the batter is out for swinging and missing, hitting the tee, or hitting into foul territory.

• If you are applying the normal rule that an inning lasts until three players are out, and this seldom happens, the batting side may have to bat through over and over again. To avoid this, the inning can be terminated as soon as a batter is caught out 'on the full' (i.e. the fielder catches the ball before it hits the ground), regardless of the overall number of outs. Alternatively, if you find that players are out too often, the batting side could bat through completely once, regardless of outs, to save time on changing over.

• In addition to the normal rules about forcing out or tagging out batters and runners, a batted ball fielded and thrown to the catcher at the home plate could halt play — that is, once the batted ball is in the catcher's hands, or has been touched by the catcher, runners must remain at the base they are on, or must stop at the base they are heading towards. (They can move again once the next batter has struck the ball into fair territory.)

• Alternatively a batted ball fielded and thrown to the catcher at the home plate could even put out all the runners who are not on base when the ball is caught at the home plate.

• The number of players per team can be altered so that everybody plays. Teams can be made up of boys and girls mixed.

COURSES AND AWARDS

To assist schools to develop teeball, the National Softball Federation and the British Baseball Federation will make coaches available to them for one-day taster courses as well as programmes of longer duration. The aim is to establish extra-curricular Youth Leagues in selected regions of the UK with regional and national competitions. The best teams will receive further high-level coaching.

The BBF is also taking part in the new National Coaches' Certification Programme administered by the Coaching Association of Great Britain. There are three levels, of which the first, Level A, is a basic coaching skills course for PE teachers and others. This course takes about six hours to complete, and includes teaching methods for primary-school players

as well as for older players. There is a written and a practical examination, and a certificate is awarded to those who pass. Attendance at the National Coaching Foundation introductory course 'Working with Children' is a precondition for entry to the course.

GOVERNING-BODY INFORMATION

Enquiries about BBF award schemes should be sent to:

Rita Collinson
Administration Secretary
British Baseball Federation
19 Troutsdale Grove
Southcoates Lane
Hull
HU9 3SD

Tel: 0482 792337

Enquiries about the BBF coaching schemes and courses should be sent to:

Jim Mortimer
BBF Coaching Association
94 Bellhouse Way
Foxwood Lane
York
YO2 3LN

Tel: 0904 783688

Enquiries about softball coaching should be sent to:

National Softball Federation
P. O. Box 1303
London
NW3 5TU

Tel: 071-356 5046
Fax: 071-356 6437

NOTES

Multi-game circuits are a good way of overcoming the problem of specializing in specific games too soon. Properly managed, they introduce the children to a wide variety of useful skills and are guaranteed to keep boredom at bay.

This example (for net games) is designed for groups of four pupils, rotating through six different stations in turn. It is essential that each station has sufficient equipment to allow all four pupils to work at the same time.

Place skill cards at the stations so that the pupils can read them before carrying out the tasks.

Dealing with odd numbers

You may have to introduce a team of two, three or five pupils to accommodate varied class sizes. Two is no problem, but the odd numbers will need to rotate within the individual stations. Make sure that you do not always have the same pupils in the odd groups.

Scoring

Provide each group with a card on which to record the group score. In this example it will be the total accumulated by all four players. If you have to compare groups of different sizes, you will have to devise a method for adjusting the scores.

Allow the children a period of practice, then give a time period in which they compete to see which group can achieve the highest score.

Skill circuit score card		Station					
		1	2	3	4	5	6
G r o u p	A						
	B						
	C						
	D						
	E						
	F						

The circuit

Note that at the stations where the pupils play in pairs, the rallies are cooperative; each individual's score is the maximum number of shots s/he gets 'in' during a single rally.

The stations in this example have been made as simple as possible. As your pupils' skills improve, the tasks can be made more challenging — for example, by marking front and back sections of the court and requiring alternate shots to be directed to different sections.

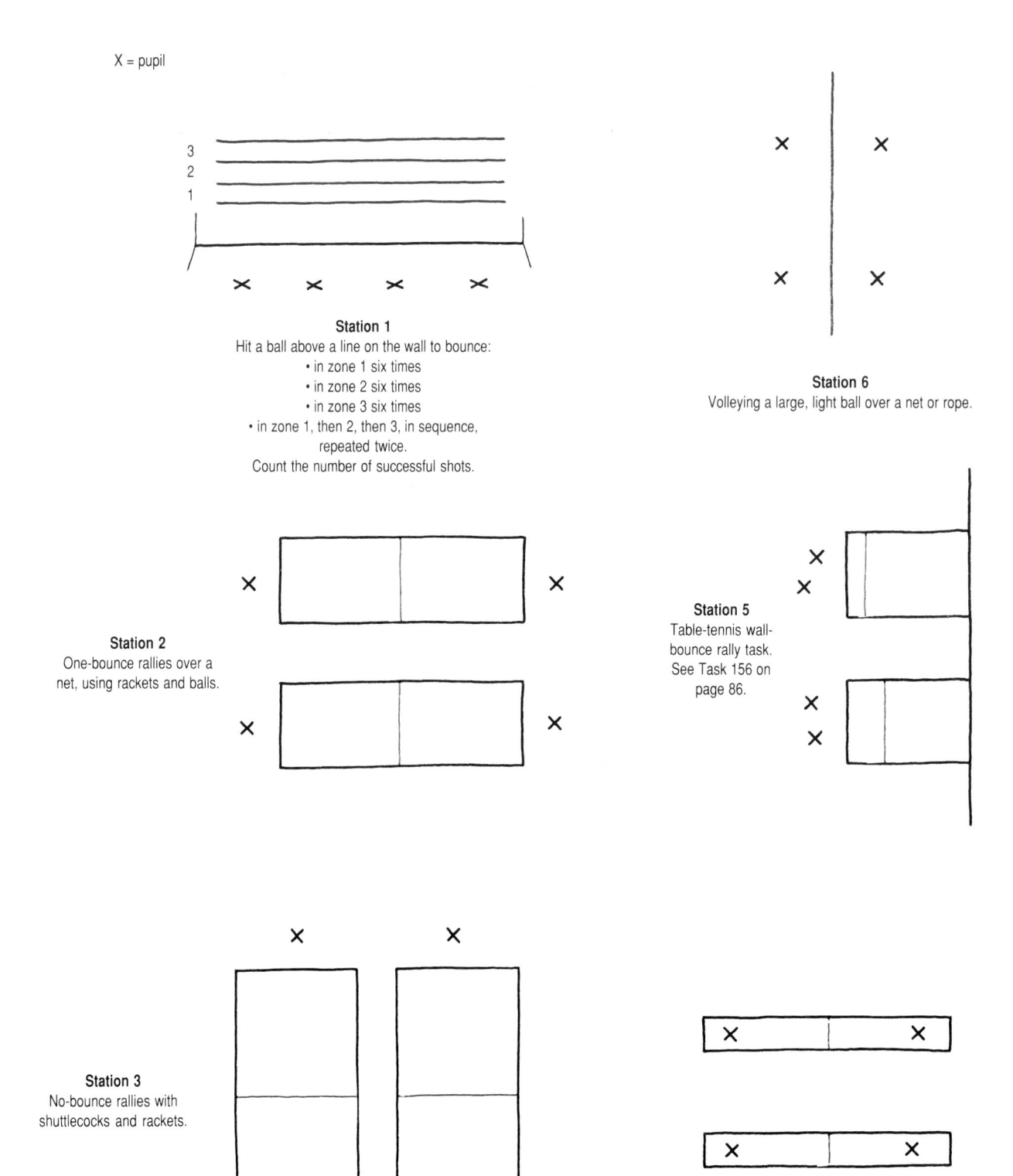

X = pupil

Station 1
Hit a ball above a line on the wall to bounce:
- in zone 1 six times
- in zone 2 six times
- in zone 3 six times
- in zone 1, then 2, then 3, in sequence, repeated twice.
Count the number of successful shots.

Station 6
Volleying a large, light ball over a net or rope.

Station 2
One-bounce rallies over a net, using rackets and balls.

Station 5
Table-tennis wall-bounce rally task. See Task 156 on page 86.

Station 3
No-bounce rallies with shuttlecocks and rackets.

Station 4
Table-tennis target serve task. See Task 154 on page 85.

The *End of Key Stage Statements* in the National Curriculum, and the related *Programmes of Study for Games*, specify levels of attainment and participation which your pupils should be able to reach. This appendix provides examples of how these elements may be interpreted as practical classwork.

Each End of Key Stage Statement begins: 'By the end of key stage *X* pupils should be able to show that they can ...'

Solo core skills

End of Key Stage Statement

• plan and perform safely a range of simple actions and linked movements in response to given tasks and stimuli

Games programme of study

Pupils should experience using a range of equipment including, where appropriate, specially designed equipment for pupils with physical disabilities.

Practical classwork

• throw or roll a ball underarm to a steady target

• throw a small ball overarm

• bounce and catch a ball

• pat-bounce a large ball by hand

• pat-bounce a small ball with a bat

• bat a slowly moving ball forwards and upwards

• play a ball against a wall, both by hitting and by kicking

• throw a ball upwards and catch it before the bounce

• throw a ball high and catch it after one bounce

• intercept and pick up a ball travelling along the ground

• run carrying a ball, showing change of pace and direction

• run, bouncing a ball against the ground with hand or bat, showing change of pace and direction

• kick a ball along the ground, or hit it with a stick

• dribble a ball along the ground using feet or stick

Pairs skills and solo skills within a group

End of Key Stage Statement

• practise and improve their performance

Games programme of study

Pupils should experience, practise and develop a variety of ways of sending, receiving and travelling with a ball; experience elements of games play that include chasing, dodging, avoiding, and awareness of space and of other players.

Practical classwork

• catch an incoming ball from a comfortable distance, both with and without a bounce

• working in pairs, pass and receive a ball using an implement such as a bat or stick: first standing opposite; then travelling in the same direction; then travelling freely; repeat travelling with throw/catch

• maintain a one-bounce rally with bat and ball against a wall, and then between you and a partner

• manipulate a ball while avoiding other pupils

• chase and tag other pupils; avoid being tagged

219

Developing personal skill

> ## End of Key Stage Statement
> - practise and improve their performance

Practical classwork

- test their developing skills by accepting simple challenges, individually and in pairs, such as: how near? how many? how far? how quickly? etc.

- play games that encourage the use of recently practised skills

Personal observation

> ## End of Key Stage Statement
> - recognize the effects of physical activity on their bodies

Practical classwork

Pupils observe that during exercise:

- they get warmer
- they breathe harder
- their heart beats more strongly
- their skin gets sticky
- they feel thirsty

Communication and invention

> ## End of Key Stage Statement
> - describe what they and others are doing

Games programme of study

Pupils should make up and play games with simple rules and objectives that involve one person and a limited amount of equipment, extended to working with a partner when ready.

Practical classwork

- watch the others and identify different actions
- play to simple rules
- make up solo and pairs games
- explain a simple game to others; watch others play a game and copy them

Solo core skills

> ## End of Key Stage Statement
> - plan, practise, improve, and remember more complex sequences of movement

Games programme of study

Pupils should improve the skills of sending, receiving and travelling with a ball for invasion, net/wall and striking/fielding games; develop their own games practices, working towards objectives decided sometimes by themselves and sometimes by the teacher.

Practical classwork

- throw, kick and hit a ball accurately to steady targets and to randomly moving targets, showing good judgement of timing, pace and direction

- receive a ball with close control

- receive and use a ball quickly

- take a ball away from an opponent

- travel with a ball under control, showing change of pace and direction

- use deception when travelling with the ball: e.g. avoid challenges by feinting

- link techniques and physical skills in fluent sequences

- initiate and perform relevant practices safely

Tactical skills

> ## End of Key Stage Statement
> - perform effectively in activities requiring quick decision-making

Games programme of study

Pupils should understand the common skills and principles, including attack and defence, in invasion, net/wall and striking/fielding games.

Practical classwork

Take a full part in both formal and informal games, making good decisions and showing knowledge of:

- in **invasion** games: when to travel with a ball and whether to keep it or to pass or shoot; whom to pass to; how to feint a pass; how to get away from an opponent; how to mark an opponent; how to support a team-mate; how to tackle and win the ball

- in **net/wall** games: how to find spaces to play the ball into; how to play a shot to move an opponent and so make a space for the next shot; how to cover the court and make return shots

- in **striking/fielding** games: bowling a ball which is difficult to hit; hitting the ball away from the fielders; deciding about running; returning fielded balls efficiently; setting a field

- in **all** games: understanding the significance of rules and playing to them; playing different roles in attack and defence as appropriate; exploring simple tactical ideas; considering options

Games-making and development

End of Key Stage Statement

- respond safely, alone and with others, to challenging tasks, taking account of levels of skill and understanding

Games programme of study

Pupils should make up, play and refine their own games within prescribed limits, considering and developing rules and scoring systems.

Practical classwork

Take part in all aspects of devising games for group play. All the following features should be considered:

- the rules

- the ideas of others

- the intention of a game and how it is to be won or lost

- how many players?

- what size playing area?

- what equipment?

- safety

- ensuring a high level of involvement for all the players

- penalties for breaches of the rules

- how changing a rule can improve or spoil a game

Physical management

End of Key Stage Statement

- sustain energetic activity over appropriate periods of time and understand the effects of exercise on the body

Practical classwork

While taking part in the games programme, the pupils should:

- appreciate the physical demands of each type of game

- use stamina, speed and strength to good effect

- recognize signs of fatigue

- know how to use energy wisely and be able to play a game from beginning to end without loss of form through fatigue

Social development

End of Key Stage Statement

- evaluate how well they and others perform and behave against criteria suggested by the teacher, and suggest ways of improving performance

Practical classwork

Through participation in the games programme, the pupils should:

- understand their roles as members of teams

- check their own performance and that of their classmates against criteria provided by the teacher, and comment on these performances

- describe and demonstrate what needs to be done to improve performance

NOTES

Indexes

INDEX 1
LIST OF GAMES AND TASKS

YELLOW SECTION

Familiarization

INDEXES

Skill Challenge Games

Avoiding and chasing games ('tag' games)

BLUE SECTION

Net and Wall Games

Net games

Invasion Games

Introduction

Striking/fielding Games

INDEX 2
ALPHABETICAL LIST OF
GAMES AND TASKS

W

INDEX 3
LIST OF SKILL CARDS

The skill cards are numbered separately from the main part of the resource; each occupies one page.

Numbers in brackets refer to the numerical designation of relevant games (**g**), tasks (**t**), work-stations (**s**) or games-making tasks (**gmt**); skill card numbers are prefixed by **sc**.

Technique-improvement Cards

(Skill Cards)

Using the skill cards

Each technique-improvement card carries information to help your pupils to perform the skills well. This takes the form of simple illustrations backed up by written criteria in note form.

The cards fulfil three purposes:

• to help the teacher to know what to look for as a pupil is performing the skill

• to help the pupils to reproduce techniques by reference to the illustrations

• to help the pupils to refine their skills and those of their classmates by checking performance against the notes

In the form in which the cards are printed here, they are primarily designed to serve the needs of the teacher. Because pupils vary in their ability to read and interpret inform-ation, we suggest that, when appro-priate, you photocopy the necessary cards with the full text blanked out, and add just a few key words to highlight the main points.

Here is an example:

Skill
18 Two-handed swing pass
card   (rugby)

1
• fingers spread
• twist at hips

2
• swing arms across body
• follow-through

18

Racket underarm service

1

• ball held out in front of body in palm of non-racket hand

2

• ball tossed up as racket is taken back

3

• racket swings through to hit dropping ball

• weight on front foot as racket follows through

1

Volleyball underarm service

3

• follow-through

2

• hitting arm swings forward past hip

• ball tossed very slightly upwards as hitting arm approaches

• ball contacted just below its centre with clenched fist or heel of hand as player's weight moves onto front foot

1

• ball held out in front of body

• hitting arm taken back with the hand closed

Racket overarm service

1

2
- ball tossed high slightly in front of body

3
- racket taken back down past hip then up behind back to 'scratch back' position

4
- racket head 'thrown' at ball
- shot timed so that body and arm are at full stretch as ball is hit

5
- follow-through

Racket forehand drive

1

• shoulders turn as racket is taken back

• player positioned so that ball approaches to side of body

2

• shot timed so that ball is hit when it is just in front of body and a comfortable distance away

3

• follow-through: racket swings from low to high

4

Racket backhand drive

1

• shoulders turn a long way as racket is taken back

2

• shoulders rotate 'into' ball as racket swings through to make hit

• knuckles face forward throughout stroke

• shot timed so that ball is hit when it is just in front of body and a comfortable distance away

3

• follow-through: racket swings from low to high

Volleyball dig

1

Ready position:

• low, knees bent, shoulders forward of hips

• hands held together

• arms held out in front of body, straight but relaxed

2

The hit:

• arms swing forward to contact ball just above wrists

• short arm swing stops on contact with ball — no follow-through

Racket volley — forehand

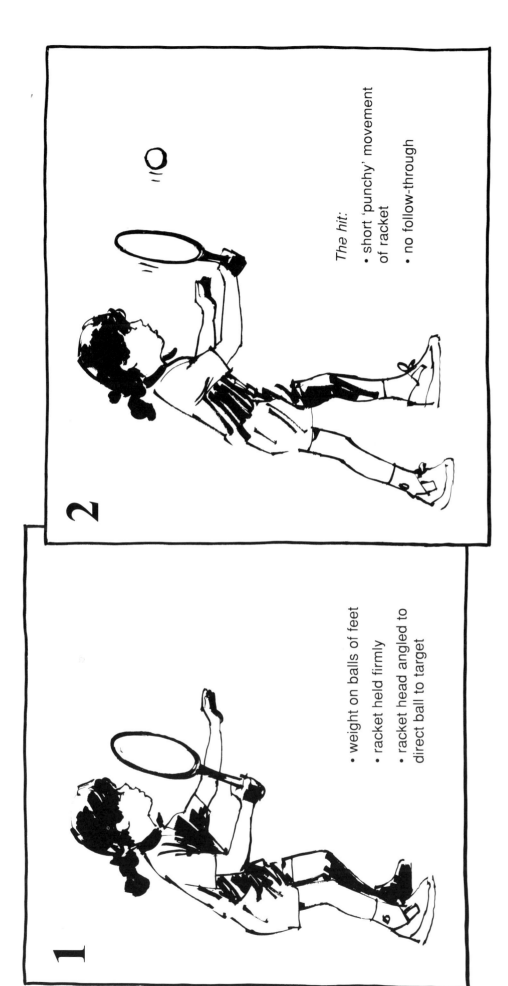

2

The hit:
- short 'punchy' movement of racket
- no follow-through

1

- weight on balls of feet
- racket held firmly
- racket head angled to direct ball to target

Racket volley — backhand

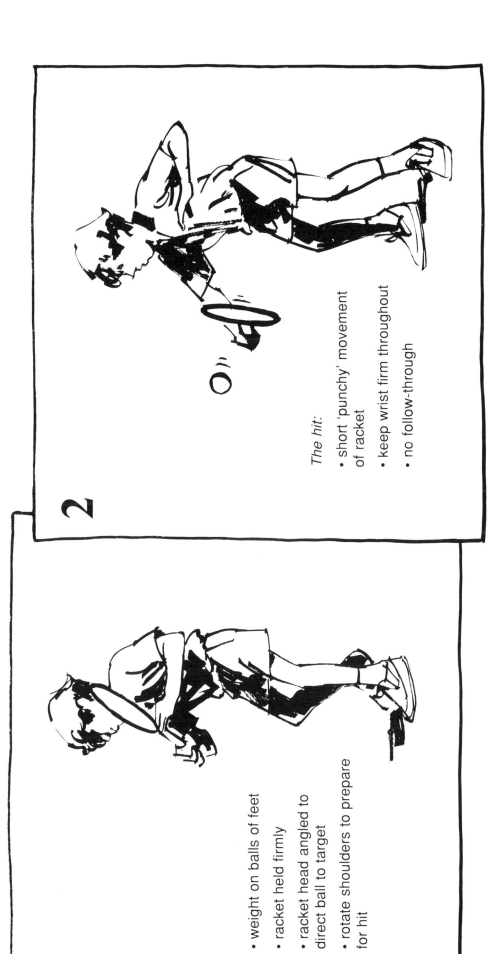

1

- weight on balls of feet
- racket held firmly
- racket head angled to direct ball to target
- rotate shoulders to prepare for hit

2

The hit:

- short 'punchy' movement of racket
- keep wrist firm throughout
- no follow-through

Volleyball volley

3

The hit:

- firm push, with ball in contact with fingers and thumbs to guide it for as long as possible

2

- arms and legs straighten to push ball away

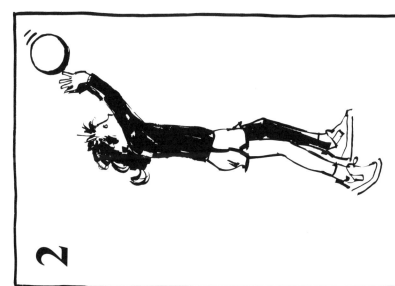

1

- face intended target
- legs slightly apart, knees flexed, one foot in front of the other
- arms high, with elbows flexed
- hands just above forehead and slightly in front; fingers spread and relaxed

Racket lob

1

- same basic action for forehand and backhand

- shoulders turn as racket is taken back

2

- swing racket head from low to high

- racket contacts ball at hip-height, about arm's length from body

- face of racket 'open' on contact with ball

3

- high follow-through

Racket overhead ('smash')

4

• ball hit forward and down

3

• body at full stretch as contact is made

2

The hit:

• racket head 'thrown' at ball

1

• racket held high

• player moves into line with ball, keeping eyes on it

• free arm points to ball

Volleyball smash

1

• three-step approach

2

• two-footed take-off into stretched vertical jump

3

• arms swing above head to help gain height

4

The hit:

• hitting arm bends at elbow before straightening to play the ball

5

• hand palm-down, fingers spread on contact

• wrist flexes to direct ball downwards

13

Table-tennis service

3

• ball hit down to bounce on table befo're crossing net

2

• ball tossed up at least 16 cm (6 in) before being hit

• forehand or backhand action (backhand illustrated)

1

• ball rests on palm

• flat, open hand with fingers together

• hand always above table-level and behind the edge

Overhead pass

(basketball/netball)

1

2

• arms raised straight above head

• ball held in both hands, with fingers spread and pointing upwards

• elbows bent to take ball back

• player steps forward and pulls ball forward over head

• strong wrist action aids throw

• follow-through over front foot

14

15

Pivot and chest pass
(basketball/netball)

3

• weight transferred to front foot
• ball pushed towards receiver and released by extending arms and fingers

2

• ball held in both hands with fingers spread
• elbows in

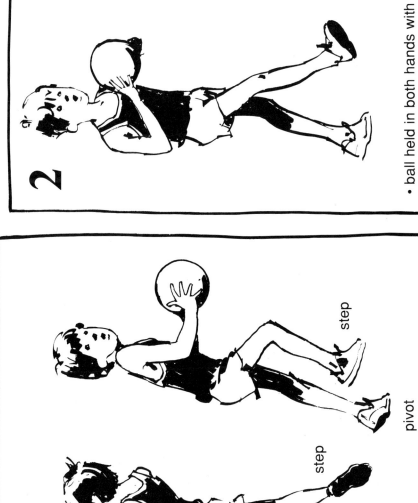

1

step   pivot   step   pivot

• player steps away with one foot and pivots on the other

Two-handed bounce pass

(basketball/netball)

2

- ball pushed hard towards the ground
- arms and fingers extended vigorously

1

- ball held with fingers spread and pointing upwards
- ball between chest and waist height
- elbows in

One-handed pass

(basketball/netball)

1

- throwing hand behind ball
- other hand supports ball underneath
- body sideways, with shoulder of throwing arm away from receiver

2

- ball taken back to shoulder
- non-throwing hand continues to support if necessary

3

- *the throw:* throwing arm thrusts vigorously while player steps onto front foo:

Two-handed swing pass
(rugby)

1

- ball held with fingers spread
- player keeps running forwards
- body twists at hips until shoulders face receiver
- ball swung back at hip level

2

- arms swing and release ball towards receiver
- follow-through: hands end action pointing to receiver

Getting free (forwards/backwards)

(basketball/netball)

- player poised on balls of feet — ready to move quickly

- hand(s) used to show where passer should send ball

- player darts in front of defender to receive direct pass

OR

- player feints to go forward and suddenly runs back to receive ball sent over defender

Getting free (side to side)

(basketball/netball)

• player poised on balls of feet — ready to move quickly

• player feints to go one way by dropping shoulders but sprints the other way

OR

• player drops shoulders but keeps going to surprise opponent

OR

• player makes several small movements to wrong-foot opponent before sprinting away

Marking facing the ball

(basketball/netball)

• player stays alert and ready to move to intercept ball

goal

Whenever possible, the player should:

• position to the side of the opponent nearest the ball

• keep opponent in view

• be slightly nearer to the defending goal than the opponent is

defender

○ ball

attacker

21

Marking facing the player

(basketball/netball)

• player keeps to one side in order to see over shoulder at incoming ball

• player matches movements of opponent

• player reacts quickly to turn and intercept when opponent goes for ball

goal

• player stays between opponent and ball

defender

ball

attacker

Standing one-handed shot

(basketball/netball)

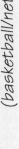

3

- knees straighten vigorously
- ball pushed continuously with arm and fingers
- ball travels in a high arc towards goal

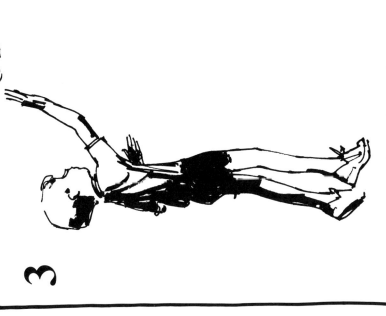

2

- knees bend
- ball taken back to shoulder

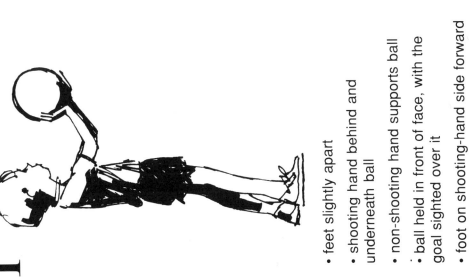

1

- feet slightly apart
- shooting hand behind and underneath ball
- non-shooting hand supports ball
- ball held in front of face, with the goal sighted over it
- foot on shooting-hand side forward

Passing backwards
(rugby)

Passer:

• ball held between hands, with fingers spread and thumbs on upper part of ball

• looks for target — just ahead of receiver and level with zone between his/her lower chest and waist

• while running, hips twist to bring shoulders square to receiver

• ball taken well back at hip level

• arms swing through

• wrists and fingers extend in follow-through to point towards target

Receiver:

• twists trunk to face passer

• hands out to receive ball and draw it to the body, ready to pass again

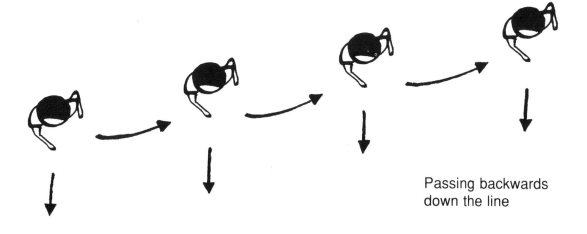

Passing backwards down the line

Roll back

(rugby)

- tackled player keeps hold of ball

- player quickly stands up and faces goal-line s/he is attacking

- one foot placed directly above ball, with the other one alongside it

- ball rolled gently backwards to a team-mate, using sole of foot

25

Chicken-scratch scrum

(rugby)

- two opposing players form scrum by facing each other and leaning right shoulder to right shoulder, with their heads side by side

- ball put between their feet by a player whose team has the put-in. This must be done from the left side of their scrum player.

- team with put-in always wins ball: their player puts one hand down to roll it back between his/ her feet

- ball picked up by player who put t in

- all other players must stay on their own defending side of the scrum until the ball is out

Three-player uncontested scrum

(rugby)

1

- two rows of three players face each other

- centre player in each row (the *hooker*) places his/her arms across shoulders of outer players (the *props*)

- rows bound together by props crossing their inside arms over back of hooker to grasp him/her just above waist

2

- keeping their heads up, the two rows of opposing players slowly interlock them right-side to right-side

- *scrum-half* of team with put-in stands one step from scrum holding ball just above ankle-height

- ball goes in straight between the rows

- team with put-in always wins ball

- hooker strikes ball with inside of his/her right foot

- ball travels between feet of left-hand prop, to be picked up by scrum-half

- all other players must stay on their own side of the scrum until the ball is out

Kicking from the hands

(rugby)

The technique shown is for the *punt*. Once learnt, the action and timing can be modified for the *drop kick*, where the ball is allowed to hit the ground before contact.

1

- ball held out at waist level with both hands

2

- ball dropped as non-kicking foot steps forward

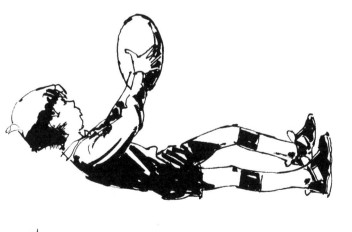

3

- kicking leg swings through, straightening as contact is made before ball hits ground
- ball contacted with upper part of foot
- follow-through with leg extended and toes pointing

28

Grubber kick
(rugby)

3

- ball kicked with either inside or outside of foot, using a short stabbing action
- ball bounces forwards along ground

2

- ball dropped as kicking leg swings down
- weight kept forward; head over ball

1

- ball held forwards in both hands at thigh-level
- player steps forward with non-kicking foot

Travelling and stopping

(hockey)

2

• player reaches over ball with stick to trap it before moving off in a new direction

1

• ball steered along ground with face of stick. If ground is bumpy or slow, ball is propelled with a series of little taps.

• ball kept away from feet — player's action should not be cramped

• player keeps looking up

• ball always kept within reach

Grip check

Start with the stick lying on the ground face-down, handle towards the player. Using a 'suitcase-lifting' grip, the left hand grasps the top of the handle, and the right hand supports it several centimetres lower down.

Reversed-stick play

(hockey)

• stick gripped with left hand; right hand forms a loose sleeve in which stick is free to rotate

• toe of stick turned over top of ball by twisting left wrist; right hand supports only

rotation of stick over ball (seen from player's left)

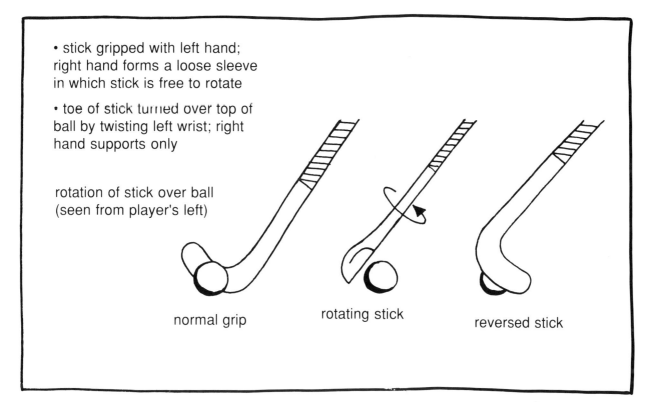

normal grip   rotating stick   reversed stick

Dribbling

Having mastered the grip change, pupils should practise moving the ball to the left and right while standing still, changing grip so that only the flat face of the stick contacts the ball. They can then progress to doing the same but while moving forwards, so that the ball makes a zig-zag pattern on the ground.

Travelling and stopping
(soccer)

3

- *simple stop:* player over-takes ball and checks it with inside or outside of foot

2

- *changing direction:* ball nudged with inside or outside of foot

- ball played with both the left and the right foot

1

- ball sent forwards using top of boot; laced area should make contact

- ball kept well in front of feet so that player can look up and cover ground quickly

Turning with the ball

(soccer)

Three ways of turning quickly to reverse direction. Players should practise with either foot.

• *trap turn* — player reaches out to place foot on top of ball, then rolls ball back with sole of boot

• *outside hook turn* — as left, but ball hooked back with outside of foot

• *inside hook turn* — ball hooked without overtaking it, using inside of foot

Turning with the ball

(hockey)

• *turning left:* ball controlled and directed with 'open' face of stick

Turning right:

• player runs around ball, leading with left shoulder; ball kept close to stick

OR

• ball trapped with stick reversed (toe down), then player pivots in required direction

Goalkeeping skills

(soccer)

• player alert, ready for shots at any time

• player constantly adjusts position to keep in line with ball and centre of goal

• player gets body behind low shots

• both hands on ball whenever possible

• ball held close to body until ready to be kicked, thrown or rolled away

• high balls taken with both hands and pulled towards body

• higher balls tipped over bar

Goalkeeping skills
(hockey)

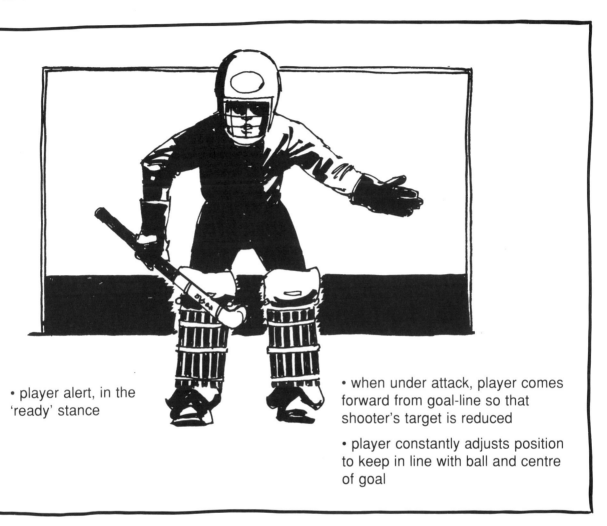

• player alert, in the 'ready' stance

• when under attack, player comes forward from goal-line so that shooter's target is reduced

• player constantly adjusts position to keep in line with ball and centre of goal

Stopping and clearing

Only the ready stance is shown here. It should be noted that goalkeeping is an active position and there are many different ways of stopping the ball. Shots can be blocked with the pads, the feet or the hands, and cleared away from the goal by kicking.

Safety

Goalkeepers must wear good protection, even if playing with a soft ball.

37

Tackling skills

(hockey)

All tackles:

- head of stick on ground throughout

- ball played, not opponent's stick

- tackler keeps contact with ball for as
long as possible

Tackling a player coming head-on:

- tackler's stick held so that its face
'looks' at ball

- tackler shadows movements of ball
until it runs onto stick

Tackling a player going in the same direction:

*The action depends on whether the tackle is
made from the stick side or the body side of the
opponent. If the right hand lets go of the stick to
allow an extended reach it should
be replaced as soon as possible.*

- *from stick side*: tackle is
sweeping action with stick,
aimed at ball, and always
keeping head of stick on
ground

- *from body side*: tackler gets just ahead of
opponent. Stick is reversed and held with
left hand only. The tackle is made by
reaching in to play the ball, taking care to
avoid body contact

Taking the ball past a defender
(hockey)

• ball kept close to stick

• ball moved quickly to one side or other to accelerate past opponent

• ball taken to left with 'open' stick ...

• or to right with reverse stick

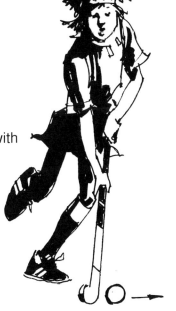

• *feint*: player pretends to go to one side and then quickly dodges to the other

• *forward dodge*: ball sent a little way beyond defender on one side, while player runs past on other side to collect it

Taking the ball past a defender

(soccer)

Using the near foot to mislead opponent:

1

- ball put out in front and to side
- player steps over ball with near foot
- outside of other foot used to move ball away

- sides of feet used to move ball to left or right

2

- ball taken other way with outside of foot
- player accelerates away from opponent

- *simple feint*: player pretends to go one way and quickly goes the other
- ball kept under control

Sending the ball

(hockey)

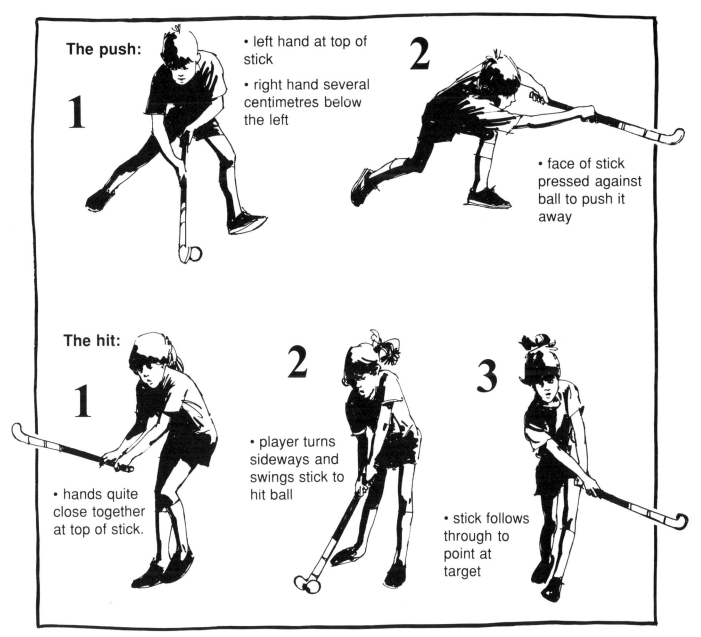

The push:

1

• left hand at top of stick

• right hand several centimetres below the left

2

• face of stick pressed against ball to push it away

The hit:

1

• hands quite close together at top of stick.

2

• player turns sideways and swings stick to hit ball

3

• stick follows through to point at target

Hitting harder

As strength and skill increase, the hands can be brought even closer, allowing a freer swing which results in a harder hit.

Sending on the move

Most players find both the push and the hit easier and more powerful if they are made while on the move, after at least a couple of approach paces.

Sending the ball
(soccer)

Long, high pass:

1

• ball level with toe of non-kicking foot

2

• kicking foot swings through, contacting ball below centre with laced part of boot

Long, low pass:

1

• ball beside non-kicking foot

2

• kicking foot swings through, contacting ball in centre with laced part of boot

Short, low pass:

• ball beside non-kicking foot, which points directly at target

• ball hit in centre with inside of foot

Receiving the ball

(hockey)

- receiver always tries to face goal s/he is attacking

- player's body must not prevent an opponent from getting to the ball

- stick kept on ground

- face of stick always turned to meet ball

- stick 'gives' on contact to stop ball bouncing away

Receiving from the left

Receiving from the right
— stick reversed

42

Receiving the ball

(soccer)

Receiving low passes:

- slow ball collected with any part of foot
- faster ball taken on inside of foot and brought under control before being redirected

Receiving chest-high passes:

- ball taken with body inclined forwards, so that ball is chested down to ground

Receiving on the thigh:

- leg raised with knee bent
- foot lowered as ball makes contact to stop ball bouncing away

43

Heading

(soccer)

1

2

• body arched back as ball approaches

• neck held firm

• head attacks ball

• ball contacted with middle of forehead

• head 'through' ball, not at it

• ball contacted above centre to play it downwards

• ball contacted below centre to keep it in the air

Marking
(hockey)

Good marking should stop an opponent from getting and using the ball. It will lead to opportunities to intercept the ball and to turn defence into attack.

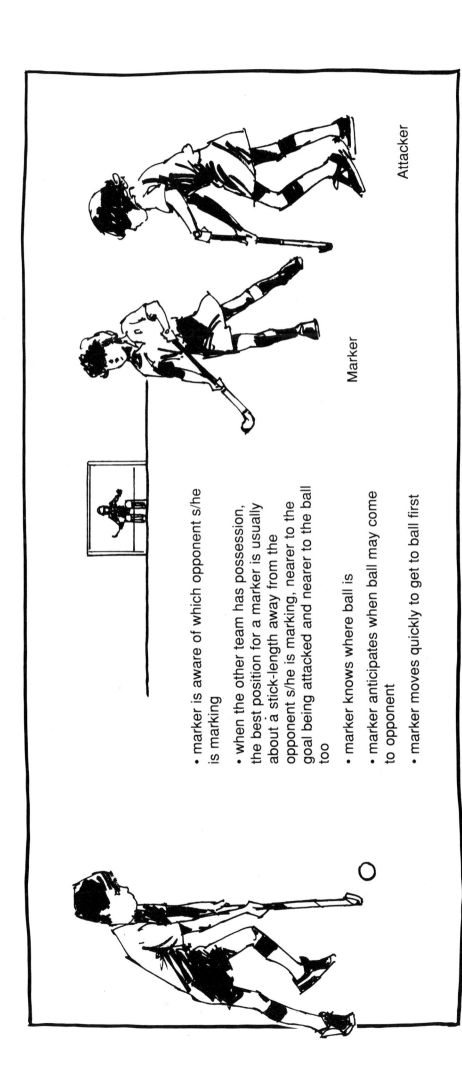

Attacker

Marker

• marker is aware of which opponent s/he is marking

• when the other team has possession, the best position for a marker is usually about a stick-length away from the opponent s/he is marking, nearer to the goal being attacked and nearer to the ball too

• marker knows where ball is

• marker anticipates when ball may come to opponent

• marker moves quickly to get to ball first

46

Marking

(soccer)

Good marking should stop an opponen: from getting and using the ball. It will lead to opportunities to intercept the ball and to turn defence into attack. Markers must always be determined to get to the ball first, and need to make it difficult for opponents to play the ball behind them.

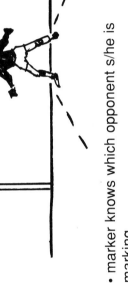

Attacker

Marker

- marker knows which opponent s/he is marking

- marker knows where ball is

- when the other team has possession, the best position for a marker is usually inside the imaginary triangle formed by ball, opponent and goal being attacked

- marker anticipates when ball may come to opponent

- marker moves quickly to get to ball first

Good running style

• weight on balls of feet

• comfortable stride length — not too long

• good fast knee-raise

• arms swing vigorously in line with direction of run — they should not cross in front of body

• body leans slightly forwards

• neck and shoulders relaxed

Starting from a base

- player in alert starting position: facing in direction of run, and watching ball

- player correctly in contact with base, post or crease

- player sprints forwards by driving off back foot as quickly as possible

- player covers ground efficiently: straight run if going to next base only, curved run to go through next base

- player finishes run by remaining correctly in contact with base, post or crease until ball is 'dead'

Fielding: intercepting the ball

(baseball/softball)

1

- player on balls of feet, ready to move in any direction
- player watches ball ...
- player moves into path of ball
- both hands stay close to ground
- gloved hand stops ball

If gloves are not available, players should stop the ball with both hands

2

- ball transferred to throwing hand while checking target

3

- no hesitation before throwing — throw on the run

Stopping and returning the ball

(cricket/rounders/softball)

1

• player on balls of feet, ready to move in any direction

• player watches the ball ...

2

• player moves into path of ball

• knee and shin form a 'long barrier' to stop ball if hands fail

• hands point down with little fingers touching

• ball watched right into hands

• player stands up as quickly as possible

• player looks at target to which ball is to be thrown

3

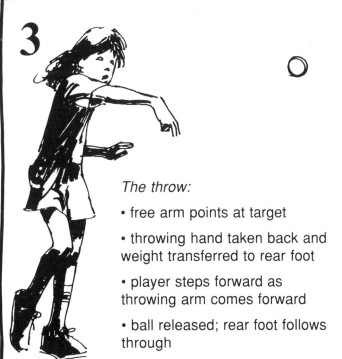

The throw:

• free arm points at target

• throwing hand taken back and weight transferred to rear foot

• player steps forward as throwing arm comes forward

• ball released; rear foot follows through

A good stop and throw is one continuous movement.

Chasing and returning the ball

(cricket/rounders/softball)

A good pick-up and throw is one continuous movement.

3

- player steps forward as throwing arm comes forward
- ball released; arm follows through towards target

2

The throw:

- free arm points at target
- throwing hand taken back and weight transferred to rear foot

1

- fast run after the ball
- long last stride taken as ball is reached
- player gets low to ground
- right-handers pick up ball with left foot forward
- left-handers pick up ball with right foot forward

Fielding high catches

(cricket/rounders/stoolball)

- ball sighted well before moving to it

- player moves quickly to get under falling ball

- ball watched very carefully

- fingers spread to make a large catching area

- little fingers close together

- hands and arms 'give' towards the chest as ball is received

card

Batting — basic forward drive

(cricket)

Instructions are for right-handed players; reverse the positions for left-handers.

1

Grip:

- bat held comfortably with hands as shown; left hand on top

Stance:

- player stands sideways with feet about 8–15 cm (3–6 in) apart; left foot forward

- hands rest against left thigh

- left shoulder and elbow point towards bowler

- player should not crouch down: weight should be equally divided between the feet

- as bowler starts to bowl, batter's body should be balanced and still

2

Action:

- bat lifted to rear, slightly above level of top of stumps

- player watches bowler's hand

- head aligns with flight of ball

- top hand guides bat

- player steps forward with left foot, swings bat vertically down to hit ball squarely with its flat face.

Batting

(stoolball)

Stance:

• player stands sideways with feet a comfortable distance apart

• shoulder of non-batting arm points to bowler

• weight on back foot

Action:

• eyes on bowler's hand

• bat raised to rear

• player steps onto front foot and swings bat with a firm grip, keeping head of bat above wrist

• ball hit as near to centre of bat as possible

Grip:

• bat held comfortably with one hand

• 'V' formed between thumb and forefinger aligns with edge of bat

Batting

(rounders)

Grip and stance:

- bat held tightly but comfortably in shake-hands grip

- batting arm relaxed

- end of bat (the head) held up higher than wrist

- batter stands sideways-on to bowler

- bat held back, ready to strike

- feet comfortably apart and weight well balanced on back foot

Action:

- player watches bowler's hand

- bat swings with a fast circular action, keeping arm parallel to ground

- player steps forward onto front foot as bat swings through to hit ball

Batting

(softball/baseball)

1

Grip and stance:

• bat held with both hands at a point on the handle which feels comfortable

• with bat pointing upwards, player's natural throwing hand should be uppermost

• little finger of top hand touches index (first) finger of lower one

• player stands sideways-on to pitcher; a right-handed batter will have his/her feet pointing to first base

• feet shoulder-width apart

• weight on balls of feet, with body bent forward slightly from waist

2

Action:

• as pitcher comes forward, wrists bend and bat moves back a little

• batter steps onto front foot, whips hands through and 'throws' body of bat at ball

3

• arms fully extended as hit is made

• ideal contact is at 'sweet spot', near centre of thickest part of bat

Simple overarm bowling

(cricket)

The 'figure 6' path

Note how the ball takes a 'figure 6' path before it leaves the bowler's hand.

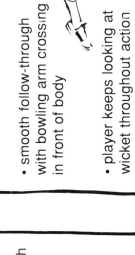

4

- while bowling arm rises up behind body, free arm moves forward and down in smooth arc
- ball released at highest point — right at top of the 'figure 6'

5

- smooth follow-through with bowling arm crossing in front of body
- player keeps looking at wicket throughout action

3

- ball pulled from under chin as front foot starts to come down

2

- bowling arm bent, holding ball beside chin
- free arm pointing upwards
- forward leg raised bent, with toe pointing at sky
- body leans backwards

Grip:

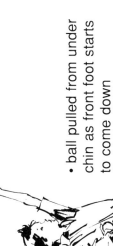

- ball held in fingers, not in palm
- seam of ball upright between first and second fingers
- thumb supports ball underneath

Starting position:

1

- body sideways-on to batter

Bowling

(stoolball)

1

The ball is bowled to the 'board', or wicket. A ball bowled to the correct length will be at least 30 cm (12 in) above the ground when it reaches the wicket.

2

Grip:

• ball held in palm of hand with fingers spread around it

Stance:

• facing wicket

• throwing arm to rear of body, leg on same side forward

Action:

• simple underarm bowling action: ball must be bowled and not thrown

• weight moved onto front foot to start action

• one step forward onto other foot as bowling arm swings forward to make delivery

• palm of hand faces target throughout delivery

• smooth follow-through

Bowling

(rounders)

The ball is bowled to the target area, which is the space just to the striking side of the batter.

1

Grip:

• ball cradled in fingers and held by thumb; ball should not touch palm

Stance:

• facing batter

• throwing arm taken to rear of body, leg on same side forward

2

An underarm bowling action, with a wrist 'snap' at the end to add speed:

• weight moved onto front foot to start action

• one step forward onto other foot as bowling arm swings forward to make delivery

• right-handed bowler's left foot should be forward as ball is released

• hand snapped forward from wrist when releasing ball

• smooth follow-through, ending with hand palm-up and pointing at target

Pitching
(softball)

The softball pitch is a fast underarm delivery in which the ball is swung from high behind the head with a powerful action. The pitcher starts facing the batter almost square-on, twists hips and shoulders sideways as the ball is taken back to start the throw, and squares up again rapidly as the ball is delivered. This body action is often compared to a door being opened and then slammed shut.

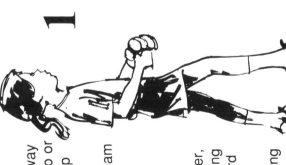

1

Grip:

- ball supported away from palm, with two or three fingers on top and thumb below

- fingers across seam where possible

Stance:

- player faces batter, with foot on throwing side slightly forward

- throwing hand in front of body, resting in other hand

2

Action:

- door opens: ball taken back and high

- door begins to close: arm swings down and forward as pitcher strides forward with opposite leg

- swing starts slow and finishes fast

3

- door slams shut: ball released with snap of wrist

- smooth follow-through; pitching hand ends up pointing directly at catcher

61

card

Pitching

(baseball)

Instructions are for a right-handed pitcher; reverse them for left-handers.

The baseball pitch is best described as a 'roundarm' throw, halfway between the underarm action of softball and the overarm action of cricket.

4

The follow-through:

- ball released with a 'snap' of the wrist

- throwing arm swings across body so that right arm ends up outside left knee

3

The pitch:

- ball taken back above, shoulder level

- player steps onto left foot as ball is delivered

2

The wind-up:

- ball brought down as right foot pivots and weight transfers onto it

- left leg raised and whole body turned sideways on

1

Grip:

- ball supported away from palm; first and middle fingers on top, thumb directly underneath, with third and little fingers helping thumb

- ball held firmly but not 'strangled'

The start:

- player stands facing the batter

- player steps back onto left foot to build momentum

- hands raised above head

Keeping wicket

(cricket/stoolball)

Stance:

- player crouches down with knees bent
- weight forward on balls of feet
- body slightly forward
- feet comfortably spaced for good balance
- hands cupped side by side
- *in cricket*: knees fully bent so that backs of fingers touch ground, with palms facing forward
- *in stoolball*: knees bent so that hands rest directly in front of them with palms facing forward

Position:

- player just to bat side of wicket (*off* side) to give clear view of bowler
- player close to wicket for slow bowler; further back for fast bowler

Action:

- ball caught and swept towards wicket as a continuous action
- keeper ready to reposition so that wicket is always between him/her and ball while the ball is being fielded

Backstop

(rounders/softball/baseball)

In the base-running games, the backstop or catcher has to catch all the balls from the pitcher which are not hit away by the batter. S/he then has to throw the ball to the base at which it is most likely to cause a run-out.

Stance:

• feet apart, one slightly in front of the other

• knees bent so that body is lowered to keep eyes in line with ball

• *for softball/baseball*: catching mitt in front of chest, fingers up; palm out; other hand (*throwing* hand) safely out of way behind back

• *for rounders*: both hands in front of chest, palms out; fingers up; thumbs touching

Action:

• alert: player aware of positions of opposing players at bases

• ball caught cleanly

• smooth transfer of ball to throwing hand

• rapid pivot on foot of throwing side; other foot points towards target

• forward step taken to throw ball with powerful overarm or sidearm action

• catch–transfer–throw is a continuous movement